T0133955

Maximizing ROI on Software Development

Maximizing ROI on Software Development

Vijay Sikka

AUERBACH PUBLICATIONS

A CRC Press Company
Boca Raton   London   New York   Washington, D.C.

Library of Congress Cataloging-in-Publication Data

Sikka, Vijay
    Maximizing ROI on software development / Vijay Sikka.
      p. cm.
    Includes bibliographical references and index.
    ISBN 0-8493-2312-6 (alk. paper)
     1. Computer software--Development. 2. Rate of return. I. Title.

    QA76.76.D47S55 2004
    005.1--dc22

                                            2004052490

Visit the Auerbach Web site at www.auerbach-publications.com

© 2005 by CRC Press LLC
Auerbach is an imprint of CRC Press LLC

No claim to original U.S. Government works
International Standard Book Number 0-8493-2312-6
Library of Congress Card Number 2004052490
Printed in the United States of America 1 2 3 4 5 6 7 8 9 0

DEDICATION

My wife, Nidhi, my two sons, Harshvardhan and Sidhdharth,
and my parents, Inder and Phool Sikka, for love, marvel, and faith.

CONTENTS

Preface xix
About the Author.. xxiii
Acknowledgments... xxv

1   A Brief Review of Software Development History....................1
  1.1   Classic Software Development Methodologies 2
      1.1.1   Waterfall 2
            1.1.1.1   Limitations of Waterfall Model 3
      1.1.2   Incremental 3
      1.1.3   Spiral.. 4
            1.1.3.1   Feasibility Determination 5
            1.1.3.2   Lifecycle.. 5
            1.1.3.3   Initial Operational Capability Milestone 5
            1.1.3.4   Risk Exposure Assessment............................. 5
      1.1.4   Prototyping... 6
            1.1.4.1   Limitations of Prototyping 6
      1.1.5   Cleanroom.. 6
            1.1.5.1   Starting Assumptions..................................... 6
            1.1.5.2   Boxes.. 7
            1.1.5.3   Steps for Cleanroom 7
            1.1.5.4   Verification and Testing in Cleanroom....................... 8
      1.1.6   Object-Oriented 8
            1.1.6.1   Key Relationships 9
            1.1.6.2   Booch 9
            1.1.6.3   Coad and Yourdon.. 9
            1.1.6.4   Object Modeling Technique by Rumbaugh 10
            1.1.6.5   Jacobson: Objectory and OOSE................................ 10
  1.2   Evolving Software Development Methodologies 10
      1.2.1   The Agile Themes 10
            1.2.1.1   Most Effort Is Spent on Design 11
            1.2.1.2   Business Systems Are Inherently Unpredictable....... 11
            1.2.1.3   Implement, Review, Iterate............................ 11
            1.2.1.4   Developers Are More Important than Processes...... 12

1.2.2 Agile Methodologies.. 12
    1.2.2.1 eXtreme Programming 13
    1.2.2.2 Advanced Software Development........................... 15
    1.2.2.3 SCRUM.. 17
    1.2.2.4 Feature Driven Development.............................. 18
    1.2.2.5 Lean Software Development 19
    1.2.2.6 Dynamic Systems Development Method................ 22
    1.2.2.7 Crystal Family 22
    1.2.2.8 Unified Modeling Language 23
    1.2.2.9 Rational Unified Process.................................... 23
1.2.3 Model Driven Architecture 24
    1.2.3.1 Interoperability between Platforms......................... 25
    1.2.3.2 Independence from Platforms.............................. 25
    1.2.3.3 Portability 25
    1.2.3.4 Improved Communication 25
    1.2.3.5 Enhanced Return on Investment.......................... 25
1.2.4 Web Service Development 26
    1.2.4.1 The Lifecycle of Web Services 26
    1.2.4.2 Design 27
    1.2.4.3 Development.. 27
    1.2.4.4 Testing 27
    1.2.4.5 Deployment in SOAP or XML Applications.............. 27
    1.2.4.6 Execution 27
    1.2.4.7 Management.. 28
1.3 Evolutionary Predictions 28
  1.3.1 The Future of Agile Development.............................. 29
    1.3.1.1 The Agile Economy.. 29
    1.3.1.2 Agile Is a Strategic Capability 29
    1.3.1.3 Application Examples.. 30
  1.3.2 Application Trends 30
    1.3.2.1 Evolving Applications and Platforms...................... 31
    1.3.2.2 Application Integration Opportunity...................... 31
    1.3.2.3 Agile Application Integration.............................. 32
    1.3.2.4 Software Reuse 32
    1.3.2.5 Management Responsibilities............................. 32
  1.3.3 Future of Web Services Development 33
    1.3.3.1 Agile Services.. 33
    1.3.3.2 Write Once Use Anywhere............................... 33
    1.3.3.3 Self-Aware Services... 33
    1.3.3.4 Easy to Upgrade Services 33
    1.3.3.5 Loosely Coupled Scaleable Services 33
    1.3.3.6 Platform Independent Services............................ 34
1.4 Summary of Chapter 34
References.. 35

2   Software Complexity Crisis 39

2.1   Contemporary Software Development Is Multifaceted
and Complex 39
    2.1.1   Old Car and Computers Analogy 39
    2.1.2   Diverse Development Locations 40
    2.1.3   Diverse Development Teams 41
    2.1.4   Diverse Platforms 42

2.2   Market Trends Favor Diversity 42
    2.2.1   Proliferation of Software Development and
Deployment Environments 44
        2.2.1.1   Microsoft Platforms 44
        2.2.1.2   Java Platforms 45
        2.2.1.3   Open Source Platforms 45
        2.2.1.4   Mobile Platforms 46
    2.2.2   Proliferation of Software Maturity Models 47
        2.2.2.1   Software Process Models 47
        2.2.2.2   Capability Maturity Model Integrated 48
        2.2.2.3   Information Technology Infrastructure Library 50
        2.2.2.4   Control Objectives for Information Technology 53
        2.2.2.5   Product Line Model 55

2.3   Changing Role of Information Technology 60
    2.3.1   Global Software Development and Test Opportunity 61
        2.3.1.1   Widely Available Technical Training 61
        2.3.1.2   Software Development Skills are a Commodity 62
        2.3.1.3   Global Software Development and Test
Reduces Costs 62
        2.3.1.4   Entire World Is Becoming a Software Consumer 62
    2.3.2   Outsourcing and Offshoring 62
        2.3.2.1   Human Factors Are Most Important 63
        2.3.2.2   Differences from IT-Enabled and Business
Process Outsourcing 63
        2.3.2.3   Governments Can Play Constructive Role 63

2.4   Business Case for Maximizing Software ROI 63
    2.4.1   Excuses for Not Calculating ROI 64
        2.4.1.1   ROI is Wasteful Number Crunching 64
        2.4.1.2   We Do Not Have the Expertise 65
        2.4.1.3   We Will Wait Until Later 65
        2.4.1.4   ROI Will Be Positive Anyway 65
        2.4.1.5   Let Us Use Someone Else's Data 66
    2.4.2   Benefits of ROI 66
        2.4.2.1   Helps Establish Business Value 67
        2.4.2.2   Helps Establish Metrics 67
        2.4.2.3   ROI gives a Healthy Dose of Reality 68
        2.4.2.4   Helps Establish Best Practices 68
        2.4.2.5   Facilitates Data Collection 69

2.4.3   Business Value Capture Using ROI 70
    2.4.3.1   Analyze Opportunities 70
    2.4.3.2   Determine Strategy 70
    2.4.3.3   Make Decisions 70
    2.4.3.4   Manage Portfolio 70
    2.4.3.5   Continuous Improvement 71
2.4.4   Getting Ready for ROI Analysis 71
    2.4.4.1   Plan Effective Timelines 71
    2.4.4.2   Establish Performance Objectives 71
    2.4.4.3   Guard Against Over-reliance on Numbers 72
    2.4.4.4   Do Not Assume Anything 72
    2.4.4.5   Make Appropriate Investments 73
    2.4.4.6   Get Stakeholder Buy-In 73
    2.4.4.7   Get Ready to Measure, Measure, Measure 74
2.4.5   Avoiding Common ROI Mistakes 74
    2.4.5.1   Missing Strategic Vision and Stakeholder Buy-In 74
    2.4.5.2   Lack of Domain Expertise 75
    2.4.5.3   Inaccurate Assumptions 75
    2.4.5.4   Incorrect Timing 75
    2.4.5.5   Missing Risk and Cost Profile 75
    2.4.5.6   Unsubstantiated Data or Supporting Evidence 76
    2.4.5.7   Overestimating Gains 76
2.5   Summary of Chapter 76
References 77

3   Software Development ROI 79
3.1   Days of "Good Enough" Software Development Are Over 79
  3.1.1   ROI Applies to Managers and Developers Alike 81
  3.1.2   Use a Business Model 81
  3.1.3   Priority of Customers May Not Match Those of ROI 82
  3.1.4   Scalability and ROI 82
  3.1.5   Use Interfaces that Are Neutral to Technology 84
  3.1.6   Financial View of Deliverables 84
3.2   Baseline ROI 84
  3.2.1   Definition of ROI 85
  3.2.2   Components of ROI 85
    3.2.2.1   ROI Percentage 86
    3.2.2.2   ROI Factor 86
    3.2.2.3   Net Benefit 86
    3.2.2.4   Net Cost 86
    3.2.2.5   Discount Rate and Internal Rate of Return 86
    3.2.2.6   Payback Period 87
    3.2.2.7   Net Present Value 87
  3.2.3   Data Collection for ROI 88
    3.2.3.1   Timeframes of ROI 88
    3.2.3.2   Mythical 1000 Percent ROI 88

3.2.3.3 Example Case: Sales Force Automation
Application 89
3.2.3.4 Summary of Case 90
3.3 Applied ROI 90
3.3.1 Phases of Applied ROI 90
3.3.1.1 Baseline ROI Is the First Step 90
3.3.1.2 Training 91
3.3.1.3 Tools and Automation 91
3.3.1.4 Processes and Methodologies 92
3.3.1.5 Cosourcing 92
3.3.2 TCO and ROI 93
3.3.2.1 Calculating TCO 93
3.3.2.2 Steps to Calculate TCO 94
3.3.3 Methodologies of Applied ROI 94
3.3.3.1 Capability and Maturity Model 94
3.3.3.2 ISO 9001 96
3.3.3.3 Six Sigma 97
3.3.3.4 Value of Methodology to ROI 99
3.3.4 Tools and Techniques for Applied ROI 99
3.3.4.1 eXtreme Programming ROI 99
3.3.4.2 Web Services ROI 100
3.3.5 When ROI Is Hard to Quantify 101
3.3.5.1 Business Values 102
3.3.5.2 Market Share and Brand Equity 102
3.3.5.3 Competitive Pressures 102
3.3.5.4 Regulatory Environment 103
3.3.5.5 Support and Serviceability Cost 103
3.4 Summary of Chapter 103
References 104

4 The Case for Global Software Development and Testing 107
4.1 Scenarios of Global Software Development 108
4.1.1 Intraenterprise Onshore and Offshore 108
4.1.2 Extraenterprise Onshore and Offshore 109
4.2 Benefits of Global Software Development and Testing 109
4.2.1 24/7 Software Development Cycle 109
4.2.2 Diversified Talent Pool 109
4.2.3 Proximity to Software Consumers and Marketplaces 110
4.2.4 Cost Savings 110
4.2.5 Reliability through Distributed Development 110
4.2.6 Handle Peaks and Valleys in Demand 111
4.3 Technology Is the Global Enabler 111
4.3.1 Project Management Tools 111
4.3.2 Communication Tools 112
4.3.2.1 Remote Conferencing 113
4.3.2.2 Case 113

	4.3.3	Distributed Code Management and Test Tools	114
	4.3.4	Emergence of Common Standards	114
	4.3.5	Component-Based Software Architecture	114
	4.3.6	Seamless and Secure Networks	114
4.4	Success Criteria for Global Software Development and Testing		115
	4.4.1	Define Execute and Measure to a Plan	116
		4.4.1.1 Aim High	116
		4.4.1.2 Find Champions	116
		4.4.1.3 Find Stakeholders	116
		4.4.1.4 Integrate Objectives	117
	4.4.2	Management Responsibilities	117
		4.4.2.1 No Second Class Citizens	117
		4.4.2.2 Establish High Quality Hardware Infrastructure	117
		4.4.2.3 Follow Best Practices for Personnel Management	117
		4.4.2.4 Follow Best Practices for Partner Management	118
		4.4.2.5 Establish High Quality Software Infrastructure	118
	4.4.3	Personal Strategies	118
		4.4.3.1 Keep Aware of Local Regulations	118
		4.4.3.2 Patience Is a Must	119
		4.4.3.3 Rely on Global Brands	119
		4.4.3.4 Avoid Driving in Developing Countries	119
		4.4.3.5 Be Prepared for Sensory Overloads	120
		4.4.3.6 Work Hours Will Not Get Shorter	120
4.5	What to Watch Out for		120
	4.5.1	Strong Cultural Currents	121
	4.5.2	Anti-Americanism	122
	4.5.3	Varying Infrastructure and Services	122
	4.5.4	Language Barriers	123
	4.5.5	Political Issues	124
	4.5.6	Business Issues	124
		4.5.6.1 Reciprocity and Investment Laws	124
		4.5.6.2 Approval Processes	124
		4.5.6.3 Taxation Laws	125
4.6	Outsourcing and Offshoring		125
	4.6.1	Outsourcing	125
		4.6.1.1 IT Outsourcing	126
		4.6.1.2 Offshoring	126
		4.6.1.3 Offshore Software Development	126
	4.6.2	Onshore and Offshore Outsourcing Myths	127
		4.6.2.1 Internal Staff Responsibility	127
		4.6.2.2 Saving Enterprise Money	127
		4.6.2.3 Responsibility Shift	127
		4.6.2.4 Investment Requirement	128
		4.6.2.5 Management Involvement	128
		4.6.2.6 Information Protection	128
		4.6.2.7 Information Sharing	129

4.6.2.8 Cheap Low-Skilled Labor 129
4.6.2.9 Poor Working Conditions 129
4.6.2.10 Old Equipment and Software Privacy 129
4.7 Summary 130
References 131

5 Software Quality and Test ROI 133
5.1 How to Minimize Risk and Maximize Quality 133
5.1.1 Myths of Software Quality and Testing 133
5.1.1.1 Quality and Cost 133
5.1.1.2 Quality and Agile Programming 134
5.1.1.3 Software and Art 134
5.1.1.4 CMM and Management 135
5.1.1.5 Wasted Time 135
5.1.1.6 ROI and Quality 135
5.1.1.7 Shortcuts 135
5.1.2 Software Inspection Techniques 136
5.1.2.1 Testing and Inspection 136
5.1.2.2 Manual Code Inspection 137
5.1.2.3 Automated Code Inspection 137
5.1.3 Organizational Measures 138
5.1.3.1 Measure Defects to Improve Quality 138
5.1.3.2 Obtain Organization Commitment 138
5.1.3.3 Measure Organizational Success
with ROI Goals 138
5.1.3.4 Use Key Performance Indicators 138
5.1.3.5 Use Successive Rings of Applied ROI
to Improve ROI 139
5.1.4 Continuous Software Testing 139
5.1.4.1 Testing Is "Designed into" Software
Development 139
5.1.4.2 Continuous Testing Stakeholders 140
5.1.4.3 Business of Continuous Testing 140
5.1.5 Metric versus Measure and a New International Standard ... 140
5.1.5.1 Information Needs Evaluation 141
5.1.5.2 Measurement Process Resource Allocation 141
5.1.5.3 Measurement Process Planning and Execution 141
5.1.5.4 Measurement Process Evaluation, Data Capture,
and Analysis 141
5.1.5.5 Measurement Process Key Learnings and
Communication 142
5.2 Software Testing ROI 142
5.2.1 Costs of Quality and Testing 142
5.2.1.1 Defects per 1000 Lines of Code 142
5.2.1.2 Fully Loaded Tester Cost 142
5.2.1.3 Developer Time to Fix Defects 143
5.2.2 Applied ROI Considerations 143

5.2.2.1 Manual versus Automated Testing..........................143
5.2.2.2 Automated Test Tools......................................148
5.2.2.3 In-House, Outsource, or Cosource?......................150
5.2.3 Calculating Testing ROI..152
5.2.3.1 Tangible ROI Savings.......................................152
5.2.3.2 Intangible ROI Savings.....................................154
5.2.3.3 Refining the Cost Savings Model.......................155
5.3 Localization and Internationalization ROI.............................155
5.3.1 Factors for ROI Calculation.....................................157
5.3.1.1 Cost of Localization..157
5.3.1.2 Cost of Internationalization.............................159
5.3.1.3 Revenue from Localization..............................159
5.3.1.4 Nonquantifiable Factors..................................160
5.3.2 Calculating ROI of Localization...............................160
5.3.2.1 Net Benefit...161
5.3.2.2 Net Cost..161
5.3.2.3 Baseline ROI...161
5.3.3 Applied ROI Considerations....................................161
5.3.3.1 Reduce Costs..162
5.3.3.2 Understand Target Market................................162
5.3.3.3 Use Automation..162
5.3.3.4 Use Effective Process and Methodology.................163
5.3.3.5 Use Cosourcing...163
5.3.4 Localization and Internationalization ROI Summary............164
5.4 Software Training ROI..164
5.4.1 Why Training Needs ROI...165
5.4.1.1 ROI Gives Valuable Insights into Training............165
5.4.1.2 Training Provides Business Value.......................166
5.4.1.3 Training Consumes Resources...........................166
5.4.1.4 Older Models of Training Are Becoming
        Obsolete..166
5.4.1.5 Selecting the Best Training Method
        Is Important..167
5.4.2 Factors for Measuring Training................................167
5.4.2.1 During Training Factors...................................167
5.4.2.2 Post-Training Factors.....................................168
5.4.3 Calculating Training ROI..169
5.4.3.1 Net Costs...170
5.4.3.2 Net Benefits..171
5.4.3.3 Baseline ROI...173
5.4.3.4 Case..173
5.4.4 Applied ROI Considerations....................................174
5.4.4.1 Online Training..174
5.4.4.2 Outsourcing Collateral and Marketing..................175
5.4.5 Training ROI Summary...175
5.5 Summary..178
References...178

**6 How Do You Implement Global Software
Development and Testing...181**
  6.1 The Global Software Development and Testing Model 181
       6.1.1 Software Development Lifecycle.. 183
              6.1.1.1 Recognize Problem.. 183
              6.1.1.2 Analyze.. 183
              6.1.1.3 Design 183
              6.1.1.4 Implement 184
              6.1.1.5 Test 184
              6.1.1.6 Maintain.. 184
       6.1.2 QA and Testing Roadmap 184
  6.2 Product Readiness and Deployment Infrastructure 184
       6.2.1 Product Readiness 185
              6.2.1.1 Functionality/Features 185
              6.2.1.2 Localization 188
              6.2.1.3 Usability.. 188
              6.2.1.4 Reliability.. 188
              6.2.1.5 Performance 189
              6.2.1.6 Supportability.. 189
              6.2.1.7 Data Migration Issues... 189
       6.2.2 Deployment Readiness... 189
              6.2.2.1 Sizing 190
              6.2.2.2 Deployment Reviews Done?..................................... 190
              6.2.2.3 Support Infrastructure in Place? 190
       6.2.3 Development and Deployment Infrastructure 190
              6.2.3.1 Define 191
              6.2.3.2 Develop.. 191
              6.2.3.3 Build 191
              6.2.3.4 Release 192
              6.2.3.5 Deploy... 193
              6.2.3.6 Maintain.. 195
              6.2.3.7 Resource Requirements.. 195
  6.3 Selecting and Managing the Outsourcer 197
       6.3.1 Selecting the Outsourcer 198
              6.3.1.1 Project Definition.. 198
              6.3.1.2 Interview 198
              6.3.1.3 Addressing Language, Culture, and
                       Time Barriers 198
              6.3.1.4 Statement of Work and Formal Contract.................. 199
       6.3.2 Managing the Outsourcer 200
              6.3.2.1 Methods and Systems.. 201
              6.3.2.2 Goals and Tasking 202
       6.3.3 Release Candidate Certification Guidelines............................ 203
              6.3.3.1 Release Guidelines 203
              6.3.3.2 During the Project... 203
              6.3.3.3 End of the Project 203

6.4 Methodologies and Measurement 204
   6.4.1 Three Columns of Best Practices and Guidelines 204
      6.4.1.1 In-House SQA 204
      6.4.1.2 Productive Experience 204
      6.4.1.3 Costs and Timelines 206
   6.4.2 Best Practices Criteria Details 206
      6.4.2.1 Productive Experience 206
      6.4.2.2 Costs and Timeliness 207
      6.4.2.3 Outsourcing Companies 207
      6.4.2.4 Outsourcing Country 208
      6.4.2.5 Hurdles for Team Communication 208
      6.4.2.6 Language Issues 208
      6.4.2.7 Types of Testing Outsourced 209
      6.4.2.8 Replace SQA Department? 209
      6.4.2.9 Required Backgrounds of SQA and
              Testing People 209
      6.4.2.10 Standards Bodies 209
   6.4.3 Experiences of Outsourcing 210
6.5 Summary of Chapter 211
References 211

7 Case Studies 213
7.1 Anatomy of Our Case Studies 213
   7.1.1 Introduction 213
   7.1.2 Sources 213
7.2 Case 1: Developing and Testing Natural Language Systems
   for Mobile Devices 215
   7.2.1 Natural Language System Profile 215
   7.2.2 Case Introduction 215
      7.2.2.1 E-Mail Interface 215
      7.2.2.2 Wireless Web Interface 215
   7.2.3 Technical Overview 215
      7.2.3.1 Agents 216
      7.2.3.2 Networks of Agents 216
   7.2.4 Supported Platforms 216
      7.2.4.1 E-Mail Clients 216
      7.2.4.2 Browsers for Wireless Handheld Devices 216
   7.2.5 Problem Definition and Solution 217
      7.2.5.1 Functional Testing 217
   7.2.6 Test Case Example 218
   7.2.7 Testing Tools Used 218
      7.2.7.1 WebLOAD 4.51 218
      7.2.7.2 Query Builder Tool 219
      7.2.7.3 TestRunner Tool 220
      7.2.7.4 Searching Functions 220
   7.2.8 Output Results from Testing Tool 221
      7.2.8.1 Log File 221
      7.2.8.2 Report File 222

7.2.9 Bug Tracking System Tools 222
    7.2.9.1 Rational ClearQuest 223
    7.2.9.2 Bug Lifecycle 223
7.2.10 Return on Investment 224
    7.2.10.1 No Cosourcing for SQA Testing............................. 224
    7.2.10.2 Cosourcing for SQA Testing 224
7.2.11 Conclusion 225
7.3 Case 2: Global Testing of Enterprise CRM Market Leader 226
    7.3.1 CRM Company Profile 226
    7.3.2 Case Introduction 226
    7.3.3 Technical Overview of Unicode 227
        7.3.3.1 What Is Unicode? 227
        7.3.3.2 Unicode and ISO/IEC 10646 227
        7.3.3.3 Encoding Forms.. 227
    7.3.4 Supported Platforms.. 228
    7.3.5 Problem Definition and Solution 229
    7.3.6 Test Case Example 229
        7.3.6.1 Testing Scenario and System Response................... 230
    7.3.7 Verification and Validation Testing Strategies 230
        7.3.7.1 Verification Strategies 230
        7.3.7.2 Validation Strategies 231
        7.3.7.3 Sequence of Testing... 231
    7.3.8 Testing Tools Used... 232
        7.3.8.1 Automated Tools: WebLOAD 4.51 232
        7.3.8.2 Manual Tools: Microsoft Project 2000 233
    7.3.9 Bug Tracking System Tools.. 233
        7.3.9.1 DevTrack 233
        7.3.9.2 RD System... 233
    7.3.10 Remote Communication Tools Used 234
        7.3.10.1 Three Testing Sites 234
    7.3.11 ROI 234
        7.3.11.1 No Cosourcing for SQA Testing............................. 235
        7.3.11.2 Cosourcing for SQA Testing 235
    7.3.12 Case Summary 235
7.4 Book Summary 236
References.. 238

Appendix A: The Quality Assurance and Testing Process............239

Index...243

PREFACE

Bob Dylan sang, "Times, they are a-changin'."

A strategic shift has been happening in the world around us. Countries are being run as businesses with the heads of state assuming the role of chief executive officers (CEOs). Trade and business in the world economy is revolutionizing global access in ways that have never been seen. Availability of resources is becoming better and cheaper in certain parts of the world with mass communication and training mediums. The structures of products that we build are evolving to be customer-centric and are absorbing change. The natures of processes that are used to build software systems have matured and are becoming efficiency plays. The ability to change with evolving requirements, to obtain quicker returns on investment (ROIs), and to achieve faster time to market are not clichés any more, but necessary ingredients to doing business.

As customer requirements are evolving at an ever-faster pace, it is becoming important to create business value for them as quickly as possible. Requirements gathering, design, planning, building, integration, and testing have to proceed quickly. Assimilating customer feedback and requirements quickly and changing the software application iteratively based on that feedback is what delivering quickly is all about. Software development organizations that do not follow these newer trends risk being isolated from customers and losing revenue streams. Care must be exercised to not sacrifice quality in delivering quickly. Quality should be an integral part of the development process and embraced by one and all. Ability to repeatedly develop and deploy high quality software indicates maturity of a good software organization. Every iteration of a software product should have a carefully planned milestone and review meetings that determine how effectively that milestone was met. Resource allocations and tasks for individual resources are monitored to empower individual team members to deliver consistently.

More corporations than ever are asking questions such as the following:

- How do I maximize my software ROI?
- What are the other successful companies like mine doing?
- What best practices do they use?
- What are the benefits of globalization?
- What are the benefits of outsourcing?
- Will my team or group lose key competency if we outsource?
- How do I maximize quality and predictability of software developed?
- What are the available software development methodologies?

This book is the result of my 16 years of experience working with large and small software groups both within global Fortune 50 corporations and 10 person start-ups. Utilizing both in-house and outsourced services from multiple geographical locations, I have gained the experience crystallized in this book.

My desire is to present one location where everything relating to software development, testing, and maximizing ROI can be viewed. This book is not a reference manual, but rather a friendly and knowledgeable guide that can help readers navigate effectively. Several references are provided for those who want more details of particular topics.

The book contains descriptions of the roles, teams, work products, activities, metrics, and so on that readers will need. Readers are encouraged to fit it to their projects. That tuning is also in the methodology.

This book contains practical suggestions for improving productivity, selecting the best global team or partner, getting a team to communicate better, and getting individuals to work better. The underpinnings of software development ROI, testing and localization ROI, training ROI, global development and testing, and why sometimes it is actually possible to combine cost savings with improving quality are discussed.

This book is about Applied ROI, a value-added methodology suited for small and large teams of software development and testing teams located in one place or across the world. This book gives tools and techniques to readers about how to execute best quality software development and testing while maximizing business value. It discusses Applied ROI in the context of Six Sigma, Capability Maturity Model® (CMM®), Total Cost of Ownership (TCO), and other relevant methodologies. It talks about what is important in global teams and how to choose the partners wisely. It provides models and metrics along with detailed case studies to explore and improve both existing and future development. It takes the view that quality improvement through software quality assurance (SQA) and testing, planning, and execution is a powerful route toward maximizing software ROI.

SCOPE

This book describes the criteria, roles, teams, values, intentions, habits, activities, policies, and work products of a software development and testing project in which time-to-market and cost are key considerations. It helps identify multiple ways in which cost dollars can be extended for increased ROI. It views quality and testing as central to software development and embraces the latest methodologies both formal and Agile. It explains to readers how to manage globalization of software development and applies to the teams already engaged in global development and those just starting out or considering it. The book will be successful if it can convey to its readers that good software development and quality are never accidents and require:

- Rigorous processes
- Meticulous planning
- Attention to detail
- Tight interaction with customers to stay focused

READERS

This book will be useful for software development and information technology (IT) managers, IT specialists, developers and test engineers, quality inspectors, chief information officers (CIOs), and users looking for best practices. Team members just starting on a project or those in the middle of a project may read this book. It may be read by those who are already using ROI methodologies or those just beginning to use it. It is equally useful to those already outsourcing or considering it.

It is not, however, an introductory text in the sense of an introductory text speaking to people who have never run a software project and want to learn the issues in running one. It is an intermediate text in the sense that readers are expected to have participated in one or several projects before and have an idea of how projects run and how they fail.

For those people, the book picks out which of the many issues confronting them are the key ones to pay attention to when setting up team conventions. Some conventions are so localized to the specific team and technology being used that it makes no sense to try to capture them in a mass-market book. The book mentions which those are. The team leader and the team are expected to create those on their own.

Some people find it useful to start with explicit mathematical formulae, spreadsheet calculators, and rules of ROI and global team development. They can review references contained herein and then return to get a global perspective and experience of how to implement Applied ROI.

For the team lead and team members of small or large teams, this book is intended to be read initially in a quick read and then later used as a reference. The average project in the ROI category can be small or large. It typically has a team lead, who acts as process designer, manager, architect, lead designer, and teacher. It has development staff and testers who may or may not all be located in the same geographical location. It may be interacting with one or more outsourcers and consultants.

ORGANIZATION

The book is written in seven chapters. Chapter 1 reviews the software development, tools, and methodologies landscape. Chapter 2 explores how complexity in software development, maintenance, and integration has exploded and will continue to diversify. We discuss the best practices for managing this complexity and discuss the business case for maximizing ROI.

After the first two chapters, ROI is examined from several sides. First there is the question of nomenclature — do we have to comply, what can we change and still say we comply, why do we care to use the correct nomenclature and calculation methods? Then there is the matter of project failure — what did we do wrong? Some people will want a full exploration of the mathematics, processes, work products, and techniques involved. Some will want to read stories of ROI in action. Some will want to know how to get started and how to extend it.

Near the end, in the examination of the global software development and testing, come key lessons based on interviews and checklists to make a global team successful and Applied ROI implementation complete. Case studies are included for software development and testing for several different types of systems including wireless, mobile, enterprise, and customer relationship management systems.

ABOUT THE AUTHOR

Vijay Sikka has worked in software development and quality for more than 16 years. This includes 8 years at Intel Corporation headquarters in Santa Clara, California, developing real-time software quality, analysis, Six Sigma, and statistical process control (SPC) systems for worldwide manufacturing. In 1996, he founded IBrain Software, Inc. and served as its CEO until its acquisition by Entigen Corp. in 1998 (later part of Roche). In 1999, Vijay started Bodha.com, Inc. and served on its board of directors until its acquisition by Peregrine Systems (Remedy), a NASDAQ traded company, in 2002. He built international software quality teams and engineering organizations with successful multiyear operations. He is an advisor and a consultant to several San Francisco bay area companies. Vijay holds a master's degree in Artificial Intelligence from Syracuse University, New York. He dropped out of Stanford University's Ph.D. program after 4 years to start his first company. He is a frequent speaker at conferences on software quality and participates in the World Wide Web Consortium (W3C) quality group. He has published journal and conference papers on software quality and applied for patents on information integration and summarization.

Vijay is the president and CEO of Sikka Software Corporation (www.sikkasoft.com), located in San Jose, California. He can be reached at vijay@sikka.org.

ACKNOWLEDGMENTS

I thank lots of people, most of whom do not know they said something of value, many of whom started off by saying, "we don't use ROI here, we just …," or "I'm sorry, we don't bother to do …," or "we do quality at the end of the project," or "what? … outsourcing improves my methodology? No I don't buy that …"

People who have commented and helped include Anurag Khemka, my friend from Nirixa days, the test case contributors in IBrain, and Gen. R.K. Joshi for his support in understanding the outsourced operation. I want to thank Professor (Emeritus) Gio Wiederhold and Professor (deceased) David Stevenson from Stanford University and Professor Pramod K. Varshney from Syracuse University for helping shape my graduate academic career.

I thank my sister-in-law Vandana and nephew Vishwakarma for intelligence and charm. Above all, thanks to Dr. Vishal Sikka, my brother, friend, philosopher, and guide, for advice and the liveliest of discussions on software, technology, trends, and the world in general.

1

A BRIEF REVIEW
OF SOFTWARE
DEVELOPMENT HISTORY

Software is defined by Cambridge Advanced Learner's Dictionary as "the instructions which control what a computer does; computer programs." Using that definition we can say that the first software was developed in 1937 by George Stibitz of the Bell Telephone Laboratories (Bell Labs), New York City, when he constructed a demonstration 1-bit binary adder using relays. This adding machine was followed in November 1939 by John V. Atanasoff and graduate student Clifford Berry's prototype 16-bit adder at Iowa State University. This was the first machine to calculate using vacuum tubes. In 1951, Grace Murray Hopper invented the first high level language compiler and then in 1957 Fortran (Formula Translation Language) was developed by John Backus and his team at IBM. Software development became possible for a large number of people. The first areas where software development was focused were military uses such as cryptography and ballistics in addition to solving scientific problems.

Several programming languages were invented in subsequent decades, including LISP (List Processing) and COBOL (Common Business-Oriented Language) in 1960, APL (A Programming Language), PL/1 (Programming Language 1) and Pascal in 1961, 1964, and 1971, respectively, and C programming language that was developed in 1972 at the Bell Laboratories by Dennis Ritchie (also a coinventor of UNIX® operating system). Widespread use of these and other programming languages ushered in an era of software development methodologies.

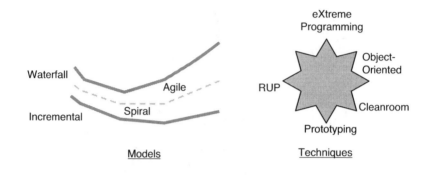

Figure 1.1   Popular Software Development Methodologies

1.1   CLASSIC SOFTWARE DEVELOPMENT METHODOLOGIES

Over the past three decades a large number of software development methodologies have been developed and in this book we will not be able to discuss all of them. Some significant software development models such as Waterfall, Incremental, and Spiral, and most recently Agile will be discussed in more details. We will also discuss in more detail software development techniques including Waterfall, Prototype, Spiral, Cleanroom, Object-Oriented, Rational Unified Process (RUP), and eXtreme Programming (XP). Together the models and techniques constitute software development methodologies as described in Figure 1.1.

1.1.1   Waterfall

The Waterfall Model was modeled after development of complex hardware systems and is a classic top-down development model. This approach to software development emphasized that software development be undertaken in phases. Each phase, once completed, established a baseline of product development and any change required a formal change management process, as shown in Figure 1.2. Phases of software development resembled the downward flow of a waterfall, hence the name of the model. Different phases are illustrated as boxes and documentation and a formal review and approval cycle was required for each phase transition. Audits were conducted with the product completion phase. The model was useful and influential in its early days. Several other models were built to fine-tune or adapt the Waterfall Model of software development, as we will discuss later [1].

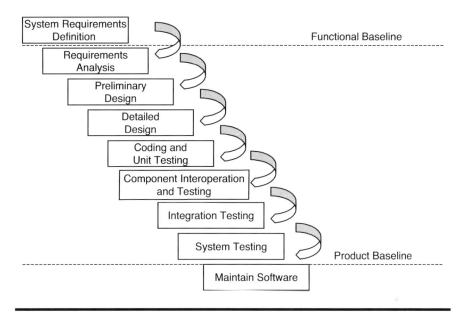

Figure 1.2 The Waterfall Model

1.1.1.1 Limitations of Waterfall Model

The analogy of hardware and software could, however, be taken only so far. Software development is characterized by several factors that are unique and different. For example, sometimes requirements are not well understood before the start of development and continuous refinement of each phase is required [2].

1.1.2 Incremental

Usable functionality is achieved quickly in the Incremental model. This happens by overlapping sections in the Waterfall Model, as illustrated in Figure 1.3. This reduces the cycle time of completion of the projects and the projects are split into several smaller ones. These small projects can be completed independently as a result of clearly defined requirements. If the requirements are not clear, projects can be completed as the objectives become better defined. As a result, the requirement on interfaces between different modules became rigid and formal reviews became difficult to implement. This was the shortcoming of the Incremental model.

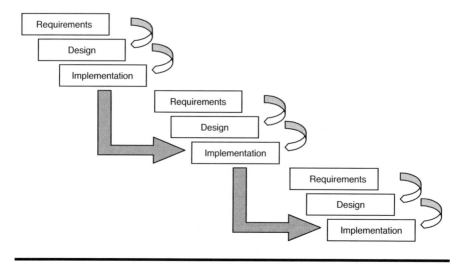

Figure 1.3 The Incremental Model

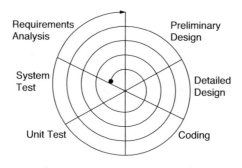

Figure 1.4 The Basic Spiral Model

1.1.3 Spiral

Aerospace, defense, and semiconductor engineering [3] software developers adopted the Spiral model effectively. The Spiral Model (Figure 1.4) embodies requirement and risk analysis followed by prototyping, requirements and design validation, development, integration test, and deployment. The resources could stay constant among these tasks or could be increased as a variation Boehm Spiral Model suggested [4,5]. Boehm's Spiral Model emphasizes evolutionary development where each step is implemented using the Waterfall Model. The system being developed does not have to be defined entirely at first and risks are better managed.

Features of the highest priority are defined and implemented first. The feedback gained from showing those features to the customers enables better definition and finer granularity implementation of features. This activity can also be represented in phases with defined milestones.

1.1.3.1   Feasibility Determination

Through customers and stakeholder meetings, determine the feasibility of the application. Get the requirements definition clarified.

1.1.3.2   Lifecycle

- Lifecycle objectives milestone — develop prototypes, plans, and detailed specifications of applications and determine architectures suitable for implementation.
- Lifecycle architecture milestone — risk assessment is done to determine whether the architecture will enable building the application using the lifecycle objectives.

1.1.3.3   Initial Operational Capability Milestone

Build a working version to show to the customers for feedback and assessment. Change management, customer expectation management and satisfaction, and business value must be taken into account at the milestones and phases of spiral model.

1.1.3.4   Risk Exposure Assessment

Risk exposure assessment is critical in a Spiral Model and is done to determine project error risk due to delay and over or under effort. This assessment applies to all phases of the spiral development described earlier. Risk assessment determines the amount of definition that needs to be prebuilt during the planning and specification phases. Higher risk activities would be those that cannot be defined well in advance or may not meet the user requirements when implemented. Examples of activities that can be deferred are graphical user interface (GUI) definitions and such. However, there are cases related to interfacing different vendor applications as well as safety applications that need a high degree of specifications even if the risk assessment may be high. A case in point is the classic Mars probe failure where two subcontractors of NASA had used different measurement systems, one English and another one metric and the software flaw caused the loss of the lander.

1.1.4 Prototyping

Most techniques described in the section below can be applied to any model described earlier. Prototyping is the process of building a mock-up or throw-away functional equivalent of a system. A requirements list or some functional description is received from the customer and the prototype is created. The prototype is then reviewed and analyzed to get more detailed requirements. The intention is to enable a lower cost feasibility phase to understand the problem better.

1.1.4.1 Limitations of Prototyping

Prototyping, however, should be done carefully because it has several limitations. These include the following:

- Prototype should never be used as a product because it is not designed, implemented, and tested to withstand rigors of actual use.
- Prototypes have poor documentation.
- Prototypes lack performance and may also promise a better feature set than what can be implemented in the product.
- Prototype is usually not well tested and so may have bugs causing a negative impression on the prospective customer.

1.1.5 Cleanroom

Cleanroom [6] was pioneered at IBM and has grown up from a good academic idea to a successful practice. The technique uses more formal notations to produce specifications and decomposes a problem into black boxes of mathematical functions. The idea is to keep software bugs out of the product by detecting them early when the costs of repair are low. Software testing in Cleanroom focuses on statistically verifying that all possible inputs to the mathematical functions are processed correctly. Cleanroom enforces that developers are not testing and need a complete set of requirements. Software development and testing is done within a statistical quality control framework. The software development process uses mathematical models to ensure correctness of design and software reliability is attempted using statistical processes. This enables formal certification when the software is ready to be delivered.

1.1.5.1 Starting Assumptions

Motivation of Cleanroom Model follows the ideas of semiconductor fabrication in a Cleanroom environment with extensive air quality and purity controls. The management has better and more objective visibility of the software development once the statistical quality control is in place.

- Spend time and resources upfront to identify and prevent defects
- State requirements formally
- Enforce and ensure quality using statistical methods

Cleanroom departs from other methods of software development because it suggests technical reviews and formal inspections before and during software development as opposed to after implementation.

1.1.5.2   Boxes

As we mentioned earlier, in Cleanroom, a problem is decomposed into several boxes. Box structures map inputs and the historical inputs into outputs. There are three key box structures that need to be mentioned here:

1. Black box — data and process implementations are completely hidden and only functional descriptions are used. A formal specification language is used for these descriptions.
2. State box — data implementation is visible, but process implementation is hidden.
3. Clear box — clear view of data and process implementation is available and the intention is to facilitate incremental refinement and continuous improvement.

1.1.5.3   Steps for Cleanroom

Software development begins with a functional and performance requirements specification. In addition, design and verification techniques are built in along with the design and usage of users functions. Verification for correctness forms an important step before software is put to work. Separate teams that have experience in statistical testing do this verification and certification. Reliability estimates are generated for final configuration and deployment environments.

- Requirements analysis — this step is the first one as discussed earlier where teams gather to describe the functions and specifications of the application.
- Detailed design — full design is produced using formal methodologies including state machines and nested functions based on the requirements analysis. The underlying tenets in Cleanroom are

that programs can be designed by decomposing their function specifications. Programs can be verified and tested by abstracting and comparing their designed functions to their function specifications in requirements analysis for similarity.

■ Coding without compiling — code generation and implementation is undertaken without compilation or inline testing. Effort is made toward verification of the code using formal and informal methods.

■ Test cases without testing — based on requirements definition step, test cases for the code are generated. The development team does not undertake testing.

■ Statistical testing — separate teams that also compile and link the code undertake formal testing. Testing and verification reports are generated based on test cases. We will discuss later in this book the CMM. Cleanroom and CMM are complementary and compatible. Both insist on software engineering driven development, high quality through statistical testing, and focus on creating correct and verifiable software.

1.1.5.4   Verification and Testing in Cleanroom

Richard Linger [7] discussed the Correctness Theorem to be met for achieving correct software in Cleanroom. This correctness verification by the development team takes place before testing can begin and is done with respect to specifications. Development team reviews are the venue for these verifications. Individual control constructs are verified instead of all the program flows. This verification step is effective in reducing defects and provides the primary thrust of quality improvements in Cleanroom.

Statistical testing and software certification is based on usage models that define all possible scenarios of use and their probabilities of occurrence. Different environments are accounted for by different usage models. The most popular model for automatic test case generation and usage model analysis is the Markov Model [8]. Statistical usage testing on randomly generated test cases from usage models detects errors with high failure rates.

1.1.6   Object-Oriented

The Object-Oriented approach to software development is becoming more popular with increasing complexity of software systems. This approach equates components in software development with real-world objects [9]. Object-Oriented includes object-oriented analysis (OOA), design (OOD), and programming (OOP) [10–12].

In comparing the definition of traditional analysis with that of object-oriented analysis and design (OOAD), the key aspect is to think about the world and the problem domain in terms of objects and classes. A class is any uniquely identified abstraction (i.e., model) of a set of logically related instances that share the same or similar characteristics. An object is an instantiation of a class (i.e., a single thing). Classes have attributes and methods. Attributes have data about the objects and methods are how the data in the object can be used. For an object class named `Account`, an attribute might be `Name` and methods might be `Add`, `Update`, `Delete`, and `Validate`. The class definition defines the `Account` class attributes and methods; a real account such as "324125" is an instance of the class. If you have different kinds of accounts, such as brokerage account, bank account, or mortgage account, you can create three new classes of accounts that are descendants of the `Account` class. These descendants use inheritance to gain access to all of the `Account` class attributes and methods, but can override any of the ancestor attributes and methods, as well as contain any required new attributes and methods.

1.1.6.1 Key Relationships

There are three types of relationships between classes — inheritance, aggregation, and association. Inheritance (also referred to as generalization or specialization) is usually identified by the phrase "is a" or "a kind of." For example, dog and cat are both a kind of animal and are therefore inherited from the `Animal` class. Aggregation is identified by the phrase "is a part of," as with a product that contains parts. If neither of the first two relationships applies, but the objects are clearly related (for example, an employee is associated with a company), then the relationship is association.

1.1.6.2 Booch

Grady Booch [13] defined one of the most popular approaches to OOAD and has since continued his work on evolving methodologies at Rational Software, now part of IBM. The approach was tightly linked with C++ in its initial days, but evolved to support newer tools and languages. Booch's design method and notation consisted of four major activities and six notations, and it was strong on requirements design and definition.

1.1.6.3 Coad and Yourdon

Coad and Yourdon published the first practical and reasonably complete books on OOAD [14,15]. Their methodology focused on analysis of business problems and used a friendlier notation than that of Booch, Shlaer, and Mellor or the others that were focusing more on design.

1.1.6.4 Object Modeling Technique by Rumbaugh

James Rumbaugh's methodology, as described in his book [16], was strong on the object-oriented analysis methodology. Design and construction was not covered in great detail. A large number of ideas and approaches formed a solid bedrock for use by analysts, architects, and programmers.

1.1.6.5 Jacobson: Objectory and OOSE

Jacobson's full OOAD methodology, Objectory, supported the entire software development lifecycle. Good examples and useful discussion enabled designers and programmers to build large-scale systems serving key business problems. Jacobson's Object-Oriented Software Engineering (OOSE) is a simplified version of Objectory, which Jacobson himself has declared inadequate for production applications [17]. Use case definitions with diagram and descriptions of single interaction between actor and a system along with exception handling formed a key part of Objectory notation. Actor was defined as an end user or some other machine object in the system. Usage scenarios and user requirements that were captured this way helped define the communication and interfaces of the programs. This was then converted into an analysis model by classifying the domain objects into three types — interface objects, entity objects, and control objects.

1.2 EVOLVING SOFTWARE DEVELOPMENT METHODOLOGIES

1.2.1 The Agile Themes

Several software development methodologies described earlier are considered bureaucratic, insensitive to developers, and overly assuming of the homogeneity of the development environment. Methodologies have been described to slow down the pace of software development and increase time spent in reviews and documentation. As an alternative to some of these methodologies, a new group emerged which people referred to as lightweight or adaptive. Since the meeting in Snowbird, Utah in 2000, they have been referred to as Agile Methodologies.

We will be looking at the Agile Model [18] in much more detail later on in this book. For the purposes of introduction, here is a summary. Agile is a collection of models that have often been referred to as lightweight and adaptive methods as opposed to heavyweight assessment standards such as CMM that we will also review in more detail later. In the context of ever-changing requirements, diverse development and deployment environments, and quicker product cycles, the focus is shifting to faster implementation methods and people rather than processes and documentation.

Agile methods are less document intensive, more people oriented, and suggest more pragmatic approach to design and implementation. Change is embraced as an inevitable, so less emphasis is given to longer term planning. Agile Methodologies embrace several common themes as outlined below.

1.2.1.1 Most Effort Is Spent on Design

As Steve McConnell suggests in his book [19], the bulk of the time spent on software development projects (more than 50 percent) is on design. Design is where most talented people should be utilized and the creativity of software development process must be acknowledged. Software development is not an engineering activity such as construction, a metaphor widely used in the previous methodologies. This leads us to the next theme about predictability.

1.2.1.2 Business Systems Are Inherently Unpredictable

Consequently, the requirements that arise out of the business systems for software development change through the product development cycle. Changing requirements should not be perceived as a surprise or a shortcoming of the business system, rather it is the norm. Software development should be adaptive enough to change with it.

1.2.1.3 Implement, Review, Iterate

Rapid iterative development has been around for a long time — Incremental, Evolutionary, Staged, Spiral, and Agile are all variations of it. The key to iterative development is to frequently implement working versions of the intended system that have a partial set of the required features. These working versions lack all the functionality, but are faithful to the demands of the intended system. They are integrated and tested just as a completed system would be.

Reviewing a tested, integrated system brings a dose of reality into any project. Documents and untested code can hide all sorts of flaws. But when people actually sit in front of a system and work with it, then flaws become obvious: both in terms of issues and features.

Rapid iterative development is essential in Agile processes because an Agile process needs to be able to deal with changes in required features. This leads to a style of planning where long-term plans are relatively fluid, unlike the short-term plans made for a single iteration. Iterative development gives a solid foundation in each iteration to base subsequent plans on. Implement, review, and iterate cycles keep the developers close to the requirements and the system being developed does not get unwieldy.

1.2.1.4 Developers Are More Important than Processes

Alistair Cockburn [20] identified how developers are better predictors of project behavior and methodology success than other methodological factors. The notion of developers as unique contributors to the success of a development project is a departure from uniform process and component-based project-planning disciplines. This also changes some of the decision making. For example, XP states that only developers may make estimates on how much time it will take to do some work.

Several techniques are grouped as Agile Methodologies. Some of these will be discussed later in this book including XP, Crystal Family by Alistair Cockburn [21], Scrum [22], Feature Driven Development (FDD), Advanced Software Development (ASD) or Rapid Application Development (RAD), and Dynamic System Development Method (DSDM) among others.

1.2.2 Agile Methodologies

In this section, we will discuss the major Agile Methodologies. Project management, collaboration, and communication are the foci of some Agile approaches such as Scrum, ASD, and DSDM. Others focus on software development and optimization such as XP. A common theme among the Agile Methodologies is testing while in development. Table 1.1 describes

Table 1.1 Agile Methodologies Key Highlights

	ASD	*FDD*	*DSDM*	*XP*	*Scrum*
Focus	Product visioning				
Plan	Project data sheet	Feature planning			
Feedback	Focus groups		Workshops	Pair programming	Daily short meetings
Optimize				Refactoring	

Agile Methodologies in a summary form. In this section, we will discuss all the Agile Methodologies in much greater detail.

1.2.2.1 eXtreme Programming

XP is arguably the most popular and high profile Agile process and was developed by Kent Beck, Ward Cunningham, and Ron Jeffries. XP evolved as a result of developers and testers seeking new ways of delivering high quality reliable software while avoiding excessively formal procedures. XP also addresses the key requirement in modern times of applications that can be quickly and flexibly developed in tune with customer requirements.

- Business oriented stories — use cases are defined based on small and manageable feature requirements from the customer. These use cases or stories are prioritized with the help of business and customer teams.
- Iteration — implementation of the top use cases forms the first iteration. Pair programming practice means two people code together on one machine. A short-term completion target is maintained for each iteration, usually a couple of weeks. Iteration is complete when the first set of use cases is tested and productized. The cycle then repeats with next set of use cases.
- Testing — unit tests are written prior to beginning coding. System level test cases are prepared with customers. Each iteration is put into production only after unit and system testing is completed. Integration of small releases is continuous and takes place every time an iteration is completed. Let us examine key drivers for XP and its impact on software development projects.
  - Simplify, do not generalize — it is not necessary to generalize if the problem can be solved simply. Testing and staying close to the customer helps determine priority of features and those should be implemented first rather than a generalized framework.
  - Change is your friend — flexibility in implementation is basic to XP. If the code can meet the customer's requirements today, it should be easily changeable to meet the customer's requirement tomorrow. Change is a way of life. Staying connected with customers and iterating early keeps the focus on business needs. Keeping regular and timely iterations going to customers for review is an essential process of development and keeping the costs low.
  - Two pairs of eyes are better than one — pair programming is an important driver for XP. Pair programming integrates code

review with development. Better adherence to coding standards, reuse, and staying close to the customer's requirements becomes possible when two developers are looking at the code. As we will discuss later, this also helps another important driver — refactoring, which is reviewing the code to be as simple and elegant as possible while meeting the requirements. Knowledge sharing, best practices, and change are better embraced using pair programming.

– Refactoring is effective — code can be simplified and made more elegant while meeting or exceeding the requirements of the customer. That is the XP belief behind refactoring. The idea is to revise code segments and refine the implementation until it becomes the simplest possible. Spaghetti code is hard to understand and causes problems with maintainability and reliability. Refactoring goes hand in hand with the fact that change is a way of life and requirements from the customer will continuously evolve. Bringing the code to the most optimal in implementation and design helps meet the requirement of continuous improvement effectively. Refactoring is the means to achieving better design while maintaining flexibility for change.

– Testing is ensuring — XP fosters continuous testing and test planning before coding. Testing does not come after coding, but rather precedes it. Features are written with test cases in mind. This enables building the library of test cases as the development is progressing and also improves the quality of code written. Coding with test planning done in advance enables regression testing because new features or optimizations in the code can be tested to comply. It is important to automate the tests so time required in testing is reduced.

– Make the customer work — traditionally customers are given the application only when it is completely developed. This often leads to making even the well-meaning customer unhappy. Requirements evolve continuously and the finished application may be too far off from what the customer was really looking for. The role of the customer in XP is reversed from being a critic to being a participant in the implementation. Customers are involved from the beginning and the features implemented with each iteration are tested by them or demonstrated to them. This keeps the customers in the loop and their feedback and buy-in is continuously maintained. Essentially the customer is working to help make the finished product. Progress is easily measured and control on the development process is better maintained with customer involvement.

- Manage expectations — managing expectations takes many forms. Programmers are required to manage expectations of their project leaders — so that they can be accurate in project planning and task completion. Managing expectations of customers is another requirement and as we discussed earlier, making them part of the testing process helps. Domain expertise of the customer helps ensure the usability of the applications being developed. Managing expectation becomes easier if project leaders and customers are involved in reviews and implementation discussions. This helps different constituencies understand the roles that the other is playing and the effort the other is putting into make the project succeed. It helps communicate the issues, roadblocks, and delays in implementation easier and provides an environment conducive to effective software development. XP advises to be upfront about communication and managing expectations. It is important to make customers and management part of the application development team and that helps improve success rates of projects.
- Prioritize for efficiency — XP fosters the discipline of efficiency. Note that this does not mean cutting corners, avoiding design, structure or documentation, and specifications. Efficiency is achieved by setting correct priorities with customer and management feedback. Staying close to the customer priorities makes the product relevant. Staying close to development priorities enables cost control and makes the product more robust. Prioritization enables focus on the lowest hanging fruits and biggest returns. It also encourages a developer to identify the most important problem areas and issues and to attack them first. Prioritization helps the developer manage his or her time effectively and helps keep project on track. XP also encourages 40 hour weeks with the philosophy that if the development team is doing things right, people will not need to spend extra long hours and burn midnight oil.

1.2.2.2 Advanced Software Development

In several ways, RAD or ASD, a notion first pioneered by Jim Highsmith, is the mother of all Agile Methodologies. This revolutionary approach of time fostered rapid development, testing, and customer feedback was intended to address the changing times with faster and better computers and compilers available as well as evolving customer requirements. Software development culture was undergoing a sea of change: going from large monolithic programs to smaller nimble applications intended to address specific needs. Older programming languages and practices changed to the newer and faster approaches that allowed individual developers to produce and deploy new applications with speed and flexibility. In this section, we discuss some key attributes of ASD.

■ Detailed planning is counterproductive — RAD or ASD developed out of prototyping (see Section 1.1.4), Spiral, and other models and appealed to quick turnaround environments. ASD asserts that planning is impossible in a fast changing business environment where several players including customers, management, suppliers, and competitors are constantly interacting and influencing. Developing mechanisms to constantly evaluate the changing technology and market-need landscape should replace large planning efforts. Teamwork should replace isolationist development efforts and constant learning should be emphasized. Change management and flexibility should be given top priorities in the sometimes chaotic environments of software development and delivery today.

■ Customer is king — ASD advocates a customer oriented and customer driven development organization. This ensures continuous improvement, successful project management, customer satisfaction, quality solutions, and flexibility. Customer orientation also enables improvements in processes and methodologies that are key to improving the quality of products. ASD advocates complete transformations of development organizations to become customer oriented. In ASD, customer orientation is managed by Joint Application Development (JAD), focus groups, and surveys. As we will see later, evolutionary product development enables customer feedback to be appropriate and timely as well as to engage the customers in the development process.

■ Rehash development process — ASD suggests removing hurdles of hierarchy and administrative approvals from software development. It was developed as a result of growing frustration with waterfall type models that insisted on reliance on bureaucratic processes in software development. ASD emphasized the speed of software completion and deployment to customers. For that reason, it suggested rehashing the software development process if needed. Visions of ASD included product orientation, smart project management skills, evolutionary product development, and continuous improvement.

■ Product development should be evolutionary — as mentioned previously, waterfall type methodologies were based on construction practices and assumed stages of software development and precise planning. Customers were only allowed to view completed products. Requirements were static and product development took long cycle times. In RAD or ASD, all of this is reversed. Product cycle times are much shorter, flexibility and change requirements are much higher, customers need to be involved in the evaluation of products and earlier versions on an ongoing basis, and plans are continuously evolving. With evolving requirements and resources, product development should also be evolutionary. Early versions are delivered to customers for feedback and evaluation. Underlying data structures are continuously refined and updated. Major failures and cost overruns are averted by diligent step-by-step implementation and testing.

ASD emphasized the need for appropriate stakeholders for a project, consultative project management, teamwork, articulated goals and objectives, and careful addressing of risks and rewards. ASD manages predictability of systems by using a complexity theory.

1.2.2.3   SCRUM

The term Scrum originates from rugby where team members come together for a quick huddle and possession of the ball. The methodology gained acceptance in the context of Agile methods, because it emphasized regular and short meetings, communication, teamwork, and change management. Scrum emphasizes key process elements as repeatable patterns. Productivity is achieved by building on these key elements. These are discussed in more detail below.

- Meetings — also referred to as Scrum meetings are the core of Scrum because they form the basis of all communication and information flow. The group comes together for Scrum meetings and discusses everything from roadblocks to issues, progress, and schedules.
- Backlog — this is a list of prioritized requirements from the customer. This list continuously evolves and should account for updated emphasis and change. Developers and business folks can add to this list and product and project management is allowed to update and change the status and priorities of the list in consultation with the customer.
- Sprints — scheduling is maintained in Sprints, which indicates the basic unit of development activity. This is usually four to six weeks. A feature set from the Backlog that needs to be completed during the Sprint is identified and worked on. Prioritization during Sprint of the feature set is maintained constant and when the development

is completed, it is shown to the customer for feedback. Backlog is then updated based on the result of the Sprint by the product manager.

1.2.2.4 Feature Driven Development

FDD advocates building an object model and then iteratively updating it using feature driven design. It consists of several steps outlined below:

1. Model development — customers or domain experts determine the scope of the system and its activities. Following that, teams comprising developers and customers build object models. These models are combined to make a composite model that will later be refined. Functional requirements are studied and discussed in peer review sessions. Alternatives are documented for use in later stages or revisions of the project.

2. Feature development — all features needed for the project using functional requirements and customer discussion are captured. Different functional areas and classifications are identified. Care is taken to keep features in manageable sizes and not too fine or not too coarse. If the features will take longer than two to three weeks, then they are split further into smaller features. This feature list is then prioritized with the participation of the development team management. The prioritization depends on resources, interdependencies of features, and implementation and refinement requirements. A detailed plan is then prepared by allocating the features to development resources. Notice that prioritization is done by the development team rather than the customer as in some other Agile Methodologies, such as XP.

3. Feature design — assigned features are picked up by the development resources and then refined. Object models are updated based on this refinement. Design implementation is begun and several features may be grouped together depending on reuse. Number and types of features may be updated at this point. All the design specifications and interface specifications are discussed and finalized. Versioning of the design is done and alternative designs are identified and cataloged with pros and cons of each. Interface documentations are prepared with the completion of all design elements of objects and methods. Reviews are held to discuss and finalize decisions as well as to generate feedback for further refinement. The development plan is then updated based on evolving assumptions.

4. Feature implementation — using the design step and all the objects and method descriptions generated at that time, coding is started. Unit testing and inspection are incorporated in the implementation activity. Individual developers take their portions of the features to be implemented and complete coding based on the requirements outlined in the first two steps. Inspections are the gates before the code is integrated and source controlled. Further iterations are undertaken based on feedback and input from the customers and domain experts. Alternative designs and development are considered if there are problems with the implementation.

1.2.2.5 Lean Software Development

Bob Charette's Lean Software Development (LD) [23] was inspired by Japanese automobile manufacturing industry's just-in-time manufacturing and other recent lean manufacturing principles. It is a top-down approach where recommendation is made to change organizational strategy to conform to radical assumptions of significantly lower costs, defect rates, and time to implement. It is suggested that the software applications should be developed quicker before the customer's requirements. LD is characterized by the belief that maturity is not measured by the administrative procedures of documentation and plans. It is measured by the efficiency of the processes and operations, which in turn is achieved by the speed of delivery of consistent and reliable products and services to the customer. LD assumes that working too hard to predict delivery schedules and quality is counterproductive. Change tends to break practices that are based on speculation of delivery schedules and milestones. LD encourages basing decisions on facts rather than forecasts and delaying decisions until as late as possible while encouraging change and quicker delivery schedules.

Lean principles can be organized into a few categories as identified below. As mentioned earlier, these have been applied over the last couple of decades in automobile manufacturing, healthcare, and construction industries. Care must be taken to adapt these appropriately to the environment.

■ Start quickly and deliver quickly — starting as quickly as possible perhaps even before all the definition is complete. Get all the stakeholders to buy into the project early and communicate often with all concerned parties. This principle does not advocate rushing in with poor requirements or incomplete specifications. It assumes that if too much time is spent on fine-tuning all the definitions and specifications, the underlying requirements may have changed. It encourages gathering requirements and user needs throughout the development. It also seeks to remove the middlemen who may be collecting requirements from customers and passing them on to the development teams resulting in lost product relevance. Software application design and architecting in lean development is a joint activity between the experts from both the customer and development teams. Source control, version control, tracking and maintaining effective control over bugs, and good software engineering practices are required for successful LD software organizations.

■ Curb wasteful practices — features that are not required by customers, defects, and too much hierarchy are examples of wasteful practices. Algorithms that are not implemented optimally and code that wastes memory utilization are also examples of wasteful practices. Flow of results to the customer should be streamlined and wasteful practices including middlemen and irrelevant interface elements and features should be removed. All user interfaces and processes should be evaluated with business value in mind, and feedback should be sought from actual users as early in the process as possible. Identifying the customer flow and walk-through should be conducted to identify problem areas and bottlenecks. Milestones accomplished should be evaluated against plans and adjustments made accordingly. Time taken to process customer requests and response times should be evaluated to identify wasteful practices and delays. Overdoing and adding unnecessary features is also a form of waste and should be avoided in applications. Commitments to future features should not be made. Refactoring should be adopted and automation should be taken advantage of. An example of automation is automated testing that frees up time from labor intensive manual testing. Programming practices that encourage too much documentation and compliance with standards should be streamlined based on their business value. Documentation should be reviewed to identify components that are not necessary and add to the learning curve of user without providing any tangible value. The scope of the software being developed should be constantly evaluated and ratified with the customer organizations to make sure that wasteful work is not being undertaken. Rarely used features should be trimmed after usability evaluations.

■ Never stop learning — software development and learning goes hand in hand. New practices, techniques, abstraction, and constant refinement are hallmarks of good programming. Part of learning is to understand what works and what does not. Learning when coupled with effective planning and follow through can be an effective tool for software development. Feedback for learning and improvement should be a part of all software development teams. Training and constant improvement opportunities should be made available to all team members. Requirements in the real world constantly change and get updated, so should the solutions that aim to address those requirements. We have all heard that a plan is not really worth anything if it is not constantly updated to reflect ground reality. Learning should similarly be continuous. Lean development intends to provide a competitive edge to those organizations that foster learning and embrace change. Development principles that include iteration and customer feedback are similar as in XP that suggests building big products in smaller chunks while not losing sight of the whole picture. Utilizing team learning effectively is another key factor of lean development and regular meetings, source control, reviews, and check-in and check-out capabilities may accomplish it.

■ Decentralize decision making — another way to look at this principle of LD is how each team member feels ownership and responsibility in his actions. As we discussed earlier, when everyone in the team knows what they have to do and how their work impacts the end product, they feel ownership and pride in their work. Commitment of individual team members is improved by providing them access to resources, plans, decisions, information, and business value. Exposure of development organizations to customers enables direct interchange and flow of ideas. Eliminating middlemen removes waste and empowers the individual team members to act. Training and constant learning let individual team members use best of class tools and practices in their work. When special circumstances arise requiring urgent action and when deadlines get closer, those same team members shine in their effective performance.

■ Quality is never an accident — a fundamental principle of LD is that quality is always planned and a result of careful and thorough effort. It is never an accident. A good quality software application will have good integrity, robustness, and performance. It will be relevant to customer needs and provide business value. Good quality begins with good testing practices. Testing needs to be integrated into the software development process and continuously updated and tuned to changing requirements. Unit testing, regression testing, integration testing, and customer usability testing should be documented and reviewed.

1.2.2.6 Dynamic Systems Development Method

DSDM was developed to formalize RAD practices [24]. DSDM enables flexible project planning by using three interactive processes for functional model, design, and implementation:

1. Functional Model — prototyping is supported in this step based on the first set of requirements from the customer. All requirements whether functional or not are gathered in this step.
2. Design Model — this process refines the prototypes by iterating over the functional requirements. Feature sets are implemented and refined in this step.
3. Implementation Model — this is the step where the system is deployed into the customer environment and feedback gathered on features, usability, and maintainability.

DSDM supports changing requirements from customers and continuously evolving functionality. DSDM controls the time required for each of the processes discussed above by a concept of time boxes. In DSDM, prototyping replaces the traditional and lengthy product and marketing requirements documents. DSDM defines 15 work products, each with a listing of purpose and quality criteria. Contracts are viewed by DSDM as counterproductive because they hinder open communication between different parties. A collaborative approach between customers and developers is encouraged. Teamwork and creating the right environment for successful collaboration are central to DSDM.

1.2.2.7 Crystal Family

Crystal Methodology by Alistair Cockburn is a family of processes each applied to different kinds of projects. Crystal admits that sometimes there are projects that require fewer rigor and development teams that may not have as much discipline as required by XP or other methodologies. Crystal supports processes for smaller teams that may have small and noncritical projects that can be developed using less rigorous methods. More rigorous Crystal processes are also available. It is intended to be the least intrusive and requiring formalism to normal working styles of individual contributors of a project. This sustains maximum flexibility and variation. Crystal recommends every software development project to be matched to criticality levels of comfort, discretionary money, essential money, and life. Based on these four, it becomes possible to find the appropriate Crystal process.

Crystal recommends the following properties in projects:

- Incremental and quick delivery
- Direct customer involvement
- Access to expertise
- Frequent integration
- Progress tracking by software developed and not documentation
- Early wins
- Continuous improvement in architecture

As we mentioned earlier, less critical projects may have a less rigorous Crystal process assigned to it and vice versa. This would affect the delivery timelines and flexibility. Delivery time frames are cast in one to four months' duration. Several iterations are pursued for each delivery increment and user reviews are conducted multiple times during each iteration. Experience gained from one iteration is applied to the next and underlying methodology is fine-tuned to accommodate this. Routine workshops for methodology tuning and reflection are held during the project. This makes the Crystal processes agile.

1.2.2.8 Unified Modeling Language

Several different variations in object-oriented techniques were combined in 1997 to create what is referred to as Unified Modeling Language™ (UML™) [25]. UML forms the basis of some more recent techniques including RUP [26], Enterprise Unified Process (EUP) [27], and most recently Model Driven Architecture® (MDA®), discussed later.

1.2.2.9 Rational Unified Process

RUP is a culmination of several individuals and teams including Grady Booch and James Rumbaugh working together at Rational Corporation. It is a process framework with several techniques built in and support for extensibility. Some may argue its inclusion as a separate technique here in this book. However, we feel that because RUP lends itself to software development, including Agile Methodologies, so well and because it is widely used by software teams across the world, it deserves to be included. RUP technique defines the following key concepts.

1.2.2.9.1 Key Concepts

- Process roles — these capture the competence, skills, and responsibilities that individuals taking part in the development may be called on to use.

- Activities — the work that each role performs, decomposed into steps. These activities operate on concrete models, code, documents, and reports.
- Guidance — guidelines, templates, examples, and tool mentors that explain how to perform a certain activity with a given tool.
- Disciplines — the organization and categories of the process definition elements discussed above.

RUP uses UML to develop use cases for the software design. Different enterprises building different applications using resources with different skill sets can effectively use RUP methodology. It is inspired by the Waterfall Model where the basic cycle is defined as follows. Understand customer business, translate the customer needs into requirements, prepare a detailed design and architecture, and implement and test it before delivering it to the customer. These are defined below.

1.2.2.9.2   Basic Cycle

Using iterations that are driven by the complexity of the project customizes this basic cycle:

1. Inception — gather requirements and put a project plan together.
2. Elaboration — define architecture and detailed plan for future iterations.
3. Construction — implement, test, and document the system.
4. Transition — deliver the product to the customer and enter the maintenance cycle.

1.2.3   Model Driven Architecture

Object Management Group™ (OMG™, www.omg.org) has recently described MDA, the Model Driven Architecture. MDA supports evolving standards in application domains, changes in technology, and the proliferation of application integration middleware. The OMG MDA addresses the complete lifecycle of designing, deploying, integrating, and managing applications as well as data using open standards.

MDA is built on UML, XML (Extensible Markup Language) Metadata Interchange (XMI®), and Common Object Request Broker Architecture (CORBA®). The basic premise is the separation of logic behind a specification and the implementing middleware. This enables development and deployment of new interoperability approaches and technologies. Integration with newer applications and platforms is facilitated while leveraging existing investments in technology infrastructure.

Key features of MDA are discussed below.

1.2.3.1 Interoperability between Platforms

Business functions can be executed seamlessly between technologies implemented in different platforms.

1.2.3.2 Independence from Platforms

This is a long cherished yet seldom real feature of architectures and methodologies in software. However, MDA presents the most compelling implementation and guidelines for saving cost and complexity associated with porting efforts to diverse platforms.

1.2.3.3 Portability

Platform independence is further enhanced by opportunity to increase reuse and refinement of application development.

1.2.3.4 Improved Communication

Key stakeholders in the software development process are empowered to communicate through common language and concepts. This enhances business value and productivity of the enterprise.

1.2.3.5 Enhanced Return on Investment

MDA enables a higher return on investment and improved quality through reduction of cost during the application lifecycle and reduced time of development. Improved cycle time enables quicker time to market and rapid introduction of new technologies.

OMG MDA enables integration of subsystems that may be built using .NET, XML/SOAP, Enterprise JavaBeans™/Java 2 Platform, Enterprise Edition (EJB/J2EE™), and CORBA. UML, Meta-Object Facility (MOF), and Common Warehouse Meta-model (CWM) are used for modeling the underlying architecture and platform independent application descriptions. New specifications, applications, and middleware are added using UML. Directory services, event handling, transactions, security, platform interfaces, and persistence are offered as common services in MDA. Standardized domain models that can be enhanced as newer technologies become available address the vertical application building.

Figure 1.5   Interviewing Web Services Capabilities

1.2.4   Web Service Development

Software development has evolved from procedural programming to OOA and OOD that enabled distributed object frameworks and further led to modular component architectures. Several newer trends in both distribution and development of software are emerging through Web services [28]. Web services divide large complex business systems into fundamental components that can communicate with each other using standard protocols. Most of the leading vendors are working together to define standards including Simple Object Access Protocol (SOAP), Web Services Description Language (WSDL), and Universal Description, Discovery, and Integration (UDDI) that together with XML and Internet-based communication form Web services [29–34]. Figure 1.5 presents an overview of Web services.

1.2.4.1   The Lifecycle of Web Services

When we review Web services from a lifecycle perspective, it helps illuminate how this set of technologies is changing the software development world. Every facet of contemporary software development including design, development, testing, deployment, execution, and management is being altered and evolved to help maximize the benefits of Web services. All major software and hardware companies in the computer industry today have strategies for developing and deploying Web services.

1.2.4.2 Design

Existing classes in case tools can be transformed into Web services using developer's decisions on compilation, deployment descriptor generation, and such. Web services are altering the design of applications and will be natively supported.

1.2.4.3 Development

Tools suites for Web services are becoming available that create generators. Generators create XML code from an object and provide conversion services back and forth. A business service can be wrapped using a Web service generator and an object. Validation strategies and format checking for XML compliance are part of the integration effort.

1.2.4.4 Testing

A Web service can be unit tested just like a regular class implementation using function and value pairs. User interfaces are not required for testing Web services and because the validation strategies and format checking for XML is built in, the extra testing layer is not required. Web services testing lends itself well to automation. Automated test tools can be used to test method sequences based on a set of test cases. Tools to do functional, unit, and load testing are becoming widely available for Web services.

1.2.4.5 Deployment in SOAP or XML Applications

A Web service is described by a deployment descriptor that may be using WSDL. Development tools such as Microsoft® Visual Studio® .NET provide this deployment descriptor. Once ready for deployment, a Web server or application server can be used to deploy Web services automatically. Web services are published when they are ready to be put into production.

1.2.4.6 Execution

If the Web service has been published in a UDDI registry, a client using UDDI can be used to retrieve the names of existing Web services, from which a specific one can be selected and invoked. Those Web services whose identities are known can be invoked directly.

1.2.4.7 Management

Setup, invocation, suspension, and resumption of Web services is enabled by management functions in a host server. Web services can be managed easily through language neutral descriptors and service implementations.

Knowing XML is a prerequisite for Web services. Currently, getting up to speed with Web services technology involves a steep learning curve, but only from a conceptual point of view. There are a wide number of tools available that offer sophisticated wizards to turn existing services into Web services. This trend is expected to continue. Those who are steeped in software development practices and object-oriented technologies are well positioned to leverage the unique benefits that Web services offer.

1.3 EVOLUTIONARY PREDICTIONS

Some of the questions that IT and development teams are asking today are listed below:

- Is it possible to build and use a cohesive technical architecture for our application platform out of the many emerging software infrastructure technologies?
- How do I use formal methodologies? Are Agile Methodologies too radical for corporate shops?
- Are Web services ready for primetime? Will they help me bring together the diverse platforms I have?
- How do we decide between long-term architecture and faster time to market?
- Should we embark on integrated solutions projects? How do we build effective integration architecture for both internal and external integration?
- What are the best ways to use business intelligence, database, and data warehousing technologies? Will we lose our focus on core business applications if we build these?
- Can we leverage our legacy systems or do we have to abandon them?

Software development platforms and applications have evolved over the last several years. As we discussed earlier, Agile Methodologies and Web services are two new key growth areas. We will review how each of these is evolving, what factors are fueling the growth, and attempt to answer some of these questions.

1.3.1 The Future of Agile Development

1.3.1.1 The Agile Economy

A strategic economic shift has been happening in the world around us. Trade and business in the world economy is revolutionizing global access in ways that we have never before seen. The structures of the products that we build are evolving to be customer-centric and to absorbe change. The nature of the processes that are used to build software systems has matured and is becoming an efficiencies play. The ability to change with evolving requirements, quicker ROI, and faster time to market are not clichés any more, but necessary ingredients to do business.

Agile development is defined by a large number of practices and techniques. Development and testing teams can use each one or a combination of these with equivalent principles. Emphasis on customer feedback and quality is universal in all of the Agile practices.

1.3.1.2 Agile Is a Strategic Capability

Most readers will agree that software applications development is evolving rapidly and Agile developments can provide a strategic capability with the following attributes:

- Adapt and respond to change
- Balance quality with value and flexibility with structure
- Empower a development team to be more creative and productive
- Lead enterprises through tough economic times with little or no job growth

In general, the increase in uncertainty requires the pace of change to accelerate. As automation is increasing in our lives, responsibility for software developers to be true knowledge workers is increasing. Following older principles of plan-driven software development is no longer an option. Knowledge workers have to stay in tune with the customers and adapt to satisfy constantly evolving requirements. Volatility and uncertainty increasingly define our business today along with changing political, security, and socioeconomic ground realities. Knowledge workers are demanding to work in environments that they can understand, change, and improve. Interaction with others is now more important than ever. Opportunities are being redefined to reward those who can be agile, flexible, reliable, and can lower costs.

1.3.1.3 Application Examples

Throughout the last ten years, the author has used the latest generation of software methodologies including Agile methods in the last few years with project teams in Ireland, India, Canada, Japan, the United States, the United Kingdom, Philippines, Malaysia, and Australia. Prototyping, exploratory projects, and outsourcing of development activities for enterprises in these countries range from pharmaceutical informatics applications, drug portfolio management and selection to financial applications, wireless and mobile applications in embedded C and Java, customer relationships management, help desk, business process outsourcing, and IT services. These enterprises are more successful by using Agile Methodologies and are creating competitive edge and market share. Creating value for shareholders and employees is not going to be possible without embracing customer feedback, rapid development, cost savings, communications, team development, and investment in quality practices.

1.3.2 Application Trends

With diverse software development platforms, models, and developer preferences, enterprises are faced with ever increasing costs. Costs of software development, cost of software testing, costs of application integration, backward compatibility with legacy systems, number of systems to be integrated, personnel training, and continuous improvement are some examples of these costs. In this section, we will evaluate some options that IT and development managers have in controlling and managing these costs while increasing productivity.

Software applications emerging out of the diverse platforms and environments discussed earlier are posing a tremendous need for application integration. According to Gartner, the market for software to support application integration and platform middleware [35] will grow by more than 100 percent — from $5.1 billion to $10.5 billion — between 2001 and 2006. IDC's 2002 Enterprise Integration Survey indicated that 55 percent of end users would currently rate the importance of enterprise integration as "critical" or "extremely important." Over the next few years, this trend is expected to intensify [36]. This growth will be driven largely by trends in mergers and acquisitions, system heterogeneity, globalization of companies, and core business needs, such as enhanced customer acquisition and relationship management. Decision support systems and the need to deliver consolidated information to employees will drive major enterprises toward development of integrated data sources and application platforms. The most challenging issues in the next few years are predicted to be integration between the new and currently operational systems (also referred to as legacy systems).

1.3.2.1 Evolving Applications and Platforms

System integrators, independent software vendors (ISVs) and IT decision makers need to consider several factors in the evolving applications, as well as software development platforms. These are listed below:

- Portability to multiple platforms
- Communication with legacy systems
- Ability to map data between heterogeneous systems
- Solutions that work on diverse application server and operating systems
- Code, process, and policy reuse

Newer Web-service-based technologies including .NET framework by Microsoft, J2EE, and Common Language Infrastructure (CLI) platforms targeted at UNIX and Linux provide a cross-platform software development and integration capability.

Based on the newer trends, methodologies, and emerging standards, we predict that the future software development will evolve as described later in this chapter. Microsoft, Sun, Hewlett-Packard, IBM, and several other major vendors are coming together to enable interoperability of Web services and platforms.

1.3.2.2 Application Integration Opportunity

As enterprises grow, application software is used to automate business processes, and integration software is acquired to link applications within and between businesses. For enterprises, integration is a continuous process that is also expensive. Gartner Group estimated that the expense of installation and maintenance can lead to a total setup cost between $2 million and $10 million. Forrester estimated this number to be $6.3 million and that less than 35 percent of integration projects are completed on time and on budget.

IT and development managers feel that enterprise integration is the most critical of the challenges they face [37]. Software complexity crises have resulted from rapid expansion and evolution of automation and IT. Web services, as described earlier, will have their most impact in addressing the application integration issue and bringing the costs down. The opportunity of Web services is to address the following major integration challenges:

- Connectivity and interoperability to a variety of legacy systems
- Data exchange between applications or storage or users with control over the integrity of the data

■ Physical transformation of data from one format to another — data mapping

1.3.2.3 Agile Application Integration

Many of the benefits of Agile Methodologies that we discussed earlier can be applied successfully to application integration. As enterprises in financial and healthcare are starting to look toward leveraging their existing investments in IT systems, they are turning to application integration as a vehicle of implementation. Business requirements are broken down into smaller subsets and mapped onto iterative development activity. This enables quicker cycles of development and better management of customer expectations and project resources. Each iterative development includes the full software development lifecycle — planning, design, development, and testing [38,39].

1.3.2.4 Software Reuse

We will discuss software reuse in the context of application integration opportunity for several reasons. The most important reason is enabling the development and IT organizations to be open to software developed by other people. Reuse cannot be taken for granted if reusable components, libraries, or applications are merely available. It has to be incorporated into the culture of the enterprise. Not invented here (NIH) for components, services, libraries, or applications are the most common reasons for failure of integration projects.

1.3.2.5 Management Responsibilities

Management can facilitate application integration and reuse by identifying resources for reuse certification, version and configuration control, application and component repository management, change management, and education [40–42]. Management should perform a business analysis and share the business vision and objectives with their development and IT organizations. Key stakeholders and management resources should be identified, and champions should be created to manage domain-specific application development effectively. Reuse and application integration should never be perceived without sound business and technological judgment, otherwise, there is a danger of costs spiraling out of control. Reuse and application integration should be pursued in a piecemeal and incremental fashion so that results and returns can be measured at every step. Management should also keep resources available for constant evaluation of market trends, integration vendor solvency, and new technologies such as Web services and standards such as model driven architecture by OMG.

1.3.3 Future of Web Services Development

1.3.3.1 Agile Services

Principles of Agile programming and Web services will be coming together evermore. The developers will involve customers at every stage of development and will constantly strive to make the Web services simpler and more general at the same time. Generalization will enable the use or reuse of Web services through broader applicability.

1.3.3.2 Write Once Use Anywhere

As the shift starts from component-based architectures to dynamic service-based software development, the separation of business logic from presentation logic will be enforced. This will enable write once use anywhere software where the developer who built the Web service will need to have no idea how it will be invoked or what it will look like.

1.3.3.3 Self-Aware Services

Every service will be aware of what information is required to access its data and functionality. So when the systems are designed, the developers will not need to know:

■ What platform or application will use the service.
■ How the service will be used.

1.3.3.4 Easy to Upgrade Services

Self-describing, dynamic services will update with underlying application programming interface (API) changes. The mandated separation of the presentation layer from the business logic layer will enable more discipline in coding. Costly and time-consuming reintegration and reinstall processes with each upgrade will be eliminated.

1.3.3.5 Loosely Coupled Scaleable Services

Enterprise software of the future will be created through dynamic loosely coupled Web services that are described by developers through registries inside or outside an enterprise. Web services will be scalable via availability of backup Web services that provide performance, fail over, security, or portable scalability as required by the situation. This is a fundamentally different model than the exposed API-based component model of today.

1.3.3.6 *Platform Independent Services*

Most widely available Web service platforms of today are Microsoft .NET and J2EE. Both of them are dependent on the platform they currently work on. Attempts at using a common language interface to extend .NET into a non-Windows platform are promising. However, to realize its full and intended potential, Web services will have to function independent of platforms.

1.4 SUMMARY OF CHAPTER

This chapter reviews the most widely used software methodologies. The models and techniques that have been used for software development over the last four decades are discussed. As the world of software applications has rapidly evolved over the last few years, so have the processes and methodologies. Newer trends including Agile processes can improve both quality and time-to-market, but are they processes that all enterprises can effectively use? The answer to this question is probably no. There is a decided preference among larger enterprises and groups to choose classic methodologies over Agile ones. Legacy techniques steeped into the development culture of enterprises prevents the adoption of newer techniques. This chapter presents details of both the classic and Agile techniques. It should be noted here that as the world is becoming a global village due to increased communication and highly qualified resource availability, newer principles will need to be adopted. Maintaining large overheads is no longer an option and large scale planning in isolation from the customer is a recipe for loss of market share. Enterprises may have to learn to use Agile Methodologies. It may be necessary for their survival. XP imposes a strict regimen of process, and RUP and Crystal allow more flexibility and multiple models depending on rigor requirements. All of them have several common threads such as iterative development, customer feedback, quick development cycles, and embracing change.

We also discussed evolving trends in application integration that are interesting. Computing infrastructures are expanding their reach in every dimension. Enterprises have considerable investments in legacy systems and are not willing to consider systems that obviate that investment. Leveraging existing investments in the tough economic climate of today is the need of the hour. In addition, enterprises are demanding better connectivity with their partners and customers. This includes development in multiple locations and multiple geographies. Internet and newer communication mediums have facilitated the need for unprecedented integration of diverse tools, teams, and environments.

Section 1.2 discussed evolving Web services technologies and their promise to help ease the integration challenge. The need for open standards and interoperability is widespread in the present diverse computing environment. As computers and networks become faster and cheaper, application software development needs to evolve. New technologies such as XML, Web services, and others are constantly appearing for addressing certain problems and introducing interesting new ones. How can enterprises ensure that their mission-critical information systems are rooted in standards that will adapt to new hardware and integration capabilities? How can enterprises ensure that their software application development, testing, quality assurance (QA), localization, and documentation teams are leveraging the best available tools and methodologies to maximize competitive edge and stay close to customer needs? These are some of the questions posed in this chapter and will venture to answer in the rest of this book.

IT spending forms a key part of any enterprise's spending. In the trying times of the current worldwide economy, enterprises across the globe are looking for ways to maximize the longevity of their current investments and balance that with the benefits of incorporating newer applications. This balancing act has been hard and ROI has become an overriding factor for both software developers and software consumers. So far we have seen how the prolific number of platforms, development environments, and models has increased the complexity of software development. We have also seen what can be done to reduce costs and increase productivity. In the next few chapters, we will be exploring each of these in more detail. We will define software ROI and discuss how, for a given investment, enterprises can maximize returns.

REFERENCES

1. DeGrace, P. and Stahl, Leslie H., *Wicked Problems, Righteous Solutions: a Catalogue of Modern Software Engineering Paradigms,* 1st ed., Upper Saddle River, NJ: Pearson Education Pod Publishing, 1998.
2. Blum, B.I., *Software Engineering: A Holistic View*, New York: Oxford University Press, 1992.
3. Weckman, J. et al., Application of Simulation and the Boehm Spiral Model to 300-mm Logistics System Risk Reduction, *31st Conference on Winter Simulation,* Phoenix, AZ, 1999.
4. Boehm, B.W., A Spiral Model of Software Development and Enhancement, *IEEE Computer*, Vol. 21, No. 5, Pp. 61–72, May 1988.
5. Boehm, B.W., A Spiral Model of Software Development and Enhancement, *ACM SIGSOFT Software Engineering Notes*, August 1986.

6. Prowell, S.J. et al., *Cleanroom Software Engineering: Technology and Process*, 1st ed., Boston: Addison Wesley, 1999.
7. Linger, R.C., Mills, H.D., and Witt, B.I., *Structured Programming: Theory and Practice*, Boston: Addison Wesley, 1979.
8. Whittaker, J.A. and Thomason, M.G., A Markov Chain Model for Statistical Software Testing, *IEEE Transactions on Software Engineering*, Vol. 20, No. 10, pp. 812–824, 1994.
9. Booch, G., *Object-Oriented Analysis and Design with Applications*, 2nd ed., Boston: Addison Wesley, October 1993.
10. Bertrand, M., *Object-Oriented Software Construction*, Prentice Hall International Series in Computer Science, Upper Saddle River, NJ: Prentice Hall, March 2000.
11. Lau, Y.T., *The Art of Objects: Object-Oriented Design and Architecture*. The Addison-Wesley Object Technology Series, Boston: Addison Wesley, October 2000.
12. Graham, I., *Object-Oriented Methods*, Boston: Addison Wesley, 1994.
13. Booch, G., *Object-Oriented Design with Applications*, San Francisco: Benjamin Cummings, 1994.
14. Coad, P. and Yourdon, E., *Object-Oriented Analysis*, Upper Saddle River, NJ: Prentice Hall, 1990.
15. Coad, P. and Yourdon, E., *Object-Oriented Design*, Upper Saddle River, NJ: Prentice Hall, 1991.
16. Rumbaugh, J.R. et al., *Object-Oriented Modeling and Design*, 1st ed., Upper Saddle River, NJ: Prentice Hall, 1990.
17. Jacobson, I. et al., *Object-Oriented Software Engineering. A Use Case Driven Approach*, Boston: Addison Wesley, 1992.
18. Ambler, S.W. and Jeffries, R., *Agile Modeling: Effective Practices for Extreme Programming and the Unified Process*, 1st ed., New York: John Wiley & Sons, March 22, 2002.
19. McConnell, S., *Rapid Development: Taming Wild Software Schedules*, Redmond, WA: Microsoft Press, 1996.
20. Cockburn, A., Characterizing People as Non-Linear, First-Order Components in Software Development, *Humans and Technology*, Technical Report TR 99.05, October 1999
21. Cockburn, A., *Agile Software Development*, 1st ed., Boston: Addison Wesley, December 15, 2001.
22. Schwaber, K., Beedle, M., and Martin, R.C., *Agile Software Development with SCRUM*, 1st ed., Upper Saddle River, NJ: Prentice Hall, October 15, 2001.
23. Poppendieck, M. and Poppendieck, T., *Lean Software Development: An Agile Toolkit*, Boston: Addison Wesley Professional, 2003.
24. DSDM Consortium, *Dynamic Systems Development Method*, Version 3, United Kingdom, www.dsdm.org.
25. Rumbaugh, J., Jacobson, I., and Booch, G., *The Unified Modeling Language Reference Manual*, Addison Wesley Object Technology Series, book and CD-ROM ed., Boston: Addison Wesley, December 23, 1998.
26. Kroll, P. and Krutchten, P., *The Rational Unified Process Made Easy: A Practitioner's Guide to Rational Unified Process*, 1st ed., Boston: Addison Wesley, April 8, 2003.
27. Ambler, S.W. and Constantine, L.L., Eds., *Completing the Unified Process Series*, San Francisco: CMP Books, December 2001.

28. Doug, K., *Review of Loosely Coupled: The Missing Pieces of Web Services,* Kentfield, CA: RDS Press, June 2003.

29. Web Services Standards Development Body. www.w3.org/2002/ws/.

30. The Web Services Industry Portal. www.webservices.org.

31. IBM Web Services Portal developerWorks: Web services. http://www-136.ibm.com/developerworks/webservices/.

32. Microsoft Web Services Portal Web Services Developer Center. http://msdn.microsoft.com/webservices/.

33. Web Services Journal Web Services Journal. http://www.sys-con.com/webservices/.

34. Hagel III, J. and Brown, J.S., *Out of the Box: Strategies for Achieving Profits Today and Growth Tomorrow through Web Services,* Watertown, MA: Harvard Business School Press, October 28, 2002.

35. McCoy, D.W. et al., Hype Cycle for Application Integration and Platform Middleware, Gartner, May 30, 2003.

36. Enterprise Information Integration, The New Way to Leverage e-Information, Aberdeen Group, May 4, 2002.

37. IDC 2002 Enterprise Integration Survey.

38. Hunter, B., Fowler, M., and Hohpe, G., Agile EAI Methods, *Loma Resource,* July 2002.

39. Fowler, M., *Patterns of Enterprise Application Architecture,* 1st ed., Boston: Addison Wesley, November 5, 2002.

40. Reifer, D.J., *Practical Software Reuse,* New York: John Wiley & Sons, 1997.

41. Lim, W.C., *Managing Software Reuse,* Upper Saddle River, NJ: Prentice Hall, 1998.

42. Poulin, J.S., *Measuring Software Reuse,* Boston: Addison Wesley, 1997.

2

SOFTWARE COMPLEXITY CRISIS

2.1 CONTEMPORARY SOFTWARE DEVELOPMENT IS MULTIFACETED AND COMPLEX

Software is beginning to cater to a wide variety of audiences throughout the world. The internationalization of software has led to a contrary localization trend. Different countries, different languages, and cultural requirements are leading the localization and optimization trends in the same software applications catering to different markets. Software development is consequently becoming more diverse and multifaceted.

2.1.1 Old Car and Computers Analogy

Rapid advances in computer hardware over the last 50 years have been a major contributor to the changes in software. We are in the age of ever increasing memory and processing power of computers. Sizes of powerful computers are shrinking and prices are falling continuously. People have often compared the computer industry to the automobile industry with the following example. If automobile innovations progressed at the same pace as the computers, today we would have a Rolls Royce that could go 16,000 miles per hour, travel to the moon and back, and could be purchased for $2.50. I like to modify this by saying that it would indeed do all of that but also have major problems twice a year perhaps even stranding its driver on the moon!

Yes, that is correct. Readers of this book will relate to this modified statement if they have used computers or if they have done any software development in recent times. We all have run into incomplete, troublesome, and buggy software that just does not work as advertised. Device drivers that do not work correctly, Web pages that do not load office productivity software, operating systems that crash, and middleware that core dumps regularly are all problems that we see on an ongoing basis.

Software developers are finding that they spend an inordinate amount of time figuring out how to work around the flaws in the software they need to use. Market pressures to get new products to market fast mean quick development cycles, quicker testing, and lax quality control with hastily written incomplete documentation. Software applications seem to be getting worse over the years while consuming ever increasing memory and processing power. As more and more software development companies are being combined in this consolidating marketplace, customers are left to deal with a devil's brew of platforms, versions, operating systems, and applications with overlapping feature sets. Constant intervention from an army of consultants and overwhelmed internal information service (IS) workers is needed to get the products barely working. There are many stories of legal action, backing out of contracts, sales drop offs, frustration, and quagmire of customers in contemporary software development and use.

However, the flip side of the story equally deserves to be told. Developers working in ISVs and IT workers in organizations are people who believe in their software and want it to work correctly. They are good intentioned people who want to do a good job in developing applications that can be used by others. They are interested in seeing their software applications succeed and generate revenue for their organizations. They are interested in minimizing problems and bugs in the solutions that they are developing and delivering. So what is it that drives the complexity of software and creates problems? Figure 2.1 shows the key factors that are causing contemporary software development to become multifaceted and complex. We will discuss these in more detail now and also present some suggestions to reduce the influence of each of these factors.

2.1.2 Diverse Development Locations

Software development today is distributed among multiple sites and multiple geographical locations. This includes onshore and offshore locations as well as development integration by vendors that could be located in different countries. Multiple time zones, network and hardware administrative policies, tool sets, development environment versions, culture, programming conventions, and language differences make development, deployment, and testing more complex. This can add significantly to the complexity of the software projects.

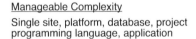

Manageable Complexity

Single site, platform, database, project programming language, application

Explosive Complexity

Multiple worldwide sites, multiple platforms, deployment on multiple databases, multiple programming languages and applications, change management, version control, remote management, bug tracking, security

Figure 2.1   Complexity Explosion in Software Development

Suggestions to reduce factor influence:

- Create, document, and maintain uniform administrative policies across locations
- Train the distributed development groups to follow uniform build, source control, defect tracking, and other conventions
- Contractually oblige the vendors to adhere to documented procedures and policies
- Locate software builds at one site
- Encourage communication and exchange of thought across time zones
- Foster respect and understanding of diverse cultures while keeping a tight focus on common goals and objectives

2.1.3   Diverse Development Teams

Multiple development teams tend to add uniqueness to their builds and methods. Teams generally also tend to use different technology platforms, development environments, project management, innovation, and integration interfaces. Development and testing teams tend to write various software tools and test harnesses during the course of their projects. Diverse development teams may also be using different programming languages. Each language would require a completely new set of software build processes that use different environments, file storage locations, naming conventions, and processes.

Suggestions to reduce factor influence:

- Standardize uniform administration policies
- Subdivide large monolithic software projects into smaller manageable ones
- Institute reviews for design, development, testing, documentation, and deployment
- Encourage and reward reuse and exchange of code, components, services, and ideas regarding integration of interfaces
- Standardize test practices and share test specifications and test plans across the development teams
- Create a uniform language independent software build process and interface to increase homogeneity in how developers will use different languages

2.1.4 Diverse Platforms

Different platforms and development environments require administration and management policies, conventions, software processes, and tool sets. This demands learning new interfaces, tool sets, procedure, knowledge, policies, and conventions. Installation and prerequisites to make the development environment work correctly also change.

Suggestions to reduce factor influence:

- Use platform independent source control and build tools
- Standardize interfaces among the different platforms
- Maximize the use of truly portable and platform independent language and development environments

2.2 MARKET TRENDS FAVOR DIVERSITY

As markets of software development, deployment, and consumption evolve, we learn that there will always be diversity of tools, methodologies, and technologies. This is known as understanding the changing development landscape. The opportunity in this situation is to understand the ever changing terminology and evolving standards, cut through the fear, uncertainty, and doubt (FUD) propagated by competing vendors and building blocks of complex applications and their interrelationships. Table 2.1 describes some of the prevalent applications, development environments,

Table 2.1   Current Software Environments

Development tools	Microsoft, IBM, Borland, Sun/Forte
Modeling and design tools	Rational (IBM), Computer Associates
Web services tools	Cape Clear, Interbind
Application platforms	BEA Systems, IBM Websphere, Sun/iPlanet, Microsoft .Net, Oracle, SAP Netweaver, and individual vendors such as Tibco, webMethods
Database	Oracle, Sybase, IBM, Microsoft, OpenSource
Business intelligence and data warehouse	Business Objects, Cognos, IBM, Oracle, SAS, Hyperion, Teradata
Data extraction and mining	SPSS, SAS, Informatica, Trillium, Ascential, Vality

and vendors who supply them. Keep in mind that this is a current snapshot and by the time this book goes to press, consolidation in these vendors may already have happened and the technology landscape may have changed again.

We are witnessing an increased dominance of J2EE and .NET as the two platforms for enterprise application development. Designers and architects of enterprise software are focusing on building their technical architecture on integrated application platforms. Web services — SOAP/XMLP, UDDI, WSDL, etc. — are emerging as flexible and dynamic means for application integration and for delivering real value over the Internet as discussed in the previous chapter. Tightening economic conditions and budgetary pressures are driving enterprise IT groups to more effectively leverage and optimize existing resources. Business process optimization and integration are drivers of continuing data exchange and integration growth. Business intelligence and data analysis are now part of any complete IT infrastructure. Agility and nimbleness of application development is becoming a crucial driving force for data warehouses and business intelligence applications. Collaboration among distributed development teams is vital and so resource portals are being deployed for both intra- and extraenterprise workforce. Development of applications for mobile devices, the frameworks available on the market (J2ME™ midlets and Microsoft's Mobile Toolkit among others), and the role of application servers is being analyzed given the current push of wireless computer, phone, and personal digital assistant (PDA) systems.

2.2.1 Proliferation of Software Development and Deployment Environments

Software development and deployment environments have evolved considerably over the last three decades:

- From procedural, proprietary, and throwaway to object oriented, standards-based, and reusable
- From compilation and execution to the interpreted and just-in-time models
- From distributed applications such as CORBA and Distributed Component Object Model (DCOM) to Web services
- From synchronous and proprietary programming solutions to component based message oriented programming and markup languages (e.g., XML)

We will discuss major software development and deployment environments in the next few sections. We have classified these into four broad categories:

1. Microsoft environments
2. Java™ environments
3. Open source environments
4. Mobile environments

Mobile is in a separate category because it is a nascent area that is rapidly evolving with multiple vendors and quick proliferation of applications.

2.2.1.1 Microsoft Platforms

Microsoft is arguably the most prolific development environment in the world. Microsoft operating systems, including Windows® 2000 and 2003, Windows XP, and Windows 98, run on about 85 percent of all computers in the world today.

- Microsoft programming languages —Microsoft's development tools and platforms in use today are:
  - Visual Studio .NET — includes support for Visual Basic®, Visual C++®, and Visual Interdev® development systems
  - Microsoft Internet information server and active server pages (ASP) technology — widely used for serving Web pages and transactional Web sites
  - Microsoft transaction server — previously on Windows NT platform has migrated to Component Object Model (COM+) services on Windows 2000 and higher

■ Microsoft .NET platform — Microsoft .NET provides support for development and deployment of Web services. Major components of Microsoft .NET include C#, VB.NET, and ASP.NET. C# is a programming language and has simper constructs than C++. Common language runtime (CLR), which is part of Microsoft .NET, facilitates development and porting from non-Microsoft operating systems such as UNIX and Linux. Visual Basic's incarnation in .NET is VB.NET and it uses ADO.NET. The learning curve between the older Visual Basic and VB.NET is not significant.

2.2.1.2 Java Platforms

Java Platform is a collection of development environment and programming language components that started from the introduction of Java by Sun Microsystems. Major components of Java Platform are Java 2 Enterprise Edition (J2EE), Java 2 Standard Edition (J2SE™), and Java 2 Mobile Edition (J2ME™) in addition to JXTA™ (Juxtapose) and Java API for XML Processing (JAXP).

2.2.1.2.1 J2EE

Java server pages (JSP), servlets, and EJBs form important components of J2EE. Other enterprise Java technologies include Java Naming and Directory Interface (JNDI) and Remote Method Invocation (RMI). IBM's Web-Sphere®, BEA's WebLogic™, and Sun's iPlanet™ are major application servers that support J2EE platform.

2.2.1.2.2 J2SE

J2SE comes with a Java Development Kit (JDK™) and is considered by several development groups as a rapid application development tool. Java Platform with its portability and write once run everywhere appeal has found widespread acceptance among software developers who are wary of Microsoft platforms. Development tools available for Java include IBM®'s VisualAge®, Borland®'s Jbuilder®, Sun℠'s Forte™ and NetBeans™, and Symantec®'s Visual Café.

2.2.1.3 Open Source Platforms

Open source platform has found widespread acceptance and support throughout the last decade and particularly in more recent times. Open source refers to software in which the source code is freely available for others to view, modify, adapt, use, and publish. Typically, it is created and maintained by a distributed team of developers across geographical boundaries. Open source is not the property of one organization or company [1–3].

2.2.1.3.1 Linux

Linus Torvalds from Finland developed Linux® operating system. A statistically insignificant presence in 1997, the popularity of Linux and the free and open source software movement has caught on. IDC estimated that Linux has 25 percent of the server market, second only to Windows NT/2000 that has 38 percent. With 4 percent of the market, Linux is also the third most popular desktop after Apple® desktops. Open source provides scripting languages such as Perl and development platforms from Apache Software Foundation such as Tomcat and Apache™ web server.

2.2.1.4 Mobile Platforms

Recent years have seen a tremendous upsurge in the usage of wireless systems. These include mobile phones, PDAs, and a suite of devices that combine the features of both. Wireless computing, or mobile computing as it is called, has given rise to a large demand for applications that support the users of these devices.

2.2.1.4.1 Mobile Operating Systems

Most popular mobile operating systems currently are Symbian™, Microsoft, PalmSource™, and SavaJe™.

Symbian has given rise to UIQ, Nokia® Series 60 and 80 platforms. Nokia is the world's largest maker of mobile handsets and, consequently, Symbian has found widespread usage. Microsoft has seen a recent upsurge in its mobile operating system use with Pocket PC phone edition, Smartphone, and Windows CE.NET versions. PalmSource has produced Palm OS® used in the majority of PDAs sold today. Embedded Linux and MontaVista® Linux CEE (Consumer Electronics Edition) have followed an open standards approach and are challenging more established mobile operating system players. SavaJe Technologies produces SavaJe OS. Java 2 Platform with its microedition architecture has also been used for mobile Java applications as well as gaming and other interoperable applications.

Among the major handset manufacturers, Nokia has driven the adoption of Symbian OS as mentioned earlier, Motorola has been driving the creation and adoption of J2ME and Embedded Linux platform, and Kyocera and Samsung have used Palm OS.

2.2.2 Proliferation of Software Maturity Models

Numerous software models, standards, and methodologies have been created over the years to cater to demand from a variety of development communities and platforms. Software maturity has emerged as a significant convergence area for quality models, product development strategies, and best practices. Both academia and commercial enterprises including Hewlett-Packard, IBM, Ford, Motorola, and NEC have implemented different models and achieved impressive improvements in productivity and predictability in software development [4–8]. In this section, we will present a quick overview of several models and then discuss a few models in considerable detail. We will also elaborate on their relationships with quality.

2.2.2.1 Software Process Models

2.2.2.1.1 Capability Maturity Model

CMM has been used effectively by several organizations to improve performance and reduce defect levels. Another software process model called Personal Software Process^{SM} (PSP^{SM}) also by Carnegie Mellon University has been used to reduce defects in software projects [9,10]. We will discuss CMM levels in more detail later.

Two of the base models including CMM and System Engineering Capability Maturity Model (EIA/IS 731) are combined to make the integrated model CMMI® [11]. There are five maturity levels representing process areas covered and six capability levels to indicate rating of each process area. CMMI standard can be used by a wider group of organizations including those that have been appraised, those that are not appraised but intend to get a formal appraisal, as well as those that are not interested in a formal appraisal.

2.2.2.1.2 Continuous Quality Improvement

Several other quality and process models have evolved from hardware world into software development. Some of these propose continued quality improvement such as Total Quality Management (TQM), Goal Question Metric (GQM), International Standards Organization's ISO 9000, and Malcolm Baldridge [12–14].

2.2.2.1.3 Six Sigma® Quality Model

According to iSixSigma (www.isixsigma.com), "Six Sigma is a rigorous and disciplined methodology that uses data and statistical analysis to measure and improve a company's operational performance by identifying and eliminating 'defects' in manufacturing and service-related processes."

2.2.2.1.4 Statistical Process Control

Traditional methods of control systems are adapted and applied to software development process in SPC [15,16]. Process capability is evaluated quantitatively based on standard deviation and sigma limits. If the process is not within designated limits, a process change may be enacted and the process resampled to determine the effectiveness of the process change.

2.2.2.1.5 Product Line Development and Reuse Model

Product Line Development Model involves the quantitative study and use of functionally valid software designs (and their variations) within vertical industries and product classes. It has been used successfully in several software development and reuse projects [17–20].

2.2.2.1.6 Defect Classification and Prevention Models

Defect Prevention is a reactive process of capturing and studying defects and defect trends, with the intention of preventing them from happening again [21–23]. The Defect Classification [24,25] and Defect Prevention models are used in conjunction to analyze and categorize defects. Design and development groups have meetings and training seminars on common and preventable defects that should be proactively avoided. Defect classification and prevention is a cost-effective method as compared to PSP and Software Inspection.

2.2.2.1.7 Software Inspection Process

Software Inspection focuses on reviewing software by designated teams and identifying defects. This process has been used effectively to eliminate software defects less expensively than waiting for the late stage testing [26,27]. Review teams are also a good method of team building and communication as we have noted elsewhere.

2.2.2.2 Capability Maturity Model Integrated

Software Engineering Institute developed the original CMM in the late 1980s. It has found widespread use for software process maturity assessment and variations have been used for everything from employee resource planning to infrastructure software acquisition, systems engineering, purchasing, and product development. However, the problems of integration, overlapping components, and incompatibility have dogged these efforts and made auditing, measuring, and streamlining attempts difficult. CMMI was initiated to establish a common framework for integration of all CMMs.

There are five discernible levels of maturity according to CMMI.

2.2.2.2.1   Initial

This first level represents unpredictability of results, *ad hoc* methods, formalizations, and tools. This is a purely team skill dominated reactive type of organization that does not document and implement specific solutions in response to problems. No attempt is made at generalization, planning, documentation, and shared learning.

2.2.2.2.2   Managed

This second level applies when processes are more mature, measurements are disciplined, and performance is repeatable. Project planning, monitoring, service level agreements (SLAs), and QA plans are in place and used consistently. This level includes the project level management. Customer requirements are maintained and updated on a regular basis and projects are tracked for performance and learning.

2.2.2.2.3   Defined

This third level applies when the group or organization works across project lines. All managed level processes are in place and the organization establishes additional performance improvement measures. Requirements are now managed across multiple projects and teams. Integration efforts are put at high priority and emphasized through change control. Quality, verification, and validation efforts are formalized to determine accuracy, relevance, and completeness of the application. Organizations at this level are aware and actively manage risks and rewards as well as pay attention to employee well-being and continuous learning. All the activities are directed at integrating the diverse teams and projects and exploiting synergies.

2.2.2.2.4   Managed through Numbers

This fourth level represents consistently improving organizations. All the attributes of the defined level are leveraged across multiple projects and the gathered feedback is used to improve performance and predictability of outcomes. This level applies to the organizational level processes and benchmarking across multiple product lines. Organizations at this level successfully employ formal quality methods and measurements.

2.2.2.2.5 Optimized

Just as in CMM, this fifth level indicates highly flexible, adaptable organizations that can conform to changes in market conditions, customer preferences, suppliers, and competitive landscapes. Process improvement is continuous and consistent. Documentation is effective and updated and used regularly. Employees are treated as knowledge workers with all empowered to expand their abilities and skills. Management is proactive about problems and conflicts as well as the business environment.

Additionally, CMMI allows a choice between two representations — staged and continuous. These stand for top-down or bottom-up goal management, respectively. Top-down is when the organization is being managed by overall goals and objectives. Bottom-up or continuous representation is when individual project level goals and objectives are shared through continuous improvement across projects and the organization.

CMMI encourages all employees of an organization to understand their roles. The roles, baseline, sizing of effort, QA, and configurations are the first steps toward applying CMMI. Assessment of the position of the company *vis-à-vis* the competition and collaborators as well as benchmarking is an important component of CMMI. Laying an improvement roadmap and aligning the objectives with CMMI levels comes next so that improvement is systematic and measurable. All best practices from individual departments and projects need to be identified and communicated with media, shareholders, employees, customers, and partners. CMMI does not differentiate enterprises with regard to their size. It applies equally to a small team of developers and large corporations with global operations that are geographically disparate. It is a powerful mechanism to guide process formalization, feedback, improvement, and repeatability. ROI, which we will be discussing in much greater detail throughout this book, is enhanced by using CMMI and other maturity models, because product development times become predictable and accelerated, defects are reduced, customer expectations are better managed, cost overruns are avoided, and competitiveness is enhanced.

2.2.2.3 Information Technology Infrastructure Library

Information Technology Infrastructure Library (ITIL) is a best practice compendium of services originally created by the U.K. government, but adopted now by a large number of organizations around the world.

Infrastructure, capacity, service level management, and release management are areas covered by ITIL. Version 2 of ITIL also includes hardware infrastructure definition, environment, lifecycle, and management philosophies for IT.

ITIL includes IT service support and delivery. These are further subdivided into several disciplines. IT service support includes the following:

- Configuration management
- Incident management
- Service desk management
- Change management
- Release management

IT service delivery includes policies on service level agreements, security risk and policy, financial management, capacity management, and availability management. SLAs form the backbone of a service relationship. For both parties — service deliverer and recipient — the SLA documents and defines the norms of relationship. For example, network availability, help desk and support response times, uptimes, error resolution, and performance indicators are all part of SLAs.

We will describe some of the service support topics in more detail below.

2.2.2.3.1 Configuration Management

In ITIL, provision and management of IT services for an enterprise are captured in a database. This configuration management database contains information on the list of items, their maintenance, issues, movement, and replacement. Information regarding the hardware and software environments; people, places, and systems; releases; documentation; and training assets is maintained in this database. The process of identification, control, status, and verification is part of the configuration management tasks. Identification includes specifications, control includes change definition and policy, status refers to the snapshot of the item, and verification ensures the accuracy of database information. Refer to www.itil-itsm-world.com for more information.

2.2.2.3.2 IT Security and Configuration

According to ITIL, configuration and infrastructure lists need to have proper controls to track moved, stolen, and lost assets. Unauthorized or illegal use could result in loss, penalties, or danger to the reputation of the enterprise. Proper planning of configuration and security procedures is critical to ensure this does not happen.

2.2.2.3.3 Incident Management

Any incident, accidental or intentional, results in loss of productivity for an enterprise. Downtime and lost time can be avoided and normal operation of an enterprise maintained if appropriate planning and management of incidents and preventive maintenance is applied. Availability of services, privacy, and confidentiality of information can be maintained at acceptable levels with proper incident management.

2.2.2.3.4 Change Management

According to ITIL, change management refers to planning, controlling, and documenting change. Configuration items and the security policies that are affected by change are part of the change management. Justification and business reasons behind each change need to be authorized and documented. After the change is made, regression testing and ensuring that there is a fall-back plan in the event of failure are included in change management. Plan to measure the business fallout of change if it is adverse. Risks need to be assessed as part of change management planning and execution. Protection from unauthorized changes and impact assessment of illegal or unauthorized changes is vital to prevent loss of shareholder value, loss of market value, loss of revenue, competitor market share gains, and private and government legal proceedings.

2.2.2.3.5 Service Desk Management

In ITIL, incident management ties into the service desk and help desk management. Successful IT service delivery depends on service desk management. Once users of a certain product or service have purchased it, the next step involves the role of the service desk. This includes product support, help desk, incident support, training, and other areas. A bad impression at the service desk could ruin the enterprise's reputation and may result in customer flight, lawsuits, and loss of market share.

Call centers and simple escalation service desks may provide event logging and incident tracking capabilities. Such services are limited and escalate calls to experts who may respond at a later time and answer questions. More sophisticated service support centers may have expert resources on hand to provide answers and customer support. Several issues that have come to light more recently relate to language skills and limited experience sets of outsourced call centers. Loss of local jobs and transfer of these jobs to outsourced countries has resulted in a number of legislations prohibiting this activity or tracking it closely in the United States.

Service desk users have access to sophisticated tracking, managing, and reporting software tools. They also include outgoing marketing and sales activities. IT security needs to be carefully managed and integrated into the service desk activities and agenda.

2.2.2.3.6   Release Management

Software development, installation, support, and change management are all components of release management. Effective control of release management results in improving the predictability of software products and reduces costs. Cost control in today's world is more prominent than ever before. Improved predictability means happier customers and better customer expectation management.

Good release management achieves effective management of multiple product lines of internal and external software and prevents piracy. ITIL specifies release management as collection of physical and logical storage into which all master copies of software are stored. This definitive software library forms the core of external and internal software distribution, respectively. ITIL toolkit provides details of management of the software items and their distribution and implementation into a production environment. A release program that is suitable for the enterprise including version control, source control, software build, update, release, and management is available from the toolkit. We will be covering a lot more details of the software development lifecycle later in this book. Better release management improves IT security. Service availability, uptime, better control and distribution, and good IT governance lead to reliable fraud and virus protection and firewalls to protect against intruders and hackers.

2.2.2.4   Control Objectives for Information Technology

Relatively recent legislation, including the USA Patriot Act and the Sarbanes-Oxley Act, has prompted the executives at most enterprises to look at security and control standards carefully. For the IT industry, one such standard, Control Objectives for Information Technology (COBIT), will be discussed in this section in more detail. Now in its third iteration, COBIT was developed as a generally accepted standard for good IT security and control practices that provides a reference framework for management, users, and information security (IS) audit, control, and security practitioners. A good reference for COBIT is www.isaca.org.

As IT has become pervasive throughout enterprises, the need for security, control, and effective governance has gained prominence. COBIT provides extensive documentation for management's control and measurability of IT processes. COBIT has 34 IT processes. These include tools for performance measurement, outcome measurement, best practices, maturity models, and benchmarking and decision improvement. COBIT assists IT organizations to prioritize external legislative requirements with internal business programs and accomplish value driven results. Senior business leaders must be part of the process for both legislative and internal priorities. More recently, several enterprises are pursuing business across the globe resulting in multiple regulatory environments. Effective prioritization, management involvement, and resource allocation leads to completion of business projects while meeting regulatory constraints.

Many organizations combine internal, external, and offshore people in different regions of the world to achieve successful completion of projects. Investments in IT should be evaluated on a continuous basis to keep monitoring, measuring, and tracking the objectives. COBIT can be applied at the product division level and regional level. It can be expanded to the country level with stakeholders and owners in business groups. Assessment and implementation of COBIT could take a few days and control objective definitions and maturity levels can be used to define improvement action plans.

Enterprise level COBIT establishes capabilities and maturity levels to identify improvement areas. Benchmarks and scoring metrics are established to track the progress over a period of time. Goals and achievements are recorded graphically for ease of communication across groups. Enterprises can customize COBIT to suit their own needs including metrics to measure progress.

2.2.2.4.1 COBIT Characteristics

COBIT has the following characteristics:

- Extensive documentation is publicly available
- It is maintained and updated as an open standard
- IT Governance Institute manages and maintains COBIT
- Ongoing support for COBIT and customizations by different organizations are available for all to share

COBIT encourages the assessment of outcomes of the process after rollout. Using the metrics and goals established, problem areas need to be identified and improvement plans laid out. Scores and benchmarking information is shared in addition to best practices across the groups. One key COBIT rule is that IT resources and components need to be managed by a set of rules and naturally aligned processes so that information needs of the enterprise are satisfied *vis-à-vis* its objectives.

2.2.2.4.2 COBIT Components

COBIT identifies managers, users, and auditors as consumers of information to support business processes for risks and controls, privacy, accessibility, and evaluation, respectively. For financial requirements, effectiveness, efficiency, and reliability of information are used for compliance. Security requirements cover confidentiality, integrity, and availability. Reliability of information so that management can use to track compliance, performance, and reporting is another key component. COBIT identifies data, application systems, technology, facilities, and people as the IT resources and defines control measures for each of them. COBIT framework has control objectives and structure for its classification. Measurable results can be achieved by activities and tasks following a lifecycle with appropriate control requirements. Natural grouping of processes to different domains is linked to the management and responsibility functions.

Table 2.2 describes COBIT framework, domains, and control objectives. Each one of the control objectives is further detailed in COBIT literature.

2.2.2.5 Product Line Model

Most enterprises spend considerable effort and time on increasing predictability of their product and service delivery and maximize long-term return on software investments. Complex software products should be managed as product lines to keep costs in check and improve time-to-market. Software product line supports large-grained intraenterprise software reuse. Product lines have been used by the manufacturing and hardware industry for a long time to reduce costs and increase productivity by exploiting commonalties between products. However, using product lines in software is a relatively new concept. A software product line is a set of software systems sharing a common, managed set of features that satisfy the specific needs of:

- Market and competitive landscape
- Mission of the enterprise
- Core assets and strength of enterprise
- Reuse of product assets

Software product lines are a good approach for achieving reuse but impose several requirements if an enterprise wishes to adopt it. Despite

Table 2.2   COBIT Domains and Control Objectives

COBIT Framework	COBIT Domains	COBIT Control
Information criteria	Planning and structure	Define plan Define architecture Define technical direction Define organization Manage investment Manage communication Manage resources and projects Manage compliance and quality Analyze risks
IT resources	Acquisition	Identify solutions Acquire software resources Develop and maintain architecture and procedures Install and accredit IT systems Manage change
IT processes	Service delivery and support	Define service levels Manage internal and external services Manage capacity and performance Enable security and service continuity Attribute costs Train users Advise partners Manage data and configuration Manage problems and incidents Manage operations and facilities
	Monitoring, assessment, and audit	Monitor processes Assess controls Get third party QA Audit

extensive time, effort, and resources spent on it, there can be several risks. We discuss what the product line risks are and how to manage conversion through design, analysis, and management.

Market forces of today are demanding fast production of new products and updates of existing ones. For software enterprises to compete effectively in rapidly changing economic conditions and to cater to demanding customers, the cost of product development and management needs to

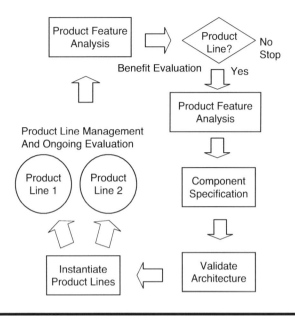

Figure 2.2 Flowchart of a Product Line Approach

be contained. Product lines enable development and marketing of multiple products instead of one at a time.

The steps below describe an outline of a product line approach. For more details, refer to Figure 2.2. The first step is to determine whether it makes sense to follow a product line approach. Before a decision is made, it is necessary to do a business analysis and understand benefits, risks, and costs. If the decision is to proceed with product lines, then it is important to identify the feature set and stakeholders of each product line. This involves interviewing users, developers, and technical support people in addition to help desk and sales staff for desired new features and feedback on existing features. This also helps identify the resources and people who will be involved in each of the product lines. Next, architectural and shared considerations need to be taken into account. This includes identifying the shared components, patterns, subsystems, platforms, and framework. Once this is done, the next step is to separate the product lines, assign ownerships, and start the management and tracking of them. Constant business analysis and feedback needs to be maintained to identify further improvements or changes.

If done correctly, enterprises can use product lines to increase competitiveness and market share as well as decrease costs, leverage shared resources, and increase customer satisfaction and reliability. The reuse and sharing does not stop at features; it extends to quality practices, test cases, test plans, quality plans, performance evaluations, scheduling, training, documentation, sales force training, marketing collateral development, and implementation.

2.2.2.5.1 When Product Lines May Not Apply

Enterprises cannot apply product line models in a blindfolded way. It is an expensive process and may not be useful or applicable to all situations. The conversion steps are usually expensive and so business analysis described earlier becomes critical. Unless there are multiple related applications that are planned or are in existence, it may not be relevant to do a product line. Product line reduces costs, but that happens later and so the initial investment and time it takes to setup product lines may not be acceptable to certain enterprises pursuing a quick to market strategy.

The first product of a product line takes longer to deploy than if product lines are not followed. Similarly, if there are not many shared resources built inside the enterprise and the code base that can be successfully leveraged across multiple product lines, then it may not be worthwhile pursuing this approach. More complex systems definitely require product line thinking because it enables sharing resources, reduced costs, improved reliability, and other benefits described earlier. Another thing that should be kept in mind before embarking on product lines is the timing of the decision and effort. Preparing for product lines before the market intensive phase of a product lifecycle starts is the right time. Doing it too soon may not yield benefits because products may not have been proven viable.

2.2.2.5.2 Evolutionary Approach to Product Line

In this approach, the enterprise would have an existing set of software products, but has not shared or reused common elements. The existing product architectures are utilized and a new architecture is developed. The products are then slowly adapted to the new architecture through shared components. This process takes more time but is less risky and the organization slowly converts. ROIs are limited, but readily realized and management is happy. In addition, there is no break in the feature evolution and development of the existing products. This has the obvious benefits of keeping customers happy. Overall, it takes more time and more investment to follow the evolutionary approach to adapting product lines. The product and feature sets developed during the product line conversion are throwaways — discarded when new product lines come on line.

2.2.2.5.3   Revolutionary Approach to Product Line

In the revolutionary approach, a product line replaces the existing set of products. This means the efforts and all resources are focused on the designing, building, and deploying the new product line. Considerable risk is involved in the revolutionary approach. However, the rewards and speed of execution is equally great. The justification behind taking this approach is to start with a clean slate and not carry the baggage of existing products. Investment in this approach is smaller, because the implementation is not prolonged for a long time and throwaway features are not implemented. However, the risk level is increased as we mentioned earlier and also the customer may not be happy if the existing product improvements and changes are not implemented.

2.2.2.5.4   Implementing Product Line

The domain engineering unit model is a classical approach to product line model implementation. A target group within the enterprise is dedicated with the task of managing core assets of the product line and distinction is made between core assets and product assets. The former includes framework, shared architecture components, and other shared resources. The latter includes applications and multiple product lines built on top of the core assets. One drawback of this approach is the separation of the core group from business units and, consequently, customers. If sufficient interaction with customers is not maintained for the core assets organization, then the development may fall out of sync with customer requirements and effort could be wasted.

If the enterprise is large and includes several product lines and vertical industries, then a hierarchical approach to domain engineering units may be used. In this approach, specialized product lines are built on a foundation product line. The foundation product line in turn is using the core assets, so the assets are being utilized across multiple levels of product lines.

Product line architecture defines a set of allowed variations explicitly. Unlike conventional software architecture where the variation is expected and unplanned, in product line architectures, it is predicted and planned. That is what forms the basis of different product lines. Integration in product lines is another fundamental component that is addressed using either the evolutionary (incremental steps) or revolutionary approach (once at the end of development). Both have advantages and disadvantages, but in the incremental approach where the integration is being pursued along with product line development, the risk of failure at the end of cycle of integration effort is minimized.

Table 2.3   Benefits of Software Product Lines to Different Stakeholders

	Stakeholder	*Benefit*
1	CEO or president	Gains in market share, competitive advantage, shareholder value, improved profits and time-to-market.
2	Operations	Efficient use of resources, nimble employees, and ability to explore better tools, technology, and processes to increase efficiency.
3	Engineering	Manageability and predictability of outcomes, well-defined roles and responsibilities, defined timelines, and support articulation. Satisfaction of high quality and reliable products. Easier integration and upgrades.
4	Marketing	High quality products, customer expectation management, and brand equity.
5	Customer	Less defects, higher quality, and better performance and delivery commitments from the enterprise. Satisfaction about the quality of documentation, training material, and technical support.

Table 2.3 describes benefits of software product lines to different stakeholders. Readers are encouraged to use this if making the case to their management. Also note that product line models are compatible with quality and ROI considerations presented in the rest of this book.

In this section, we discussed how numerous maturity models have contributed to helping build and manage better software systems. We have not covered all the approaches that are out there, because it is outside the scope of the current context. Our intention has been to identify approaches that are most popular and contribute the most to software quality and ROI discussion. We discussed these approaches to also highlight a key point that developers and IT professionals are witnessing an explosion of software platforms and maturity models. Navigating all these and managing to maximize software quality and ROI is the objective of this book. In the next sections, we will discuss how IT has gained center stage in enterprises and how this changing role is resulting in new sets of challenges and opportunities.

2.3   CHANGING ROLE OF INFORMATION TECHNOLOGY

Not so long ago, IT departments were cost centers that were a necessary evil. Accountability was not great and results were often fuzzy with reworks dominating the deployments. Today the situation has been reversed: IT departments are a competitive asset and a key part of global growth strategy. As IT groups evaluate which software projects and applications to prioritize in their budgets, they need tools for measuring ROI. Traditionally, labor cost savings were the primary metric used by IT departments for investments in applications and solutions. Indirect benefits include improved system availability, performance, and qualitative improvements in productivity.

As the role of IT changes to get more strategic and business value oriented, the justifications for investments are becoming increasingly sophisticated. Ability of IT to enable increased revenue, improved market share, better margins, competitive advantage, first mover advantage, and time-to-market are being quantified and measured. As the Internet has become ubiquitous, enterprises have capabilities to leverage the new medium in a big way. This has increased the pace of IT investments and it has also provided the ability to interact with customers in real-time, track inventories, purchases, information, and improve customer service. As we will see in more detail later, the ability to link different departments of an enterprise, such as sales with inventory, marketing with product development and customer service have provided unique opportunities to IT departments for adding value. The simultaneous challenge and opportunity for IT departments to obtain business-value investments is to start defining and measuring ROI and associated key metrics before a new solution is implemented.

2.3.1   Global Software Development and Test Opportunity

Internet and modern communication systems have enabled unprecedented globalization. Today, unlike just a few short years ago, developers in one part of the world can work seamlessly on projects across multiple geographical locations. Work can now be distributed across many locations and developed units can be integrated together in one place. Software development and project management has evolved considerably over the last decade.

2.3.1.1   *Widely Available Technical Training*

Business schools and commercial and private colleges specialize in IT training and coursework that can be pursued part-time and in night classes. Enterprises encourage their employees to acquire new skills, take classes, and continue education. Incentives for this include better job functions and tuition reimbursement programs.

2.3.1.2 Software Development Skills are a Commodity

Programming and general software development is not a rare skill any more. Over the past decade, universities and colleges across the world have produced quality computer science and computer application graduates.

2.3.1.3 Global Software Development and Test Reduces Costs

Many enterprises have established development centers throughout the world to take advantage of this growing trend. SAP as a case in point now has development centers in China, India, Israel, France, and Japan. EDS has development centers in Brazil and India. Microsoft has development centers throughout the world. As these development centers have performed over the last decade, enterprises have realized significant cost savings and benefits. Wages and benefit levels outside the European Union and the United States are generally lower and the costs of maintaining development centers are attractive. We will see in later chapters how development organizations can leverage global software development and test opportunity for reducing costs while maintaining productivity and quality.

2.3.1.4 Entire World Is Becoming a Software Consumer

Globalization has enabled enterprises to create markets for their software applications worldwide. Traditional consumers of software applications such as North America, Japan, and the European Union continue to expand. However, the fastest growing markets are those in Asia, including China and India, as well as South America.

2.3.2 Outsourcing and Offshoring

Changing economic conditions and requirements on corporations to manage their bottom-line more efficiently and derive maximum ROI from software development have resulted in emergence of outsourcers. Outsourcing, which extends from business process outsourcing to IT outsourcing is now central to 80 percent of Fortune 500 businesses. Companies such as IBM, EDS, ACS, InfoSys, Wipro, and others have firmly established themselves in what is referred to as providing their customer a "best shore" strategy. Best shore referring to IT and business specialists providing service from the most effective geographical location. Let us look at some of the success drivers for outsourcing.

2.3.2.1 Human Factors Are Most Important

The keys to success in outsourcing and offshoring are largely human factors. Even though most of the work is conducted across the Internet, it is project management expertise, communication style, culture, and familiarity with western business norms that do more to influence software development outsourcing decisions than cost and other quantifiable factors.

2.3.2.2 Differences from IT-Enabled and Business Process Outsourcing

Software development is a distinct industry when compared to other activities such as call centers, data entry, medical transcription, or other business processes. Requirements, skill sets, and numbers of people involved are generally different and not interchangeable. IT-enabled and business process outsourcing (BPO) markets are rapidly growing and several multinationals such as GE have established successful outsourced operations. IT-enabled and BPO services are not the focus of this book.

2.3.2.3 Governments Can Play Constructive Role

Local, state, and federal governments can play the role of a facilitator for outsourcing and offshoring growth. Creating the right telecommunications infrastructure, competitive environment, education and training system, intellectual property regulations, and immigration policies are all steps to creating good business conditions. Unfair trade policies, legislation to regulate pricing, block movement of business people across countries, and other steps stifle growth and cost saving opportunities for enterprises.

2.4 BUSINESS CASE FOR MAXIMIZING SOFTWARE ROI

As computers are playing an increasingly central role in every sphere of life, software development of high quality and reliability is becoming imperative. QA and testing have formed an important component of the software product lifecycle and delivery for a long time and now more than ever. As the age of mainframes gave way to personal computers and more recently always-on computing systems, the requirements for quality, testing, and verification have become more complex and demanding. Software is constantly being developed by multiple development teams with several products in different stages of their versions and lifecycles. With enterprise software and e-business systems, business users and consumers across the entire globe are accessing and using applications

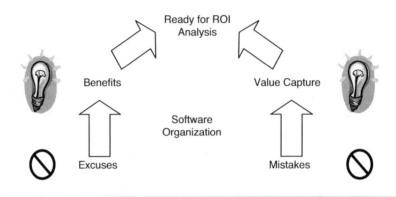

Figure 2.3 Path to Getting Ready for ROI Analysis

on a 24/7 basis. The always-on application usage and continuous software development has posed increased requirements on reliability, accuracy, and performance of systems. There have been countless technology and software application rollouts that failed miserably. A good project may have indirect benefits in addition to direct quantifiable ones. Even the best of the projects may not succeed if a good business case is not built and updated continuously to evaluate it. The role of software development and IT organizations in nearly every industry is shifting from supporting back office operations to being a key driver for creating value through increased revenue, increased competitive advantages, increased ROI, and reduced costs. Figure 2.3 describes how we will approach building the business case for ROI by identifying the excuses and mistakes to avoid and identifying the benefits and value capture of ROI analysis.

2.4.1 Excuses for Not Calculating ROI

Before we start discussing the business case for ROI, let us first elucidate most common reasons people give for not calculating or using ROI.

2.4.1.1 ROI is Wasteful Number Crunching

"Too much time and resource will have to be spent on number crunching. We are very busy with the product development and timely launch and it will be wasteful to do it at this time. If you want us to stay under budget and on time, don't ask us to do ROI right now."

ROI calculation may have some initial time and resource cost, but as time goes on and the project matures, these costs are lowered and accuracy improves. Resources spent on analyzing ROI will be better informed and aligned with the business goals and objectives and will actually help get the project completed on time and under budget.

2.4.1.2 We Do Not Have the Expertise

"We are not expert economists and financial people! Why should we be doing the ROI calculation? It should be someone else's responsibility. Our work is software development, we are good at it, and that is what we should focus on."

We are attempting to simplify and explain ROI calculation in this book so it is not only addressable by the economists and financial people! Readers of this book will be better equipped to calculate ROI with only the basic knowledge and understanding of financial benefits and costs. As we have discussed elsewhere, software developers and managers who are involved in ROI calculation and business objectives are better informed and make better decisions.

2.4.1.3 We Will Wait Until Later

"ROI numbers are not perfect anyway, so why do it now. Let's wait until our software application is completed and when customers start to use it. We will use them as case study and 'back into' ROI numbers from there. We will have better data at that time."

It is true that the ROI numbers at the beginning of projects may not be perfect. However, the process established due to analyzing and calculating ROI is extremely valuable for the enterprise. It is another positive step toward improving the methodology and achieving predictability and reliability in software development. Waiting for customers to use the applications may be a flawed strategy, because initial positive response of customers could quickly turn negative with lack of reliability, supportability, and predictability of the software. In addition, if the initial customers present a number of bugs and features, the development and deployment process could break down trying to chase moving requirements and customer dependencies. A proper ROI analysis is the key to understanding how to effectively manage the entire software development process.

2.4.1.4 ROI Will Be Positive Anyway

"ROI in our type of software application is positive anyway. That is why we are in business right? So why do it?"

All software applications do not necessarily have positive ROI. Sometimes application development starts with positive ROI given market, competition, and estimates on cost, but along the way due to a variety of reasons, costs may mount and revenue potential may fall. A constantly evolving landscape and mix of tools, platforms, technologies, applications, and market economics ensure that no single formula of success will apply forever. Businesses lose their competitive edge if they ignore ROI to reinvent and constantly improve themselves. ROI analysis for every enterprise is unique and can only apply to that enterprise.

2.4.1.5 Let Us Use Someone Else's Data

"Let's get some statistics from other companies in our industry who are doing it. That should be good enough, because someone else has already done the analysis and spent time and resources."

Every enterprise is different. Every department with its unique mix of development, deployment, and testing resources is different. Sharing the same marketplace and applications is no indicator that all competitors will have the same ROI. Successful enterprises in the software world differentiate themselves by their better margins, lower cost, predictability, innovation, and reliability. It is not advisable to adopt ROI analysis of a different enterprise, because it will most likely not be applicable to yours. Differences in internal environments, technology platforms, software tools, employee skill sets, cash and capital outlay, profitability, customer base, and other factors result in unique ROI analysis for each company. Using someone else's data could lead to a counterproductive situation of mismanaged expectations, unhappy employees and customers, and missed revenue targets.

2.4.2 Benefits of ROI

Major development and IT projects of our times need unique ways of justifying investments and resources. Benefits and business cases of the software application development have to be presented to decision makers who are emphasizing cost control. Managing development projects no longer is about meeting timelines of deliverables and budgets. It is about selling the business case to management, shareholders, and customers. Successes and failures of large-scale development and IT projects have negative repercussions on stock prices and market capitalization of the enterprise. It also impacts existing and future customers' perceptions about the enterprise. Employee morale could be impacted resulting in further erosion in innovation, sales, service, and support functions of the enterprise. ROI and other financial metrics are becoming mandatory tools to convey effective decision making and value creation ability of a successful enterprise.

As an example, a publicly traded customer relationship management (CRM) software maker's CIO did ROI analysis to justify a $40 million expense to implement a new business value chain system. He was able to show a projected bottom-line cost savings of $120 million and projected additional cash availability for capital expansion, acquisition, and market share purposes. Additional cash availability meant improved shareholder value and consequently increased capitalization for the enterprise. The analysis helped the CIO convince his management and board members that the $40 million investment was a sound one.

2.4.2.1 Helps Establish Business Value

Small-scale software development and IT investments may not need a lot of analysis. A simple total cost of ownership and basic benefit analysis may be enough. Examples of such cases are making a single computer or small application purchase decision or a two to three month development effort to build a quick prototype. However, any longer duration projects or investment decisions require rigorous business value analysis. In the current environment of fiscal prudence, every significant project is reviewed and analyzed by customers, employees, suppliers, and shareholders alike.

ROI analysis helps establish the business value drivers. It helps put milestones and metrics in place that can be used to measure progress over the duration of the project. It helps in review and decision making. It enables management and developers to participate in a shared common vision of business success and to identify risks. The data collected and analyzed during the ROI calculation is useful tool for future projects.

2.4.2.2 Helps Establish Metrics

When ROI analysis and calculation is used correctly, it provides milestones and targets for benefits and cost reductions. These targets can be subdivided into yearly, quarterly, and monthly goals for teams to achieve. The business case of ROI is facilitated by asking questions about the market, the competition, and core focus area of the enterprise. Metrics established as a results of ROI analysis can be developed for all stages and all processes of the enterprise. This may include spending and cost centers, purchase and capital assets, working capital, accounts receivables, general and administrative functions, and human resources. In addition, benchmarking among similar businesses for each of these processes leads to additional measurable metrics and comparison basis. If the enterprise is well run with better margins and cost controls than its competitors, it will have more respect among employees, shareholders, suppliers, and customers.

ROI analyses can be extended to measure and govern other metrics such as days sales outstanding (DSO), receivables outstanding, excess inventory, inventory cycle rates, and collection efficiency.

2.4.2.3 ROI gives a Healthy Dose of Reality

One of the characteristics of a good ROI analysis is identifying risks, trade-offs, and challenges associated with maximizing benefits and minimizing costs. Care should be exercised that risks are properly weighted so that they are not marginalized and similarly a healthy dose of skepticism should be exercised with rewards. Once the ROI analysis is completed and areas of potential improvement identified, it becomes a perfect opportunity to step back and look at the entire scenario. The business value benefits, the new environments, the software applications, the resources, the cost outlay, and the processes will become clear. A good ROI analysis injects a healthy dose of reality. All new methodologies and processes should function within the metrics and benchmarks identified as part of the ROI analysis. Successive improvements and constant updates to the ROI model and planning should be undertaken to keep it current and accurate. Business values are constantly evolving and changing, as we discussed earlier, which should also update and change the measurements and actions. There may be situations where some practices and methodologies may be counterintuitive and may not make sense. Every such situation should be carefully evaluated with the proper business values mindset and acted upon.

Successful project managers will constantly seek feedback from customers, financial sponsors, and management to keep faithful to their requirements and metrics. Suppliers and contractors should be constantly evaluated with the same set of objectives and their products and services used accordingly. Every contributor to the project should be evaluated, keeping in mind equitability and highest quality standards. If regulatory approvals are a requirement, such as for government systems, appropriate adjustments should be made to account for them. This will substantially raise the level of confidence in ROI analysis.

Prototyping and pilot studies should be undertaken wherever possible to ensure the success of the intended project. These will highlight the needs, costs, and benefits of the proposed system better than any theoretical analyses. It also helps make a better business case for the required investment.

2.4.2.4 Helps Establish Best Practices

Metrics established as a result of ROI analysis (as discussed earlier) and analysis of the competitive landscape enable an enterprise to identify best practices. These best practices include published and widely available ones to those that are developed internally and are unique to the enterprise. Some best practices would include hiring and resource management practices for a certain market and geographical area. Others may identify the suppliers, prices, and strategies for negotiating best deals. Third-party vendors have established process libraries and designs that assist in capturing these best practices. Different departments of the same enterprise should be sharing best practices among themselves and benefiting from each other's experience instead of inventing them from scratch. An example of a nonbest practice is different departments in the same enterprise using different software applications to do nearly same set of work processes. This would mean different vendors are being used with different contracts, supply, and support strategies. It also means nonoverlapping training requirements, different resource requirements, multiple platforms, and communication gaps. A good ROI analysis process would identify such weaknesses and capture the cost burden.

2.4.2.5   Facilitates Data Collection

The process of ROI analysis starts with data collection. Accurate collection and representation is crucial for dependable ROI results. This helps developers and IT departments to define, analyze, and capture key quantifiable elements of their development and deployment process. Accurate data collection enables managing changes and surprises later and it helps keep the project on track. Data collection processes should also anticipate failures and disruptions as well as reasons that may contaminate data. Making a ROI business case helps an enterprise realize value from its investments and is only as accurate and workable as the underlying data collection methodology.

Data collection for ROI analysis includes value computation, IT project, and application lifecycle estimates, benefit realization tracking, scorecard for intangible and real benefits, and cost estimates from deployment, service, and capital expenditures. Dependability of data collection methodology is crucial to management's ability to select and maximize business value from software projects and applications.

Sound data collection for ROI analysis also facilitates capture of intangible and soft dollar benefits of a project. These intangible payoffs tend to yield the most ROIs. In the discussion on ROI in the next chapter, we will discuss the intangible and hard to quantify ROI factors in more detail.

Once the data collection methodology has been established, IT management is able to deliver quantifiable numbers to the senior management and board members with confidence on an ongoing basis. A disciplined approach toward data collection offers better customer and employee expectation management and increases the credibility of the entire enterprise.

2.4.3   Business Value Capture Using ROI

ROI analysis helps capture the business value to the enterprise. It does this in several ways. In this section, we will discuss this business value capture in more details. We will start by describing business value capture phases and then understand how they interrelate to each other and to ROI analysis.

2.4.3.1   Analyze Opportunities

As we will see later, ROI is all about net benefits and net costs. The first phase of business value capture using ROI involves an analysis of the landscape. Market pressures, economic opportunities, government regulation, labor markets, currency stability, and supply pricing are some of the opportunities that enterprises can avail. These opportunities will lead to changing benefits or changing cost situation.

2.4.3.2   Determine Strategy

This phase focuses on using the opportunities and determining a corporate strategy around them. Identifying milestones and guidelines and measuring progress at the milestones should be an integral component of the strategy. Strategy determination should include all constituencies, including marketing, sales, development, deployment, and support organizations of the enterprise.

2.4.3.3   Make Decisions

Taking all the data into account and with the agreed-upon strategy, it is time to chose appropriate tools, software systems, applications, and resources. Decision making should be impartial and again should involve all constituencies. Decisions made should be documented and revisited often for follow-ups and updates. A project should be modified based on feedback from participants and abandoned if it is not meeting the desired opportunity criteria.

2.4.3.4   Manage Portfolio

The next phase is the implementation phase. Investment decisions and projects should be managed just as a financial portfolio is managed. The intention is to utilize full value and potential of all projects, effort, time, and money. This phase involves implementation of appropriate projects and processes, design, development and deployment of systems, documentation, and testing efforts as well as training and localization services.

Throughout this phase, the strategy that has been laid out should be adhered to and followed in letter and spirit.

2.4.3.5 Continuous Improvement

This phase, as the name signifies, should really not sit at the end but is an ongoing process. Continuous improvement includes communication and distribution of key learnings to all constituencies. It includes measurement and feedback for refining opportunity and decision phases as discussed earlier. Continuous improvement includes updating analyses and refinement of the strategy. Business value that is gathered as these phases progress is fed back into the overall process as part of the continuous improvement step. Continuous improvement includes communicating to the marketplace, shareholders, suppliers, employees, and customers success stories and achievements. This increases their confidence in the enterprise and increases its value.

2.4.4 Getting Ready for ROI Analysis

2.4.4.1 Plan Effective Timelines

It is important to realize that it may be possible to calculate ROI as a number, but the process of maximizing ROI takes time. Benefits of incorporating IT-enabled software and applications will only be realized by upgrading the process and methodology to use them effectively. Effective timelines incorporate when the process and methodologies will be upgraded, when the resources using these tools will be trained, and when the business value of the project will be established. Effective ROI analysis will be achievable in years, not overnight. It is important to lay out the plan on a timetable and establish milestones to measure the plan. Include details of when the constituencies will be introduced and trained, when the results and changes in the process will be expected from them, and when performance improvements will be communicated to the management. A realistic timeline that is constantly updated with changing priorities and business conditions is an effective timeline.

2.4.4.2 Establish Performance Objectives

Developing measurable objectives and working toward them will bring about important process improvements in an enterprise. This is an important step in the initial and ongoing ROI analysis. Business value measurement is possible if measurement of performance objectives is in place. Performance objectives should not only be restricted to technical components, they should also include business objectives. Even development organizations should think about how they are contributing toward business objectives of the enterprise. Funding decisions of new development projects or software applications should be tied to successful performance objectives. Past records of teams undertaking new projects should be used to measure success rates. The approach to be followed for establishing the performance objectives is what we refer to as the forest, trees, and leaves approach. Each department level objective should be divided into group objectives and further into team and individual contributor objectives. This helps in establishing accountability and ability to measure performance. At each step, it is important to have both technical merits and business merits articulated. This helps establish overall business values of the project.

Here is an example: a software application is intended to allow sales personnel to make more customer contacts per day with better marketing collateral. In addition, this application will also help the sales person get more up-to-date information about and to each customer. The quantified effect of the application in the form of customers reached per day, productivity in the form of lead conversion, and improved customer response time and revenue increase is captured. Now, put numbers against each of these effects and calculate them independently of other applications. This will give you the business merits.

2.4.4.3   Guard Against Over-reliance on Numbers

Management by numbers is a great thing, but over-reliance on numbers from ROI analysis may lead to problems. It should be understood that ROI is a means to a bigger cause — improving productivity, reliability, and business value. Similarly, too much reliance on monetary benefits and percentages takes the focus away from performance objectives rooted in teamwork, innovation, and success. Individual achievements and recognition are lost when too much emphasis is placed on net dollars. Being focused on numbers will invariably lead to failure, because the environment in which those numbers are being measured is constantly changing. Changing market conditions, competitive landscape, employee morale, customer satisfaction, and any other business environment changes may affect the project.

2.4.4.4   Do Not Assume Anything

Get ready to understand, analyze, and measure everything. Consult with domain experts for verticals that the application or software is intended to address. Make sure that any assumptions are verified and validated before proceeding. Understand how technology will affect the lives of those who will use it. Know what the boundary conditions and benchmarks are and use them effectively. Many times, the intended use of the application or project gives way to something completely different. Be prepared to adapt to change and upgrade the benchmarks and business value guidance. Review project and business values with the rest of the team. Several times it will lead to useful ideas and suggestions for improvement. Business need is usually a good benchmark to compare things against and track improvements. Evaluate and measure progress often to keep the projects under control.

2.4.4.5   Make Appropriate Investments

Allocating adequate resources to the analysis, planning, measurement, and benchmarking activities is important. Funding just the hardware and software applications and development resources is not enough. Project managers should realize that in the initial stages of a software project, analysis and measurement setup may be time-consuming and results not readily obvious. However, establishing this activity as part of the methodology is an important initial step that pays off handsomely later. For a ten-person development or IT team, it is important to keep one-half as a dedicated resource for measuring progress against business values and milestones. The work to be done by this resource could be distributed among all the team members. It may also be necessary to budget for some tools and training for team members so they can be part of the measurement process and feel empowered.

2.4.4.6   Get Stakeholder Buy-In

All ROI analysis and calculation projects need appropriate stakeholder buy-in. The stakeholders could be the senior management, the employees participating in the analysis, and, in several cases, suppliers and customers. This is a team activity and making sure that appropriate stakeholders are participating in the process enables funding, feedback, ownership, and responsibility. To get appropriate stakeholder buy-in, it will be important to gather the appropriate domain expertise and ask relevant questions. Different stakeholders need different ways of information presentation. Management, for example, is happy with dollar values, others including shareholders and analysts may be interested in increased capitalization and market value, employees are interested in recognition and how it helps make their jobs easier.

Let us look at an accounts payable (AP) department. For example, the new application for tracking AP is intended to give a 40 percent increase in productivity. If there are five AP personnel, then this will help do the work of two extra resources. If the number of AP requests for suppliers that are processed is 1000 a month, then the new application will enable processing 1400 AP requests a month. This will lead to a saving of approximately three months of checks processed and a dollar value of $60,000 with the current set of resources. Existing AP personnel will be happy that it makes their jobs easier with the productivity and speed increase. Management that may be looking at cost savings would be happy with the dollar savings, improved cycle times, supplier satisfaction, training cost savings, and other benefits.

2.4.4.7 Get Ready to Measure, Measure, Measure

Effective measurement is key to tracking project performance and ROI analysis. As we have discussed earlier, projects that will maximize ROI will be the ones that are constantly tracked, measured, and adjusted. Measurement will include establishing baseline, keeping score, and comparing the difference with targets on an ongoing basis. Changes and updates should be reflected and impacts on different business values should be evaluated. New targets and baseline updates should be recorded. A simple table or a spreadsheet will be adequate to do the initial calculation and ongoing measurements. The measurements will be useful in making the business case to management and other constituencies. Different people in different areas of responsibility could be assigned to the tasks of measurements appropriate to them and polled on an ongoing basis.

2.4.5 Avoiding Common ROI Mistakes

As the need for ROI analysis and calculation becomes recognized, the practice is becoming widespread and there is an increased likelihood of mistakes. We will discuss the common ROI pitfalls to avoid and steps to ensure reliability in ROI initiatives.

2.4.5.1 Missing Strategic Vision and Stakeholder Buy-In

The most common mistake is to embark on ROI analysis without the stakeholder buy-in and participants who can give you accurate data. It is equally dangerous to not take full scope of the analysis into account and just follow a quick and dirty piecemeal analysis without adequate data capture. The effort and energy spent in doing ROI analysis this way is not going to be utilized well. Getting stakeholder and constituency buy-in will help remove sticky spots from a process that will last for a number of years.

2.4.5.2 Lack of Domain Expertise

Calculating and presenting ROI analysis is only relevant if:

- It is made in conjunction with participants who know about the application or product that is being analyzed.
- It is done in a format that is appropriate to the audience the case is being made to.

Champions that should be enrolled for making a successful business value case of ROI have different priorities and preferences. Their styles of presentation are different and so are their requirements. All this means that the ROI calculation should be tailored to the audience using appropriate domain expertise.

2.4.5.3 Inaccurate Assumptions

The ROI analysis will only be as strong as the assumptions and data it was based on. If the assumptions are overstretched, the ROI analysis will not be accurate and will not hold up to the scrutiny of different constituencies. It should not be a halfhearted attempt; the research to get the data and assumptions correct should be thorough and credible. There should be room for assumptions to evolve over time and for different stages of the project.

2.4.5.4 Incorrect Timing

Sometimes it may be premature to present ROI analysis results. As we mentioned before, if the strategic vision and stakeholder buy-in is not in place, it may be too early. Similarly, if the appropriate resources to backup the analysis are not in place, the desired outcome of ROI analysis may not be possible. Similarly, if ROI analysis is done and presented too late into the life of the project, it may be difficult for a course correction or motivating people to comply.

2.4.5.5 Missing Risk and Cost Profile

Every application or software project has risks and costs associated with them. If the management is not made aware of the appropriate risks, their assumptions in budgeting and resource allocation will not be correct leading to inadequate results. Similarly, if a good analysis of benefits and costs has not been done and a cost profile is not available in concrete terms, then the chances of runaway costs increase, potentially jeopardizing the project. The ratio of risks to rewards and upfront costs should be carefully analyzed and articulated. Dependencies and slips in schedules should be made part of the analysis and evaluation. Resource uncertainties and integration of technologies should be highlighted and made part of the equation. The numbers should be evaluated by each stakeholder and domain expert for feedback and updates. Feedback should be incorporated in the ROI analysis and calculation.

2.4.5.6 Unsubstantiated Data or Supporting Evidence

Any attempt at ROI analysis and calculation should be supported with key pieces of data and evidence to substantiate claims. The management that will be making project go or no-go decisions usually is savvy about numbers and will greatly appreciate proofs and case studies to backup ROI analysis. Any metrics or benchmarks used should also be carefully analyzed and supporting evidence should be gathered. It may sometimes be useful to get a third-party perspective or an independent evaluation of data and claims. A sound investment decision from management is forthcoming if the presentation is substantiated with verifiable proof and examples of success in other enterprises or industries.

2.4.5.7 Overestimating Gains

ROI calculation and analysis should guard against overestimating the benefits of application or technology. Usually the productivity gains and resource time savings are not as high as they may initially seem. Value adds of letting resources do more complex work will not always stack up as predicted. Some of the cost overruns will be involved in training and learning curve issues and benefits may be less than predicted. All these should be taken into account and overpromises should be avoided. It is better to be conservative in making the gain predictions due to a certain application, technology initiative, or new process.

2.5 SUMMARY OF CHAPTER

In this chapter, we discussed how market trends favor multiple software development deployment environments and diversity. We discussed different popular platforms for application development for enterprises and the emerging class of mobile wireless systems. Diversity is also prevalent in software models that include CMM, Six Sigma, product line development, and several others. We discussed eight of these software models. These diverse trends are also supplemented by trends in the marketplace to cost containment. We discussed how application integration opportunity has presented itself and how attempts are being made at containing the runaway costs in integration. We discussed how software reuse and Agile application integration has helped. Cost savings have also been achieved by several enterprises using global software development and test teams. Globalization has helped because technical training and software development skills have become commodities. Education and communication mediums have further facilitated this. In Section 2.3 regarding the changing role of IT, we discussed outsourcing and offshoring in more detail. Finally, we have presented the business case for maximizing software ROI that forms the basis of this book. We discuss how the changing role of IT is impacting rethinking along these lines and what the most common excuses are for not calculating ROI. In Section 2.4, we discuss the benefits of ROI and the most common ROI mistakes to avoid. We also elaborated on the business value capture using ROI through effective analysis of opportunities and decision making. Section 2.4.4 on getting ready for ROI analysis is useful for teams that have embarked on similar projects or those who are just starting out. We discussed how to plan effective timelines, establish objectives, get stakeholder buy-in, and get ready to measure.

REFERENCES

1. Open Source Initiative. www.opensource.org.
2. Stallman, R., *Open Sources: Voices from the Open Source Revolution,* Sebastopol, CA: O'Reilly & Associates, Inc., January 1999.
3. Raymond, E.S., The Cathedral and the Bazaar: Musings on Linux and Open Source by an Accidental Revolutionary, Sebastopol, CA: O'Reilly & Associates, Inc., February 2001.
4. Diaz, M., How Software Process Improvement Helped Motorola, *IEEE Software*, September/October 1997.
5. Kan, S., Metrics and Models in Software Quality Engineering, Boston: Addison Wesley, 1995.
6. Mays, R., Experiences with Defect Prevention, *IBM Systems Journal*, Vol. 29, No. 1, 1990.
7. Billings, C., Journey to a Mature Software Process, *IBM Systems Journal*, Vol. 33, No. 1, 1994.
8. Reed, D.L. et al., Institute of Defense Analyses, Ford Motor Company's Investment Efficiency Initiative: A Case Study, April 1999, http://www.acq.osd.mil/io/se/ippd/fordcase.pdf.
9. Ferguson, P., Results of Applying the Personal Software Process, *IEEE Computer*, May 1997.
10. Humphrey, W., Introduction to the Personal Software Process, Boston: Addison Wesley, 1996.
11. Ahern, D. et al., *CMMI Distilled*, Boston: Addison Wesley, 2001.
12. Moriguchi, S., Software Excellence: A Total Quality Management Guide, New York: Productivity Press, 1997.

13. Tingey, M., *Comparing ISO 9000, Malcolm Baldridge, and the SEI CMM for Software: A Reference and Selection Guide,* Upper Saddle River, NJ: Prentice Hall, 1996.
14. Van Latum, F., Adopting GQM-Based Measurement in an Industrial Environment, *IEEE Software,* January/February 1998.
15. Burr, A., *Statistical Methods for Software Quality,* Boston: International Thomson Computer Press, 1996.
16. Owen, M., *SPC and Business Improvement,* IFS Limited, 1993.
17. Macala, R., Managing Domain-Specific Product-Line Development, *IEEE Software,* May 1996.
18. Dikel, D., Applying Software Product-Line Architecture, *IEEE Computer,* August 1997.
19. Investment Analysis of Software Assets for Product Lines, CMU/SEI-96-TR-010.
20. A Case Study in Successful Product Line Development, CMU/SEI-96-TR-016.
21. Kajihara, J., Learning from Bugs, *IEEE Software,* September 1993.
22. Mays, R., Experiences with Defect Prevention, *IBM Systems Journal,* Vol. 29, No. 1, 1990.
23. Gale, J., Implementing the Defect Prevention Process in the MVS Interactive Programming Organization, *IBM Systems Journal,* Vol. 29, No. 1, 1990.
24. Chillarege, R., Orthogonal Defect Classification — A Concept for In-Process Measurements, *IEEE Transactions on Software Engineering,* November 1992.
25. Bhandari, I., A Case Study of Software Process Improvement During Development, *IEEE Transactions on Software Engineering,* December 1993.
26. Fagan, M., Advances in Software Inspections, *IEEE Transactions on Software Engineering,* July 1986.
27. Weller, E., Lessons Learned from Three Years of Inspection Data, *IEEE Software,* September 1993.

3

SOFTWARE DEVELOPMENT ROI

If there is one concept that is spoken and written about a lot and yet is the least understood, it is ROI. Sales and business people use it, developers use it, managers use it and yet often it is hard for them to really express how to calculate it. We discussed the business case for maximizing ROI in the previous chapter. In this chapter, we will define and describe ROI in more detail and discuss why ROI along with TCO are good mechanisms for minimizing risk and maximizing benefits of software development and new application adoption.

3.1 DAYS OF "GOOD ENOUGH" SOFTWARE DEVELOPMENT ARE OVER

Software applications have enjoyed an immunity of sorts when it comes to reliability and quality. So many people have seen the core dumps or blue screens in computer applications indicating bugs or problems that it was an accepted part of the process. It would take an army of software consultants to make sure new software versions of the same product or new product introductions could work with legacy or existing systems. Even after that, if there was a problem, the knowledge of how to identify the cause of the problem and solve it was delegated to a few who would treat it pretty much like black magic. The amount of funds spent by enterprises to address the Y2K issue was enormous and if anything it highlighted how little understood our software systems are. Software bugs or errors cost the U.S. economy an estimated $59.5 billion annually or about 0.6 percent of the gross domestic product according to a newly released study commissioned by the National Institute of Standards and

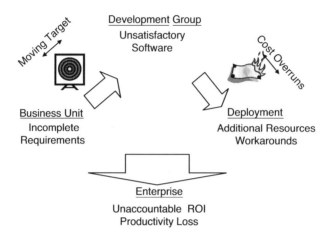

Figure 3.1 A Vicious Cycle

Technology (NIST) [1]. At the national level, over half of the costs are borne by software users and the remainder by software developers and vendors.

A vicious cycle (Figure 3.1) that has emerged for over a half century for software development can be described as follows. The enterprise sought software applications based on incomplete and inaccurate requirements. The business unit that produced the requirements was responsible when the software application failed to perform satisfactorily. The software development team stuck to code by feature style of development. A moving target situation was created and it became harder to satisfy requirements. The enterprise had to continue funding enhancements to an unsatisfactory solution. The business needs evolved faster than the code by feature could keep up. The bugs, errors, downtimes, and workarounds became the norm. The software development team continued to get funding and was not delivering solutions that were relevant at all. There is no accountability for ROI and blame is passed around without ownership to fix the problem.

As the dot.com bubble burst (or did it?) and the market shifted its focus away from excesses, a reality began to emerge. There was going to be less budget and emphasis on getting the latest and greatest. Instead, software applications had to withstand much greater scrutiny of testing, reliability, quality, and productivity. This has led to a reemergence of ROI and TCO metrics. It has led to companies becoming acutely (and rightfully) deserving of software applications that work and are worth it. It has led to software development becoming more responsible toward productivity, reliability, and accountability.

Most development and IT managers are considering adopting newer applications and technologies. Marketing messages abound for these newer applications and technologies touting all the benefits, ease of deployment, and improvements in performance, maintainability, and accessibility. However, IT managers keep asking tough questions so that their investments and resources are spent on the most optimal applications and technologies. Some of these questions are listed below:

■ Why is this the right time to use and budget for this new application or technology?
■ What are the real benefits?
■ Does this lower costs?
■ How mature is it?
■ Who are the other vendors supplying this technology or application?
■ What will be the time it takes for application integration and deployment into my existing environment?

ROI is one such metric that helps development and IT managers evaluate the usefulness and effectiveness of a new application or technology.

3.1.1 ROI Applies to Managers and Developers Alike

Myth: ROI is only for managers and those odd business folks.

Reality: ROI applies to developers, testers, and every stakeholder in software development.

Most times, development teams are insulated from business view and customer contact. One of the reasons ROI has not been acknowledged and used as a means to increase productivity in development groups has been a lack of guidelines or rules of ROI. The rules of ROI described below are geared toward development teams.

3.1.2 Use a Business Model

Management should discuss and share business models with development teams. Quarterly business updates or e-mail exchanges are usually not enough. There should be a concerted effort at discussing and sharing business environment, business model, customer feedback, and customer requirements on a repetitive and regular basis. Business plans and models should be shared and discussed.

A clear business model will make the developers better informed about the capability of the application they are developing. It makes them better informed about usability, scalability, and extensibility of their application in a real-world usage scenario. Better appreciation of the real-world usage scenario and business model gives the developers the motivation to design, architect, and develop with thoroughness that in turn produces more robust and relevant applications. Another key outcome of this exercise improved delivery timelines. Prioritization of feature upgrades should be made using bottom-line business considerations such as increased top line (increased revenue) or improved margins (decreased costs). Objectivity established with these business considerations results in better prioritization and feature development.

3.1.3 Priority of Customers May Not Match Those of ROI

We have all heard that "customer is king." Indeed, it is true that if the application development stays close to the customer requirements, it will spell success for the application and the enterprise. However, there are situations when it is important to step back and think about the overall business objectives. This ties back to the earlier point. What is important in software development is to take both a big picture and business-oriented view of what the customer is looking for and developing accurate requirements. However, getting too tied into quick fixes to satisfy every feature nit of the customer may lead to a short term gratification but a cost overrun in the long term. As described elsewhere in this book, XP and newer concepts emphasize quicker development cycles, prototyping, and customer participation. These lead to less capital invested and faster time to market and faster realization of revenue. Cost cutting projects and revenue driven projects sometimes have different requirements when it comes to feature sets and prioritization. Figure 3.2 illustrates this interesting inverse relationship. If a clear business model is not articulated, ease of use features may be added to revenue intensive projects and latest and greatest new features may be added to cost cutting projects. Similarly, the low cost of maintenance is a higher priority for cost cutting projects as opposed to revenue intensive projects.

3.1.4 Scalability and ROI

Several commonly used terms in the software development world have different meanings at different times of the software development and deployment lifecycle. For example, performance in the development phase means software developers producing acceptable code in a given amount of time. Performance at the deployment phase indicates ability of the

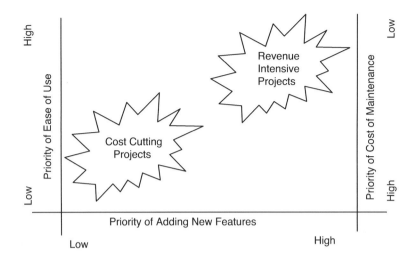

Figure 3.2   Differing Project Requirements

software application to handle a number of concurrent requests or multiple input and output calls or some other metric indicating the response times during higher usage. Other such words are testing, which generally means unit and functionality testing in the development phase, and black box, which is stress and performance testing during deployment phase. Similarly, scalability indicates numerical increase of developers on a given project, and during deployment it means the increase in usage the application can handle. Productivity and ROI generally improve with software developers who follow the guidelines listed below.

- Software quality and software productivity are closely related. Both have to be simultaneously improved. More software development does not translate to better quality and vice versa, and a balance of both must be constantly maintained.
- Working long hours on a project does not signify success or higher productivity. When the business model and requirements are not greater, more effort is spent in writing the code.
- Automation tools are used where appropriate at each stage of the project. Manual and repetitive component building and testing leads to lowered productivity, efficiency, and developer dissatisfaction.
- Better tools in the hands of bad developers does not make better code. There is no magic — the best people should be driving the most crucial aspects of software application development.
- Define and manage interfaces at the design level and not at the code level.

3.1.5 Use Interfaces that Are Neutral to Technology

Code automation tools are becoming widely available and commonly used these days. The efficiency of the software process can be measured as the size of the technical and business interface *vis-à-vis* the size of code or code base. The smaller the business interface file for larger code base, the more efficient the software process. As the earlier description of Web services indicated, better interfaces enable technology elements to be swapped without taking down the software application.

3.1.6 Financial View of Deliverables

Software development is not about the type of tools or hardware; it is about people. The more the merrier is not always productive. However, if the productivity is high, ROI is good, cash flow is available, and the feature set is demanding, it makes sense to add more developers on a project. Finding the right developer with the right skill set in a timely fashion becomes critical in this situation. We will discuss how outsourcing and offshoring contribute to enhanced ROI and better results later in this book. Deliverables should be laid out in such a way that they make financial sense. Eight to ten weeks for every key deliverable makes financial sense, because most budget and financial cycles proceed in quarters.

Getting a product build done and released quickly places requirements on the support and administrative functions in a project. Several project planners and developers never take the financial costs and timelines of this into account. ROI-based projects need to account for, and involve, support and administration logistics right up front in a project. Sometimes ordering and installing equipment may take a couple of months and may completely stall the release process.

From a financial perspective, employing permanent developers creates an ongoing headcount and benefits liability. The result is that a percentage of projects cannot be undertaken because they require the same ROI at development time. Improved ROI can be achieved when outsourcing or contract staff is used for expanding the project during development and then slimmed down after deployment.

3.2 BASELINE ROI

ROI, as we will define it in subsequent sections, is the classic or baseline definition and has been reported widely in literature. We will see later in this book how the baseline ROI can be enhanced with several techniques such as methodology and process improvements, automation, and outsourcing. Collectively, we will refer to the baseline ROI with these improvements as Applied ROI. More details of that will be in later chapters. Let us look at how ROI is defined and measured.

3.2.1 Definition of ROI

ROI is defined in the Dictionary of Modern Economics [2] as:

> A general concept referring to Earnings from the Investment of Capital, where the earnings are expressed as a proportion of the outlay.

In mathematical terms:

$$ROI = (Net\ Benefits/Net\ Costs) * 100$$

Net benefits can be either direct, in terms of incremental revenue generated, productivity gained, or expense saved, or indirect, the redeployment of resources or tasks that the organization would alternatively have had to hire new and like resources to perform. Net costs include recruiting, salaries, benefits, software licensing, and general and administrative overheads.

The ROI for each project is compared with the net costs on a yearly basis. ROI analysis means that where expected benefits and costs are realized within the same year of implementation of the project, the project is more likely to proceed. Sometimes ROI is not used as a percentage but as a numerical number (Net Benefits/Net Costs). That is referred to as ROI Ratio. This ratio is equal to 1 (or 100 percent) when net quantifiable benefits equal net quantifiable cost, which represents a break-even condition. Those projects having a ROI less than 100 percent may not be undertaken.

A 400 percent ROI over five years indicates a return of four times the original investment over a five-year period. Break-even analysis is used to indicate how many months after investment that the investment is recouped (100 percent). Not all benefits or costs are easily quantifiable. However, the approach to ROI taken in this chapter seeks to identify and quantify all significant net benefits and costs.

3.2.2 Components of ROI

We defined ROI earlier in this chapter as a ratio of net benefits to net costs. This ratio is equal to 1 (or 100 percent) when net benefits equal net cost. That indicates a break-even situation. A ratio of less than 1 reflects a negative growth and a ratio of greater than 1 indicates positive growth of investment.

3.2.2.1 ROI Percentage

ROI is frequently expressed as a percentage, in which case the ROI result is multiplied by 100. The percentage ROI calculation can thus be represented as:

$$\text{ROI Percentage} = (\text{Net Benefits}/\text{Net Costs}) \times 100\%$$

3.2.2.2 ROI Factor

The ROI factor is the ratio of net benefit to net cost (NB/NC) expressed as a real number instead of a percentage.

3.2.2.3 Net Benefit

In the early stages of software projects, there is development cost, but no benefit. This makes ROI undefined with negative net cash. Net benefit (NB) is the benefit to the enterprise from the implementation of the application. Implementation can include the relative benefits in the development, deployment, operation, support, and maintenance of the software applications. NB can be either direct, in terms of incremental revenue generated, productivity gained, or expense saved, or indirect, from the redeployment of resources to tasks that the organization would alternatively have had to hire new and equivalent resources to perform. NB can be either positive or negative and can be expressed in currency.

3.2.2.4 Net Cost

Net cost (NC) is the difference between the total cost and expenses associated with the application and the similar costs associated with the most likely alternative solution. The alternative solution could be manually doing the work done by the application or none at all. Typical NC components include software licensing and maintenance costs, product consulting costs, training and education costs, and any added hardware costs associated with implementing the application. NC can also be expressed in the local currency. Both NC and NB should be expressed in the same units.

3.2.2.5 Discount Rate and Internal Rate of Return

The discount rate is the expected rate of return that could be obtained from other projects of similar risk. If there is an investment that requires and produces a number of cash flows over time, the internal rate of return (IRR) is defined to be the discount rate that makes the net present value of those cash flows equal to zero. In other words, the discount rate that makes the project have a zero net present value (NPV, which is defined later) is the IRR.

The IRR method of analyzing investment in a new technology or using a technology in a project allows a company to consider the time value of money. IRR enables one to find the interest rate that is equivalent to the dollar returns that are expected from the technology or project under consideration. Once a company knows the rate, it can compare it to the rates that it could earn by investing money in other applications or technologies or investments.

3.2.2.6   Payback Period

Management generally prefers to measure the effects of budget allocations and returns in a fixed period of time. The percentage value of ROI should generally include a payback time to make it more effective. For example, if a $200,000 investment in Web services technology is generating $400,000 a year in profit, it pays for itself within half a year. Costs divided by years in which benefits are realized gives the payback period in years.

3.2.2.7   Net Present Value

NPV is the present value of an investment based on a discount rate and a series of future payments and income. It is the difference between the NC and the ROI measured in today's dollars. In other words, NPV calculations account for the time value of money. This is done by discounting the future cash flow of the investment at some rate, which varies with the risk of the investment. NPV is widely used by the investment community as a calculation to determine the present value of an investment.

$$NPV = \text{Initial Investment}$$
$$+ [\text{Net Benefit for Year } 1/(1 + \text{discount rate})]$$
$$+ [\text{Net Benefit for Year } 2/(1 + \text{discount rate})]$$
$$* 2$$
$$+ \ldots \ldots$$
$$+ [\text{Net Benefit for Year } N/(1 + \text{discount rate})]$$
$$* N$$

For example, if enterprise integration technology costs $200,000 and will result in NB of $50,000 per year for five years, there is a $50,000 net

ROI. The NPV of the investment, however, is actually less than $50,000 due to time value of money.

3.2.3 Data Collection for ROI

ROI is a relative measure in that the benefits and costs of an application are generally compared with those of an alternative solution. An alternative solution could be:

- What the organization had been doing to address this business problem before
- Manually doing what the application is supposed to be doing
- Purchasing an application (i.e., buy versus build)

NB and NC are defined differently for each situation and, in some cases, the results are not as quantifiable as in others. Increased productivity of a workforce is often a result of implementing a new software application. Whenever productivity gains are achieved, we assume that the resulting extra time is either used for some other value added project or task, or it leads to a reduction in workforce (RIF). To collect the data, we suggest the following methodology:

- Understand the business opportunity
- Understand what problem the application will solve
- Identify and quantify all components of ROI defined earlier
- Use a consistent set of questions and analytical techniques across interviews

3.2.3.1 Timeframes of ROI

The timeframe for assessing ROI can be different between applications, between different projects, and between different business units. ROI measurement timeframes can be in years and we suggest timeframes that are longer than two years. Longer timeframes result in a ROI calculation that has better accuracy and, based on our experience, two years is the least amount of time required for a project's evaluation. If a significant amount of accurate historical data is available, the ROI calculation will be more precise. Management usually also has projections on how NB and NC will evolve over time. This future data is also relevant to ROI calculation.

3.2.3.2 Mythical 1000 Percent ROI

Although gains of 1000 percent may be possible in some extreme circumstances, the reason we refer to it as mythical is because people have often abused ROI calculation and definition. As we defined earlier, ROI is the ratio of NB to NC. The key is the use of the word net. Often even reputed authors and studies have ignored the net in the calculation and presented ROI as simply the ratio of benefits to costs. This leads to significantly high ROI percentages — read as mythical 1000 percent ROI gains — and may be used to impress the management that they have been presented to. However, using the correct definition of ROI is crucial. NB means the total benefits minus the costs of those benefits. This leads to a more reasonable ROI calculation and presentation.

3.2.3.3   Example Case: Sales Force Automation Application

A multinational enterprise software manufacturer wanted to evaluate how to move its legacy sales force automation applications to a new wireless and natural language-enabled one. The first step was to start with how the business units using the sales force automation application saw the new technology. There was a danger of the project stalling because business unit managers did not see any operational benefits and only a newer learning curve of training, installation, and maintenance. A corporate ROI perspective at this stage would involve identifying the business benefits of the new application.

- Increased mobility of sales force
- Elimination of a legacy system with higher maintenance costs
- Ease of use through natural language interface
- New features and benefits such as tracking by account, demographics, customer, and product
- Faster updates of marketing department documentation and information
- More efficient tracking, with systematic controls to minimize marginal prospects and accounts
- Delivery of real-time data to sales representatives for quotations to customers when they are in the field
- Sales quota and targets visibility through real-time delivery of information

Most of these benefits are easily quantifiable and a dollar value is put next to them. A technique of scoring and weighting [3] is used to further enhance business objectives for development and support staff. NB and NC numbers are collected and timeframes for ROI and historical data is collected. Cross-functional groups prioritize each business goal and scores are assigned to each benefit indicating how it helps the business goal. Results are added up and distributed along with plots illustrating the benefits. This exercise yields several revelations. Many business benefits identified earlier are aligned with the business unit's goals. ROI numbers generated are higher than originally estimated and even hard to quantify benefits turn out to be important players in turning the mindset of business unit managers.

3.2.3.4 Summary of Case

Development, business, or IT managers can leverage their enterprise's business goals to highlight the benefits of their proposals. The use of business goals also helps improve the ROI process. Remember that ROI analysis is a comprehensive improvement indicator and should not be used just as a budgetary approval vehicle. Business value of a proposal should not be based exclusively on cost savings that sometimes are not enough to justify change. Strategic benefits of ROI analysis should be related to all the key stakeholders and different groups. This eliminates misconceptions and fear of change. Empowerment of different groups creates a wider body of support for the change and improvement.

3.3 APPLIED ROI

We have reviewed the concepts of baseline ROI analysis. In this section, we will compare several other interesting approaches to improving software development productivity, management, and planning. We will also review ROI of several newer technology approaches including XP and Web services. Collectively, we will refer to these as Applied ROI. Applied ROI refers to increased leverage of the same investment or cost and higher returns or NBs. Several techniques include better development and test methodology, development and test automation, and globalization of software development and testing including cosourcing work in outward rings to increased returns for the same investment. Let us look at some of these methodologies in more detail in this chapter.

3.3.1 Phases of Applied ROI

As Figure 3.3 illustrates, Applied ROI is concentric rings of successive improvement of technology, automation, methodology, and processes for increasing baseline ROI.

3.3.1.1 Baseline ROI Is the First Step

We refer to the definition of ROI that we have presented earlier as baseline ROI. Many authors have extensively written about ROI and one of the

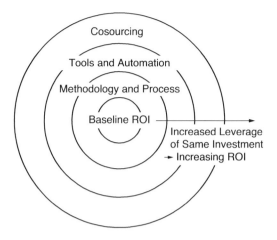

Figure 3.3 Rings of Applied ROI

major problems has been how ROI has been defined. As we discussed earlier, ROI should be defined in terms of NBs and NCs. The numbers calculated thus form the baseline ROI. Baseline refers to the fact that based on a current study of the processes, technology, and methodology, a given investment will be worth so much.

3.3.1.2 Training

This phase involves training on the specific technology and tools. Training costs involved are part of the cost metrics used later for ROI calculation. Training leads to increased familiarity with tools and technologies that in turn improves the returns. We will be discussing training ROI in more detail in a later chapter.

3.3.1.3 Tools and Automation

It has often been said that technology is a great equalizer. It can help improve the performance level of resources and increase ROI. Including technology, tools, and automation in the overall strategic vision should be the priority of every CIO, IT and department manager, and individual contributor. Software development and quality can both benefit from the technology, tools, and automation. Applications for personal productivity improvement are included in this category. Use of automated test tools, code generation, and design automation tools and analysis tools is critical for effective teams. Large-scale returns of 200 to 300 percent have been reported through the use of technology, tools, and automation. Other examples of tools and automation are remote monitoring, secure remote access, virtual private networks, security and networking, communication and conferencing, and remote customer assisting. Executives rely on business intelligence tools that give an accurate snapshot of the state of business, competitors, customers, and investor sentiments. They enable executives to make decisions that enhance the value of the enterprise.

3.3.1.4 *Processes and Methodologies*

Project and financial management methodologies, quality and processes definition, and repeatability are all critical in the success of development organization. Major technology investments are of no use or consequence unless good processes and methodologies are in place. Strategic business vision is implemented through processes and methodologies. Businesses are reorganized and transformed to the next level of performance using these processes and methodologies. Enterprises are constantly seeking new innovation while leveraging existing applications and customers. Process- and methodology-driven enterprises are the most successful in achieving these goals. Combining process and methodology improvements with technology catapults an enterprise to the next level of performance and brings about a sea change transformation. The impact and improvement on ROI is unlimited. Improvement of quality of service, reduction of costs, employee satisfaction, and increased capacity are all results of a successful combination of technology with processes and methodologies.

3.3.1.5 *Cosourcing*

Given today's business climate and global competition, keeping costs low is a must. Globalization has resulted in several countries and companies located offshore supplying high quality, low cost resources. This has been called offshoring and outsourcing. However, the author has found through years of experience that offshoring in isolation cannot be successful. It is important to combine an element of local — on-site — stakeholders to truly enjoy the benefits offered by outsourcing and offshoring. This combination of local and remote is what we refer to as cosourcing [4,5]. We believe that cosourcing offers another significant layer of increased ROI and forms an integral component of Applied ROI.

In subsequent chapters, we will visit automation and globalization of software development. We will discuss how cosourcing facilitates improvements in quality and business value. We will consider cases that provide backing for the Applied ROI concept that we have outlined here and we will calculate some actual numbers of Applied ROI. We will compare Baseline ROI with Applied ROI and identify key learnings.

3.3.2 TCO and ROI

Traditionally, TCO analysis has been used to determine the justification of buying computer hardware systems. Technologies, hardware, and software assets are evaluated and a cost is assigned to them in addition to processes and people. More recently, TCO has also been applied to IT and software assets [6]. All costs associated with a capital investment and operating costs are taken into account. TCO has been used in the past to determine the best value between several alternatives.

In the software world, the development and execution environment is one asset and the application itself is the other. TCO has been applied to evaluating automation software, training, and streamlining processes to increase efficiencies. Although TCO dominates discussions when companies plan to roll out new technology, ROI should be seriously looked at as well. Costs by themselves are not the whole picture. The savings that complete the picture are available from ROI analysis. Consequently, TCO forms the first step in ROI analysis

Determining ROI can be a time-consuming and expensive process. Striking a balance between immediate costs and long-term savings is not easy. That is due in part to the nature of ROI, which includes benefits that can be hard to quantify, such as increased productivity and less downtime. So productivity gains and benefits are important to consider, but cannot be used in the absence of cost savings, especially in today's environment. On the other hand, some companies can easily quantify ROI based on productivity gains; for example, in the case study of wireless natural language sales force automation system, the company realized 15 percent revenue increase on average for each sales representative when deployed. This resulted in an immediate buy-in from management for subsequent rollout based on productivity benefits alone.

The next steps toward Applied ROI are the methodologies and processes. As methodologies and processes get defined, implemented, and followed through, the same amount of investment in software gives more NBs. This results in increasing ROI.

3.3.2.1 Calculating TCO

TCO calculation is straightforward. The costs of initial acquisition of software and hardware are added to the cost of support, consulting, and setup. Maintenance and upgrades in the post-purchase phase along with training and ongoing support are factored in as continuing costs. Yearly TCO can be used for budget planning and it is a good metric for comparing similar applications. In summary, the three costs are:

- Acquisition costs — hardware, software, management, support, development, and communications
- Management costs — budget and resource expenses, administrative and office costs
- Intangible costs — unplanned costs, downtime, user costs, and miscellaneous costs

As discussed earlier, TCO is a great tool for budget exercises, but is not very effective in investment returns and bottom-line analysis, because it ignores benefits. TCO supports only the strategy of reducing costs and may be inadequate by itself.

3.3.2.2   Steps to Calculate TCO

It is difficult to account for all the intangibles when calculating TCO. These may include unexpected hurdles and costs or payoffs and benefits involved in a software application implementation. The steps to calculate TCO are listed below:

- Determine period of analysis
- Collect all the relevant financial, resources, and costs data
- Determine the changes in the costs data over the period of analysis
- Identify potential issues and make educated guesses and action items
- Understand change control by doing what-if analysis
- Set a process of accounting for ongoing costs, maintenance, and support cost management
- Use the numbers to determine costs and get the TCO number

3.3.3   Methodologies of Applied ROI

In this section, we look at methodologies in greater detail. Others mentioned elsewhere in this book and literature are equally applicable and useful to Applied ROI.

3.3.3.1   Capability and Maturity Model

Development and IT departments continually search for methodologies to improve reliability, maturity, performance, and scalability of their software deliverables. Delays and quality deficiencies are a constant hurdle to overcome without a consistent and repeatable software development process and methodology. CMM is an application for software engineering

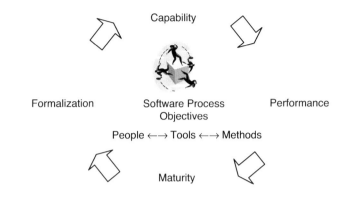

Capability

Formalization   Software Process   Performance
Objectives

People ←→ Tools ←→ Methods

Maturity

Figure 3.4   Guidelines of Capability and Maturity Model

that was introduced by Carnegie Mellon University's Software Engineering Institute (SEI) [7]. It is designed to guide software organizations in selecting process improvement strategies by determining current process maturity and identifying the issues most critical to software quality and process improvements as shown in Figure 3.4.

CMM consists of five levels:

1. Initial — *ad hoc* and chaotic process. No requirements.
2. Repeatable — basic requirements management, project planning and oversight, software quality assurance, and configuration management
3. Defined — process focus, definition, documentation training program, integrated software management, product engineering, and peer reviews
4. Managed — process management, software quality management, and control
5. Optimizing — continuous process improvement, process change management, defect prevention, and technology change management

3.3.3.1.1   Initial

This CMM level signifies individualistic artist-like approach with no guidelines or standards in the use of tools and no metrics gathered. Small groups of highly skilled developers may produce good software, but a large development team cannot. Support for reuse does not exist and no standards for development are applied consistently.

3.3.3.1.2 Repeatable

At this CMM level, projects are using a common set of tools and there is some level of teamwide integration of tools. Local metrics for level of effort are gathered and standards are used among the project participants. Limited reuse of design and code is practiced and training is standardized.

3.3.3.1.3 Defined

This is the level that several enterprises reach and stop improving. This level uses standards across the organization and reuse is practiced at enterprise level. Metrics are gathered, stored, analyzed, and applied to software development in a consistent fashion.

3.3.3.1.4 Managed

In CMM Level 4, processes used by the organization have been standardized and training for them is continuous. Metrics are analyzed quantitatively and used to improve the processes.

3.3.3.1.5 Optimizing

The highest level of CMM, Level 5, signifies the capability of an enterprise to proactively seek and adopt innovative tools, technologies, and processes.

3.3.3.2 ISO 9001

ISO 9001 is a global standard for quality and process improvement. It is also a widely used certification criteria in the European Union. ISO 9001 is composed of five broad categories of requirements for the design and certification of quality management systems:

1. Quality management system — documentation and general requirements
2. Management responsibility — commitment, customer focus, quality planning and policy
3. Resource management — human resources, infrastructure, and environment
4. Product realization and management — planning, design and development, customer processes, purchasing, and services provision
5. Measurement, analysis, and improvement — monitoring, analysis of data, and continuous improvement and control

All subsequent discussions that use CMM as the basis also apply equally well to ISO 9001 and other methodologies in this book.

3.3.3.3 Six Sigma

Six Sigma uses a set of strategies, statistics, and methods to improve the design and manufacturing processes. Marketing, sales, and service as well as help desks can use Six Sigma to help both internal groups and external customers. Six Sigma allows significant improvements in quality processes and financial performance. It is a methodology rooted in statistics and the objective of Six Sigma is to reduce process variation. The intention is to reduce the defects to less than 3.4 per million. Several companies including GE, Honeywell, and Motorola have been reported to have saved more than $1 billion using Six Sigma methodology. In addition to DPMO, there are several Six Sigma nomenclatures that we will describe below.

3.3.3.3.1 Defects per Million Opportunities

Defects per million opportunities or DPMO is described as the boundary of Six Sigma. A Six Sigma process should have less than 3.4 DPMO.

3.3.3.3.2 Design for Six Sigma

Design for Six Sigma or DFSS is a systematic methodology utilizing tools, training, and measurements to design products and processes that meet customer expectations and can be produced at Six Sigma quality levels.

3.3.3.3.3 Define, Measure, Analyze, Improve, Control

Define, measure, analyze, improve, and control or DMAIC is the process for continuous improvement. As mentioned earlier, it is a statistical and fact-based systematic process. As we will see later, DMAIC can be applied to software development lifecycle appropriately. The intention of this closed-loop process is to remove inefficient and wasteful steps and apply new techniques, measurements, and technology for improvement. This is the key behind our inclusion of this important process for Applied ROI.

Six Sigma includes several quality tools to help participants (also known as associates) monitor and improve the process.

3.3.3.3.4 Statistical Process Control

SPC is the application of statistical techniques to monitor and analyze data and control the process variations to help continuous improvement and contain defects. The analysis component includes understanding the reason for process nonconformance so it can be fixed.

3.3.3.3.5 Control Chart

Control chart is a statistical process control tool to monitor variance in a process over time. Control charts have unexpected variance detection measures built in that trigger alerts and help detect defect-causing conditions. Limits such as Three Sigma and also trend lines can be measured as part of variance detection.

3.3.3.3.6 Pareto Chart

Pareto chart uses the rule that 80 percent of problems are caused by the 20 percent of root causes. It shows relative frequency or size in a descending order bar chart. This highlights the problems that have the highest potential for resolution.

3.3.3.3.7 Defects

Defects or bugs cause problems to the users of the software application. Bugs are expensive to detect and fix when the application is in the hands of the user. It is important to find and fix them earlier in the software development lifecycle.

3.3.3.3.8 Black Belts and Green Belts

Black belts are full-time leaders of the team responsible for DMAIC. Black belts are teachers and mentors to associates and green belts. Green belts are not full-time positions.

3.3.3.3.9 Six Sigma and Software Development

As we discussed earlier, software development can be enhanced through the use of Six Sigma. The continuous improvement and defect and cycle time reduction are both results of successful application of Six Sigma principles to software development. Typically, benefits exceed cost within a year of the start of a Six Sigma program for software development with cost reduction to the tune of 25 percent in two years' timeframe. Several significant changes in culture of the development organization need to be implemented to make this happen. The training needs to be pursued top-down, so that a good proportion of IT and development managers are exposed to Six Sigma. A good mix of black belts and green belts need to be engaged for this purpose. The team should be involved in training and improvement and empowered to plan and implement it. Best practices and key learnings need to be shared and applied across the board. Project management, market development, and resource utilization should be evaluated and updated, and in-process metrics and root cause analysis should be implemented throughout the software development lifecycle.

The objective during the software development lifecycle should be to bring defects or software bugs down and software rework time reduction. Customer focus, as advocated by Agile Methodologies including LD principles discussed earlier and feedback to measure deliverables, is crucial to the Six Sigma process. Application costs can be lowered by appropriate reduction in wasteful practices and failure avoidance including reduced hardware downtime and installation streamlining.

3.3.3.4 Value of Methodology to ROI

Methodologies such as CMM, Six Sigma, and ISO 9001 provide several quantifiable improvements in Applied ROI.

- Reduction in software development and maintenance costs
- Improved quality of deliverables and reductions in rework and workarounds
- Improved morale and accountability of developers
- Sustainable improvements on everything from design, development, and deployment
- Improved enterprise image as an embracer of standards and good practices
- Improved customer expectation management and satisfaction
- Management visibility into the software development process
- Improved tracking of costs, schedules, and functionality

Each one of these improvements can be quantified. IT reports from Verizon listed in good detail some quantifiable gains for several categories. These included software productivity gain (35 percent), improved defect detection gains (22 percent), reductions in reworks and workarounds (20 percent), and ROI (500 percent) [8]. Other gains that are not readily quantifiable include customer satisfaction and expectation management as well as time-to-market improvements.

3.3.4 Tools and Techniques for Applied ROI

3.3.4.1 eXtreme Programming ROI

XP, as described earlier, enables the management of software development to focus on developers. It has introduced the notion of treating software development as a more creative and flexible process, unlike models based on building construction. Applications are now being built rapidly and deployed globally in a matter of months rather than years and the newer methodologies in this Agile programming group are geared to address that.

XP has empowered the developers, but with that has come increased responsibility toward business models and reasons behind software development. ROI now has to be understood by every developer because value is not in the quantity of programs they write, but in the quality and appropriateness of a few programs that are profitable. XP as laid out on the CMM process addresses Level 2 and Level 3 organizations [9] and focuses on colocated teams of usually less than ten developers. To develop ROI models for XP, one has to compare invested capital with the expected benefits on a yearly basis. If the project has a positive ROI, then it is more likely to proceed.

Two ways in which enterprises can conduct ROI analysis of new technologies, such as XP and Web services, are:

■ Discounted cash flow
■ Payback period

Both of these techniques have their origins in the investment community. They have been used in the past to determine whether or not money should be invested in a company. Applied to XP, discounted cash flow will work as follows. Expected cash flows relating to investment in XP tools, development environment, and methodology over the next few years are discounted using a discount rate to determine NPV. If NPV is positive, then XP is undertaken. For payback period analysis, the time it takes for XP to yield enough returns to pay for the initial investment or to break even is considered. Usually if it is less than a year, it is considered to be a favorable investment. As readers may have observed, XP usually measures favorably with ROI in projects where requirements are changing rapidly and development and market introductions cycles are shorter. Development of real-time and large-scale systems as well as situations where there are virtual teams through outsourcers or remote sites are less conducive to use of XP due to lack of clearly defined ROI.

3.3.4.2 *Web Services ROI*

With several large companies developing and adopting Web service standards, there are several usage scenarios and delivery mechanisms emerging. By construction and design, a typical business function could be handled by several Web services served by internal IT groups as well as outside vendors. ROI calculation for Web services is particularly challenging for these reasons and adopting a standard approach hard. In this section, we will discuss some more details of how Web services ROI can be calculated. Later we will give examples.

3.3.4.2.1 Net Cost

To get to the ROI calculations and methodology for Web services, we should first understand what are the typical costs of developing and deploying Web services-enabled applications:

- Cost of buying software license and maintenance
- Cost of installation, configuration, setup, and maintenance
- Cost of development — including indirect costs
- Cost of training
- Cost of vendor consulting

3.3.4.2.2 Net Benefit

NBs include such things as cost reduction, increased revenue, faster time-to-market, etc. ROI analysis is more of a guideline than gospel and should not be assumed to be always accurate. As we will see throughout this book, ROI calculations help identify the mechanism of improving processes, eliminating risks, and identifying business value creators that can be replicated.

ROI as we defined earlier is NBs that accrue from a given cost. The ROI on Web services is derived by the automation of business processes and ease of integration, which results in reduced application development time and maintenance. ROI measures the amount of reduction in operational and developmental costs and not just the reduced paperwork or reduced need for building data interfaces. ROI of Web services should take training and consulting costs into account because at the current time, those are significant cost factors. In addition, several tools for Web services are not completely developed and do not integrate all the capabilities. This requires increased setup and maintenance costs and development costs.

3.3.5 When ROI Is Hard to Quantify

What we have discussed so far are quantifiable aspects of ROI analysis. Several business values of ROI are hard to quantify. These include the improvements attained in customer satisfaction, customer service, and support organizations. Additional issues such as business brand name and equity in the marketplace, market share, and value of the company are hard to quantify.

3.3.5.1 Business Values

ROI analysis and the improvements to the organization it imparts enable enterprises to improve business agility through outsourcing of business services, business processes, and functions. Scaling business to cater to increased customer demand at a lower cost becomes possible through successful outsourcing relationships as this book discusses. Measurements and monitoring of the outsourcing relationships become possible through a better understanding of what drives ROI and how NBs can be maximized while keeping NCs in check.

Some of the harder to quantify business values of ROI analysis are:

- Time-to-market improvements
- Improvements in customer service and support leading to overall improvement in customer expectation management and satisfaction
- Improved business agility
- Reduction in uncertainty that may have existed due to lack of business process automation
- Improvement in brand name and value of the enterprise
- Increased business-to-business collaboration

3.3.5.2 Market Share and Brand Equity

As market share of an enterprise's applications increases, so does the brand value to the customer. However, this may not always be true. There can be applications from well-known enterprises with a lot of brand names that are not market leaders in their specific category. This ROI factor is difficult to quantify. However, in general, as the application quality, usability, service, and support increases, market share increases and brand equity increases. This leads to better customer retention and loyalty that in turn triggers better word of mouth and improved customer acquisition. All this has the effect of increasing NB for the steady cost level and consequently increased ROI.

3.3.5.3 Competitive Pressures

Multiple applications geared to the same marketplace and providing similar feature sets increase competitive pressures. If more than one enterprise is offering applications catering to the same need, there will be a downward pressure on cost and increased requirement of reliability, serviceability, and support. This tends to consume more resources of enterprises providing and supporting those applications. This in turn leads to increased costs while NBs are decreasing, leading to decreased ROI.

3.3.5.4 *Regulatory Environment*

Another factor for ROI that is hard to quantify is the government or regulatory environment. Several countries in this world impose specific requirements and restrictions on software applications. These restrictions may be user-interface-related or documentation-related or compliance-related (such as Section 508 by the U.S. government), privacy-related, encryption-related, national-security-related, or export-control-related to name a few. Sometimes these are initiated by protectionist regimes that want to increase local development and discourage outside software applications and products. Any one or a combination of these factors can quickly result in costs escalation related to paperwork and approval bureaucracy. ROI could be adversely affected in such situations.

3.3.5.5 *Support and Serviceability Cost*

As software applications begin to be used worldwide, costs of support for native languages, localization, and serviceability in diverse distant countries is becoming important. Sometimes these costs are difficult to quantify and predict in advance. Customer retention could be adversely affected if the support and serviceability is not up to the mark leading to further deterioration in revenue. The key to increasing predictability is to use consistent methodology and training for support and service resources and carefully evaluating partnerships from ROI perspective.

3.4 SUMMARY OF CHAPTER

ROI is used to measure the benefits and value of a new and improved process or application or technology. ROI is also used for measuring the economic value of popular approaches to software development. However, ROI continues to be an exploited word with several people using it and few completely understanding the appropriate techniques for determining the ROI and relationships of ROI to TCO, CMM, XP, and Web services. This chapter explains the ROI of software development and introduces practical metrics and models.

As we identified in Section 3.2, ROI is the ratio of NBs to NCs, expressed as a percentage. ROI is a simple and powerful tool for analyzing costs and benefits. Costs and benefits are most often expressed in currency or other monetary terms. A positive ROI indicates money well spent, a negative ROI indicates losses and ROI when the numerator (NBs) is equal to denominator (NCs), then it is a break-even situation. Readers are introduced to the author's concept of Applied ROI that defines and measures how ROI can be maximized given a constant investment or cost level using several applied techniques described as concentric rings of Applied ROI. Baseline ROI, as defined, forms the core of Applied ROI rings. It signifies an enterprise's commitment to maximizing returns on software investment.

As methodologies and processes begin to be defined, established, and enforced by the enterprise, NBs (numerator of the ROI equation) start to increase. The increase in the NB is generally higher than the increase in NC. This helps improve the ROI. Next come automation and tools. Successful application of this second ring of Applied ROI results in enterprise saving costs, increase employee satisfaction, and improve reliability and predictability of software applications produced. Successful application of automation and tools requires upfront infrastructure and training investment. This adds to the NC (denominator of the ROI equation). However, after a brief period, the NB again starts to increase faster than the NC. This helps further increase ROI. In Section 3.3, we explore the relationships of CMM, ISO 9001, and Six Sigma methodologies to Applied ROI in this chapter. We also look at Six Sigma terms and its relevance to software development lifecycle.

Finally, the third ring of Applied ROI is cosourcing. We define cosourcing as an organization's effort to globalize its software development and testing. This includes establishing development subsidiaries as well as partnering with third-party companies that have experience in software development and testing. Successful cosourcing results in a reduction of NCs (denominator of the ROI equation) and boosts the ROI further. It is important to note here that successful cosourcing requires that the organizations have developed good methodologies and processes and identified appropriate automation and tools. Without these necessary ingredients, cosourcing will not be successful. Communicating with teams located geographically separately and making sure that the software application can be developed and tested effectively, on time and within budget requires maturity in processes and methods. In the subsequent chapters, we will see how to effectively globalize software development and testing.

REFERENCES

1. Software Errors Cost U.S. Economy $59.5 Billion Annually. NIST Assesses Technical Needs of Industry to Improve Software-Testing, June 28, 2002.
2. Pearce, David W., Ed., *The Dictionary of Modern Economics*, 4th ed., Cambridge, MA: The MIT Press.

3. Kepner, C.H. and Tregoe, B.B., The New Rational Manager: a Systematic Approach to Problem-Solving and Decision-Making, London: J Martin Publishing, 1981.

4. Sikka, V., Maximizing Outsourced Software Quality and ROI: Selecting and Managing an Outsourcer, *Systems Development Management*, Boca Raton, FL: CRC Press, 2003.

5. Sikka, V., Realizing the ROI of Outsourced Development. *Systems Development Management*, Boca Raton, FL: CRC Press, 2003.

6. Hornby, D. and Pepple, K., *Consolidation in the Data Center: Simplifying IT Environments to Reduce Total Cost of Ownership*, Upper Saddle River, NJ: Prentice Hall.

7. The Software Engineering Institute, Carnegie Mellon University, *The Capability Maturity Model, Guidelines for Improving the Software Process*, Boston: Addison Wesley Longman, Inc., 1997.

8. Verizon IT department report, Using the Capability Maturity Model for Software Development March 7, 2003, Verizon Information Technologies, Inc. whitepaper.

9. Paulk, M.C., Extreme Programming from a CMM Perspective Software XP Universe, Raleigh, NC, 23–25 July 2001, Engineering Institute Carnegie Mellon University.

4

THE CASE FOR GLOBAL SOFTWARE DEVELOPMENT AND TESTING

The world is becoming a global village. Increased communication capabilities, computer networks, and language compatibility are challenging older models of doing all software development and testing in one large in-house location. Enterprises and independent software vendors (ISV) are following a distributed development model where there are development offices around the world and development as well as testing is happening round the clock. For example, Microsoft, SAP, and others have development centers in the United States, Europe, Israel, and India; IBM, Hewlett–Packard, and Electronic Data Systems are developing software and outsourcing support from Mexico, India, and Brazil; BearingPoint, formerly KPMG Consulting is serving software development out of China. There are numerous other examples of development centers located in Ireland, the United Kingdom, Singapore, Canada, Russia, and others.

This fundamental change in the current software application development process has accelerated. The reasons for the acceleration are as follows:

- Downturn in the market and economy in the last few years
- Rising complexity in technology
- Stringent customer requirements

The dramatic increase in the number of development centers around the world is growing faster than ever, yet several ISVs continue to trail behind and fail to utilize this opportunity of cosourcing development and

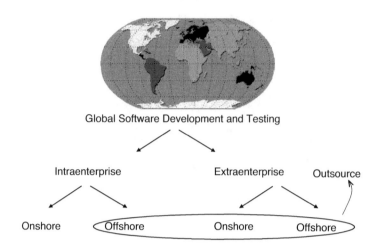

Figure 4.1   Scenarios of Global Software Development and Testing

testing. In this chapter, we will discuss the benefits of distributed software development and the value proposition derived from it. We will discuss background behind globalization and cosourcing software development for current and future projects that readers may be wishing to undertake. We will discuss myths of global software development including offshoring and outsourcing. We will discuss benefits and types of projects that are best suited to this environment, and we will also address the enabling technologies and the success criteria for effective global software development.

4.1   SCENARIOS OF GLOBAL SOFTWARE DEVELOPMENT

In this section, we will describe different global software development and testing scenarios used throughout this book. Figure 4.1 shows the nomenclature we use for the different scenarios. All the metrics and methodologies described in the book apply to all of these scenarios. We will refer to global software development for an organization also as cosourcing. Cosourcing signifies the fact that the company has internal software development and also may be interfacing with third parties that outsource parts of software development.

4.1.1   Intraenterprise Onshore and Offshore

Enterprises may have two sites in two different countries. We will call this intraenterprise onshore and offshore development. In this scenario, ISVs and enterprises that globalize software development, establish a subsidiary and a development center in the country of choice. This development center is in addition to one existing locally. The development teams are located in both the centers and share the same project plan and may share the same administrative and cost center resources.

4.1.2 Extraenterprise Onshore and Offshore

This has been referred to as outsourcing or best shoring (by IBM, EDS, etc.). If an enterprise seeks to use a third-party vendor to get software development or testing done, then they establish a partnership or joint venture. In this scenario, the third-party vendor could have a local office in the same city or it could have an offshore location in a different country. Development teams are located in both the centers and may share the same project plan but not the same administrative and cost center resources.

4.2 BENEFITS OF GLOBAL SOFTWARE DEVELOPMENT AND TESTING

There are several benefits to global software development and testing. Several of these are listed below.

4.2.1 24/7 Software Development Cycle

Development centers located throughout the world provide an opportunity to continue development through day and night. Development teams distributed across different geographies can make use of source control, bug tracking systems, and project management tools and cooperate in making the builds and picking up from where the other team left off. In addition, different countries follow different holidays, so development work continues throughout the year with practically no downtime. This continuity imparts extra momentum to the development effort.

4.2.2 Diversified Talent Pool

Several years ago, with the lack of travel and communication, cultural and language barriers were almost insurmountable. These cultural and language barriers around the world are becoming irrelevant these days. English is widely spoken and technical education and training is becoming standardized. All of this has led to growing opportunities of hiring talented and qualified software developers and testers. Job market decline or glut in one country does not hurt the prospects of maintaining and adding to the workforce of the company. Fluctuations in economies of different countries have less overall effect on the global software development. Vastly improved broadcast (television, radio), print, communication (telephone), and Internet have enabled an understanding of different cultures among people throughout the world and that in turn has enabled better comingling of teams in different countries.

4.2.3 Proximity to Software Consumers and Marketplaces

Several countries have growing software and technology systems demand with their growing economies. Chinese IT and software market increased four times that of gross domestic product (GDP) in the last ten years according to Lou Qinjian, vice minister of information industry in China. The number of Internet users in China is now second only to the United States. Similarly, Indian IT and software market was ranked by Gartner as the fastest growing IT market in the world. According to Nasscom (www.nasscom.org), the IT market in India employs more than 700,000 people domestically, is growing at about 35 percent annually, and is currently more than $17 billion in size. In addition to North America, the European Union, and Japan, countries in Asia and Latin America are rapidly becoming major software and IT product consumers. The need for localization and internationalization of software and systems is increasing and the development centers of major companies located in these countries are performing these tasks for local software consumption.

4.2.4 Cost Savings

Easy availability of a talented and educated workforce in countries such as India, Brazil, China, and Mexico and reduced cost of communication infrastructure is enabling companies to enjoy reduced cost of software development. Coupled with the market slowdown and economic pressures in the United States, the European Union, and Japan, this has provided an opportunity for expansion of outsourced development centers to these countries. This has enabled an increase in extraenterprise offshoring that provide great price to value ratios for software development in addition to high quality. We will discuss more of these advantages later in this book. We will also discuss how there is a strong growing backlash against outsourcing that has resulted from job loss and a shift of key competencies.

4.2.5 Reliability through Distributed Development

When development centers are distributed in diverse places and teams are working in unison, software development is relatively uninterrupted and more robust. Natural calamities, terrorist attacks, or political conditions

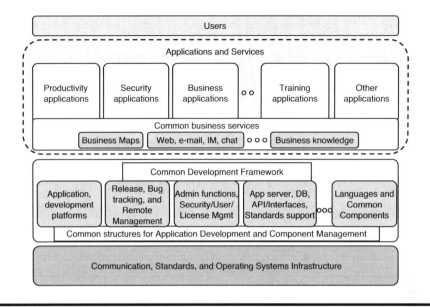

Figure 4.2   Global-Enabling Technologies and Applications

in one country will not shut down the development effort in an organization with distributed development.

4.2.6   Handle Peaks and Valleys in Demand

Software development and testing has its peaks and valleys. Sometimes with impending new releases, the activity level for both development and testing is increased and at other times when planning and design is involved it slows down. The required resources and the amount of work done by resources can change sharply over a small time period. Flex resourcing in global development centers is one approach for the enterprise to follow to handle the demand peaks and valleys.

4.3   TECHNOLOGY IS THE GLOBAL ENABLER

Ubiquitous availability of software and hardware throughout the world has led to the adoption and use of the latest tools. Technology has empowered teams to communicate and manage global teams. Figure 4.2 describes several of these global-enabling technologies.

4.3.1   Project Management Tools

As the project management and test tools expand, it is becoming easier to manage tasks across teams in different geographies. Code management and bug tracking systems are increasingly global in their deployment, maintained and updated in real-time. Software development for diverse platforms is increasingly being standardized. Software architecture is becoming increasingly component-based with a rising number of object-oriented development environments (e.g., Microsoft .Net, Sun ONE, SourceForge™, and others). The emergence of common standards is facilitating the use of standardized third-party components, for example, J2EE for application servers, JSP/ASP for the presentation layer, Lightweight Directory Access Protocol (LDAP) for directories, and public key infrastructure (PKI) for security.

4.3.2 Communication Tools

Global computer and telecommunication networks are enabling faster and cheaper communication including video, audio, and data. Communication vehicles have become reliable, seamless, and secure over the last decade. The Internet has facilitated a cheaper medium to communicate through instant messaging, chat, and sharing.

We all know someone who is a marathon flyer, a person who has logged more than 30,000 miles in a year. Although there is a distinct value in meeting people face to face and getting to know them, newer communication mediums are enabling the rest of us participate in distant meetings. Video conferencing, Web conferencing, and phone communication are facilitating that now more than ever. The events of September 11 have rekindled the debate and made people ask the question: Is the meeting important enough for me to be there in person? A not-to-fly sentiment has been taking hold and enterprises are eager to conduct global business meetings remotely. Holding global meetings among diverse audiences needs a phone and an Internet connection. Video conferencing, teleconferencing, and Web conferencing (where files, workspace, and pictures are shared using the Internet) are three popular ways of conducting global meetings. Videoconferencing uses dedicated lines and television-based meetings where remote participants can see and hear each other. Teleconferencing uses phone-based communication with speakerphones for groups of people to communicate with each other. More recently, companies such as Placeware (now Microsoft LiveMeeting) and WebEx have facilitated Web conferencing. It should be realized that the budget for conferencing technologies generally comes from the IT budget and not travel and selling, general, and administrative (SG&A) expenses. CIOs and IT managers are encouraged to pursue a thorough evaluation in appropriate remote communication technologies before making investment decisions. Training in new equipment and related processes is another crucial area because just the investment and purchase of the communication tools are not enough. The trade-off between in-person meetings and remote meetings should be carefully considered and evaluated on a case-by-case basis.

4.3.2.1 Remote Conferencing

As we have discussed earlier, the remote communication tools such as videoconference and Web conference enable inclusion simultaneously of many geographically distributed teams. Recording the proceeds of the conference is easier and tracking questions, comments, answers, and statements becomes possible. Effective publishing and presentation tools can be combined with the video or Web conferencing format for successful meetings. Internet has enabled several of these mediums to cost less and provide significant business value.

Teleconferencing exacerbates language and comprehension problems among the participants. For this reason as well as the reason of being able to see the person, share documents, and share a common workspace, Web conferencing is preferable as a communication medium for meetings of global teams. Teleconference may be an acceptable medium if people have worked with each other for a long time and are comfortable with language and communication abilities.

Videoconferences sometimes tend to get unwieldy and counterproductive if there are large teams meeting. Participants may need to spend more time on setup and learning how to use it. Communication problems may surface and time delay in the pictures could make the meeting less effective. It does not easily replace an in-person meeting. Also, the meetings should be kept on schedule without much free form style discussion, otherwise some participants may keep talking and others become passive.

4.3.2.2 Case

Let us consider a group of 40 developers and 15 quality engineers located in Vancouver, British Columbia; Mountain View, California; Bangalore, India; and Pune, India. These four locations are in two time zones — Pacific Standard Time and Indian Standard Time. The four teams' typical communication volume will be as follows when a major release is approaching. There will be 20 to 30 e-mails relating to daily updates, project planning, status, and methodology. Alternate day Web conference calls starting at 7:00 PM Pacific Standard Time and 8:30 AM Indian Standard Time. Sharing of bug fixes, feature updates, and test specifications by sending reports in advance before the Web conference. Occasionally, a PC-based videoconference would be used when new members are being introduced or group problem solving becomes necessary. Overlap of development and testing time would be exploited for two to three instant messengers and chats. Builds developed in Mountain View would be completed by the end of day and certified by Vancouver. Test cases would then be run in Bangalore and Pune, and bug tracking systems updated via a virtual private network (VPN) before developers returned back at work in the morning of the next day.

4.3.3 Distributed Code Management and Test Tools

Most of the effective project management and planning tools are distributed in their implementation these days. Code management, build management, and source control tools such as Source Safe, CVS, Perforce, Revision Control System (RCS), and ClearCase® are designed so that diverse teams can interact and maintain uniform builds and a codebase. Testing tools enable testing the same product from multiple locations and error-tracking tools enable managing bugs at one central location.

4.3.4 Emergence of Common Standards

Common standards for software development planning, design, architecture, and development have enabled widespread use of good software engineering practices. Sharing designs and development versions across different geographies is not only possible, but also practical and commonplace these days. RUP, OMG, MDA, and other methodologies have enabled universal language of planning, design, and development. This has helped bridge boundaries between diverse teams.

4.3.5 Component-Based Software Architecture

Shared class libraries and patterns have long been used in good software engineering practices [1]. Standardized data access components, model, view, and control paradigm that separates data from user interface and logic have helped build robust applications. More recently, Web services, MDA, and others described earlier are facilitating global software development and testing.

4.3.6 Seamless and Secure Networks

The Internet has provided many low cost or free and reliable mediums to communicate across different geographical locations. E-mail, Voice-over Internet Protocol (VoIP), chat, and Instant Messaging are some of these mechanisms. Quality of telecommunications infrastructure, prevalence of wireless and mobile technologies, and other mechanisms facilitate direct one-on-one communication between team members across regions and

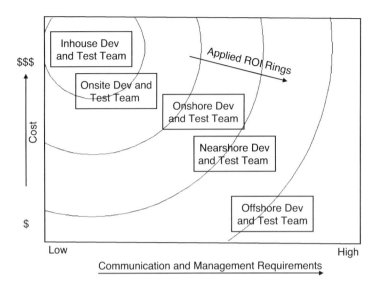

Figure 4.3   Types of Outsourcing and Cost/Management Requirements

continents. Security protocols such as IPSec, PKI, VPN technologies, and others enable protecting confidential information and increase confidence in communications.

4.4   SUCCESS CRITERIA FOR GLOBAL SOFTWARE DEVELOPMENT AND TESTING

Intraenterprise and extraenterprise (outsourced) offshore locations are no longer cheap labor suppliers. Successful companies have integrated their global offices as partners in a common development program. They have successfully added partner networks to this program and made them joint stakeholders. In addition to executing to a well-defined strategy, it is important to build and manage effective partnerships, implement best of class communication and network infrastructure, and stay competitive with local human resource practices to retain best talent. Figure 4.3 shows cost savings with need for effective communication and management for intraenterprise and extraenterprise vehicles. The cost management requirements are laid out with the current models of software development location. Rings of Applied ROI are laid out on the cost saving matrix. As readers can see, teams that are onshore and on location tend to be near baseline ROI; however, as teams are distributed and cost advantages of offshore start to be realized, the enterprise is traversing outward on rings of Applied ROI and benefiting.

Regardless of which scenario is chosen by enterprises to pursue software development in today's environment, success in software development globalization is also dependent on several additional factors. These include a well-defined plan to leverage a globalization platform and development and execution strategy. Beyond this, following best practices, methodologies and proven models, and evaluation processes are important. These factors are described in more detail below.

4.4.1 Define Execute and Measure to a Plan

The first step is to define the business objectives and next a global software development strategy and plan for meeting those business objectives. Successful plans are only those that are constantly updated and revised to reflect the realities of the project. If the plan is not kept up-to-date, it will lose relevance. Prepare to measure to the plan and stick to it. Suitable communication channels related to the plan updates and reviews should be established.

4.4.1.1　Aim High

When setting up the global software development initiative, plan big and build excitement and management support. This will enable overcoming hurdles of finding the best talent as well as the budget and resources to support it.

4.4.1.2　Find Champions

Obtaining management buy-in and ensuring success of the global software development strategy needs a strong champion and management stakeholder. Onshore and offshore development centers should always be on the agenda and in focus. People and resource issues should be discussed frequently and inclusively.

4.4.1.3　Find Stakeholders

People who will manage global software development should have experience and real interest in coordinating development across geographical boundaries. It will require an unprecedented commitment and focus to balance and achieve success between onshore and offshore development activities. Payment and incentives of the management should be aligned with the success of the global software development initiative.

4.4.1.4 Integrate Objectives

As discussed earlier, onshore and offshore development centers should be treated as equal. This integration of objectives enables team building and better dissemination of latest techniques and methodologies. It also enables responsibility among different parties to perform and support each other.

4.4.2 Management Responsibilities

Software development and testing team's management has to share special responsibilities to make sure that the global teams can function well together. Developer groups with the best of intentions can still form islands of interaction. One group does not feel responsible to help the other group in times of need and learnings are not shared between teams. Sometimes, there are misperceptions or misconceptions about outside resources. This may be true independent of whether the offshore development is part of the same organization or being supplied by a third party. Management should actively follow the steps outlined below to encourage effective and productive team building.

4.4.2.1 No Second Class Citizens

Most enterprises and ISVs have traditionally looked at extraenterprise locations as low cost, low importance, labor-intensive locations. To fully leverage the advantage of an offshore platform, enterprises should instead look at the offshore location as an integral part of their software development effort and planning. This means that the remote teams should work together with the main development centers to create new products, localize existing products effectively, and identify, build, and adopt capabilities in newer technologies.

4.4.2.2 Establish High Quality Hardware Infrastructure

Investment of financial and technical resources upfront on the infrastructure for the offshore development center is as important as for an onshore one. Better hardware infrastructure that includes state-of-the-art computers, networking and security equipment, and communication facilities is key to ongoing success. Offshore centers should not be treated as stepchildren when it comes to facilities and infrastructure.

4.4.2.3 Follow Best Practices for Personnel Management

Human resource and personnel management facilities should be geared to attract and retain the best technical and management resources. Incentive plans should be tied to individual and development center success. Benefits, training, policies, and facilities should be uniform across onshore and offshore development centers as much as possible. Cross-cultural language and customs training should be provided and exchange programs established to facilitate seamless team building.

4.4.2.4 Follow Best Practices for Partner Management

Enterprises pursuing global software development through outsourcing partners should focus on the quality and processes of the partner. The same criteria should be applied to selection and the ongoing management of the partners as would be to in-house teams. Intellectual property and proprietary information management should be established and agreed upon. Partner privacy practices and infrastructure should be carefully evaluated from security considerations. Subsequent chapters will discuss the ongoing partner management in more detail.

4.4.2.5 Establish High Quality Software Infrastructure

Software infrastructure plays a crucial role in the management of ongoing software development across distributed teams. Build management, code management, bug tracking, and project management tools should be selected carefully. Appropriate training should be provided to teams for enhanced workability. Plans should be followed up with regular meetings and updates. Change management should be carefully integrated into overall development program.

4.4.3 Personal Strategies

In this section, we will discuss the things that people should be mindful of if they have to directly interface with international travel and work together with global teams. This section is geared toward CIOs and IT and development managers as well as individual team members who find themselves leveraging global teamwork.

4.4.3.1 Keep Aware of Local Regulations

In several countries and states or regions of our world, regulations may be unique or different. Some places do not look favorably on chewing gums and some places have prohibition — meaning carrying alcoholic drinks for personal consumption or gift giving is against the law. Some places will not look favorably on any explicit or sexual materials. A visa and registering with local police during stay may be required and violators could get into trouble despite their best intentions. When business and teams go global, one can inadvertently run into problems even without looking specifically for them. It is best to consult fellow employees or consultants who are familiar with regulations and legal requirements of that country. Sometimes, a foreign employee may have to pay duties at customs for products that they may be bringing in for personal use such as stereo or a laptop computer. Business people are encouraged to be aware and careful of excise, local tax regulations, and custom and immigration formalities in the country of business.

4.4.3.2 Patience Is a Must

In the destination country, everything may be different. This includes air travel, procedures, transportation, time required for travel, documents required, on-board facilities, food, hygiene, and so on. It is important to be patient and keep one's cool. Security checks, armed guards, frisking, and the examination of bags and contents are part of routine air or ground travel in many countries. Giving plenty of time for travel and getting to the place of work is important. Another thing that may be different in the country you are visiting may be the weather. Some places will be much colder than what you are used to and some others may be hot and humid. It is important to familiarize oneself with the weather and bring gear to help protect against it.

4.4.3.3 Rely on Global Brands

As one reaches the destination country, it is important to rely on global brands. This includes staying with better known albeit pricier hotels and using familiar brand consumables. If it is a short business visit, staying in better hotels will generally provide safety, convenience, and access that are needed. Larger rooms, more workspace, business and laundry services, and conference facilities are available. In addition, concierge service and parking are ensured and food is better prepared. Catching a food- or waterborne illness such as diarrhea or vomiting is a common condition that can easily put anyone out of commission for several days. Drinking bottled water and eating well-cooked food is important for good health.

4.4.3.4 Avoid Driving in Developing Countries

In general, it is not advisable to rent a car in a developing country and drive on your own. Rules and traffic laws are different and streets tend to be congested with different types of vehicles. Driving on a different side of the road, roundabouts, traffic signals, and posted signs that may have different meanings in the destination country could cause distractions, extra time spent traveling, and accidents. It is sometimes better to have the hotel where one is staying arrange transportation that may come fairly cheap along with a chauffer. It is good to be familiar with metered taxi procedure before jumping in a cab and sometimes prices need to be fixed upfront. Beware of overcharging cab drivers and check with local employees of the company or hotel concierge with fares and rules.

4.4.3.5 Be Prepared for Sensory Overloads

Sights, sounds, and smells in a new country could easily overwhelm an outsider. Pollution, dust, blaring horns, the number of people, music playing, and unfamiliar aromas and language could be greatly unnerving. Most developing countries that are currently oases of low cost, high quality talent pools and sites of globalization will have these sensory overloads. Music and culinary tastes will be different. Lunch breaks, tea breaks, afternoon breaks, prayer breaks, and other customs of the local workforce may seem strange at first, but need to be accepted for business success. The sheer number of people may be unnerving for westerners visiting a subsidiary office in a developing country. It is important to accept that life goes on differently in different parts of the world and one set of standards may not apply in all places. Signs of poverty, social stigma, and economic or social castes may be prevalent and at times disturbing. Gaps between the underprivileged and rich may be obvious and it is important to understand that in certain countries this is an unfortunate legacy that governments and societies are attempting to improve.

4.4.3.6 Work Hours Will Not Get Shorter

One influence of globalization is that work hours everywhere are getting longer. People are interacting with teams in different time zones and need to routinely work outside normal business hours. In the global offices this is more true and applicable than ever. If one is traveling to a subsidiary or a contractor of a large U.S.-, E.U.-, or Japan-based company, chances are that people in the destination country work longer hours as well. Notions of no calls after 10:00 PM, for example, do not exist and the workday begins as early as 6:00 AM. Cell phones mean that anyone can call you any time and one has to learn to manage this effectively.

4.5 WHAT TO WATCH OUT FOR

In this section, we list several things that a CIO, IT manager, or a development manager needs to be aware of to succeed in setting up and managing a global effort.

4.5.1 Strong Cultural Currents

Any CIO who has attempted to globalize, or plans to in the near future, needs to be sensitive about cultural currents. Every country in our world has different cultures and customs. Understanding and respecting them is an enabler for good business. Software, applications, company brands, and other considerations typically cannot be force fitted among different countries. Antiglobalization sentiments are still prevalent and it is wise to be aware of and adapt to the specific culture and situation to succeed. Worldwide offices have to share and adopt cultural sentiments, local holidays, and sensitivities to increase collaboration and momentum. Several good books [2–5] discuss how companies that work effectively in a global environment often make choices that may sometimes compromise or bend standardization rules.

Heightened political tensions, wars, and corporate scandals have similar effects on people and countries. Some events may have a tendency to polarize certain countries or certain groups. In situations such as those it is important to be sensitive and aware of political, cultural, social, and personal reasons of business partners. Follow an inclusionary approach to globalization that includes best practices and methodologies from each global office. Also, include global teams in any effort at standardization and administrative control. That will enhance local support for the initiative. Business group leaders should be involved in helping drive projects that need to be implemented at global levels. This ensures a business level buy-in from both local and global teams. The global teams should see themselves as the part of a bigger whole where the whole is greater than the sum of its parts. This will help discourage the isolationist approach that tends to creep into global offices.

Years ago, this author was working for a large publicly traded U.S. manufacturing corporation with sales offices in nearly all countries and manufacturing and test facilities in several. It was a complex network of suppliers in one country and consumers in another. One such event was the completion of the manufacture of first batch of units in one country that were shipped to be assembled to another. What was not realized was that there were no official religious or trade or even political contacts between the two countries. People of the two countries had no experience working with one another and their respective governments did not even acknowledge each other diplomatically. It later turned out that this problem was solvable with the assistance of a third country that was friendly to both. The office in that third country acted as the conduit for manufactured items being shipped for final assembly.

Mass entertainment mediums like films and TV as well as communication and Internet have facilitated a perceived cultural and language homogeneity across the world. However, it is much like thin ice in several cases. Someone assuming U.S. culture, perception, and values could easily fall in cold water if they are not careful. The outside façade of similarity and familiarity among business partners or employees from different countries may not be deep. It is important to understand the underlying cultural and interpersonal details.

4.5.2 Anti-Americanism

For a variety of historical or political reasons, people in some places may have strong anti-American feelings. We are not referring to travel advisories and such issued by the State Department. Even friendly countries that have democratically elected governments can sometimes have sections of society that have such feelings and express it. Watch out for historical antipathies, national pride, and discrimination against multinational companies, labor disputes, protectionism, and discrimination based on color, race, or religion. It is better to steer clear of controversial statements, political comments and debating, or teaching rights and wrongs. Staying focused on the business objectives and values as well as professionalism toward employees and coworkers in that country is the best way forward. Following guidelines by the human resource and legal departments of the company regarding travel and local customs is suggested.

It should also be noted that some countries might have a more relaxed pace of business than in the United States. Country differences must always be taken into account and ways of doing things that would not be at all normal in the United States may have to be accepted as standard practice. If the focus is maintained on business goals and objectives and care and understanding are exercised, things will generally go well.

4.5.3 Varying Infrastructure and Services

Beyond testing CIOs and IT departments for people skills and cultural issues, globalization also means grappling with varying infrastructure and facilities. All countries will not have the same bandwidth availability for Internet connection or power availability or software versions. Basic services that are assumed as always available in the United States including food, electricity, water, and communication may have shortages. Transportation services including public transportation, flights, trains, airport access, and roads may not be the same. Travel between centers may take longer than expected and be more tiresome due to road conditions.

Lower cost offshore countries that currently are supplying the bulk of development and testing resources have power outages, unreliable phone lines, road and transportation problems, and unsanitary conditions including lack of potable water. Most enterprises with offices in these countries:

- Incorporate elaborate battery backups and banks of generators
- Lease or buy private lines for communication
- Employ their own water filtration systems
- Have buildings housing the development and testing groups
- Have controlled environments for the equipment
- Have security details at main gates
- Provide transportation that carries employees back and forth between the workplace and home.

Additionally, recreation, healthcare services, shopping, and residential communities have to be created to provide a good environment for employees to live and work in. Investment in infrastructure is usually much more than investment in people resources. This is in contrast to the United States, the European Union, and Japan where human resources are the key budget item.

Wireless communication has made inroads in many of the global countries and that has enabled better communications. CIOs may also have to deal with fairly obvious shortages in expertise in addition to the weak infrastructures. These limitations are usually not hard to accommodate: a little more patience with the government official issuing a permit, a good diesel generator, or standing in a line may be useful to get the desired service or purchase a specific item.

4.5.4 Language Barriers

We all know about language barriers between countries. Different countries may have different languages that are used for work. However, there is also a semantic language problem. Even though English may be spoken by all global centers, the understanding and colloquialism may be different. Meanings of certain phrases and words would be different and vocabulary may be limited. In addition, sometimes the speed of spoken English is dramatically different and so are the pronunciations. Accented English may sometimes be difficult to understand and the speaker might as well be speaking in his native language. This problem is exacerbated during teleconferences and distance meetings. Understanding the spoken English is different among different countries as well. It is well advisable to slow down and adopt clear pronunciations. Speaking the sentences in a couple different ways and asking whether or not the statement was understood helps. Patience, courtesy, understanding, and perhaps even a writing pad go a long way in easing communication. Use of phrases, colloquialisms, and metaphors with certain sports should be avoided. Many sports played in the United States may not be common in other countries and vice versa. The author knew an executive who loved to cite baseball analogies such as "batting a thousand" and "getting men on base" that made no sense to people in a country that played cricket instead of baseball.

4.5.5 Political Issues

Many countries in the present time have opened up their insular regulations and barriers to business. Tariffs and import duties have been slashed and sweeping reforms and deregulation implemented to facilitate improvements in the business climate. This has been an incredible force in the growth and worldwide cost advantages that enterprises are now enjoying. Manufacturing, software services, call centers, business process outsourcing, and other business functions are increasingly being done globally. However, everything is not smooth from a political and business environment, yet. In spite of incredible strides in improving business climate, there are still pockets of uncertainty and danger that exist. Developing countries that provide the best sources of cheap labor and eager consumers are also places where there may be destabilizing political and separatist forces. Conflicts along the lines of religion, ethnicity, poverty, beliefs, and antiglobalization persist and sometimes get out of control.

4.5.6 Business Issues

Several countries have made it easier to do business, but there may still be several remaining issues. Below we highlight some of these issues. It is advisable to consult the Department of Commerce updates and the respective country's consulate for more information.

4.5.6.1 Reciprocity and Investment Laws

International companies opening branch offices in some countries may not be allowed to earn income in that country. Their expenses must be paid exclusively from funds received from the parent company. Any profits made by that company must therefore be funneled back into its country subsidiary. Even visiting businesspeople may be forced to produce documentation that their parent company will assume their expenses while visiting that country. Another example is some countries require significant minimum investment before allowing a company to set up a subsidiary office. Sometimes there are requirements of reciprocity: some governments will only allow operations in their country if a similar facility is provided on a reciprocal basis from the parent company's country.

4.5.6.2 Approval Regimes

Considerable regulatory and financial approvals may need to be obtained from the Federal Reserve banks or equivalents from some countries. There may be fast track approvals for company majority owned by the returning residents of that country. Similarly, obtaining export control permits, building and office permits, business permits, accounting and foreign exchange regulations, and others may be a time-consuming process. Readers are encouraged to read economic policies and Web-based information resources that many countries seeking investment are now offering.

4.5.6.3 Taxation Laws

Dual taxation, most favored nation, free trade laws, tax laws, and other laws apply to doing business globally. Many of these depend on bilateral treaties between the country of the parent company and country where the subsidiary is established. World Trade Organization (WTO, www.wto.org) is a great resource for understanding some of these treaties and their applicability to doing global business. Some federal, state, provincial, and local governments offer lucrative packages if a company employs a significant number of resources. Special economy zones or technology parks are commonplace in India and China in addition to other countries for helping companies with reliable infrastructure, duty free, and tax reduced zones. State and provincial governments also offer discounts and incentives and subsidies in the form of land, office buildings, registration fee waivers, faster processing, reduced power, communication and Internet tariffs, and zoning regulation costs.

4.6   OUTSOURCING AND OFFSHORING

One option available to enterprises seeking to establish global development is to partner with a third party that provides software development resources. Enterprise software development including stand-alone applications, client–server systems, business systems, network applications, and Web-based applications can now be done easily and inexpensively offshore. This section discusses outsourcing and offshore software development and how it can be leveraged by enterprises for global software development.

4.6.1   Outsourcing

The global market for IT services was $439 billion in 2001 and that figure is projected to rise to $700 billion by 2005. Of this total, about $64 billion was outsourced (domestically and internationally) in 2001. The outsourcing market for other IT-enabled services (e.g., call centers, data processing) is about $10 billion a year currently, with projections for this figure to top $100 billion by 2006. In addition, the BPO services market is estimated to be about $173 billion by the year 2007. Outsourcing has garnered considerable media attention in recent days. First, the cost control measures and economic downturn saw acceleration in outsourcing projects. Later, as the job market started to get soft in the United States, the United Kingdom, and elsewhere, there has emerged a backlash against outsourcing as a job stealing activity by low cost and developing nations. There has been considerable confusion and politicization of what it means to outsource.

4.6.1.1 IT Outsourcing

IT outsourcing has been a growing reality for all Fortune 500 companies recently. IBM, EDS, Oracle, PeopleSoft, Computer Sciences, Infosys, Wipro, and several other companies have closed successful billion dollar multiyear outsourcing contracts with large financial, banking, retail, and manufacturing clients. In IT outsourcing, all the development, deployment, support, and maintenance functions are turned over to an outsourcer. The outsourcer maintains the resources, hardware, software, integration, and all the necessary functions to keep IT functioning.

4.6.1.2 Offshoring

Most of the outsourcers now also have development centers located in countries such as India, China, Russia, Ireland, Israel, Brazil, Mexico, the Philippines, and others. In this situation, the work is being done outside the country and is referred to as offshoring. Enterprises gain the benefits of cost reduction and resources that are specialists in the task being outsourced. Outsourcing IT helps the enterprise focus on its core competency and targeted customer base. Offshoring software development from the United States and the European Union to Ireland, Israel, and India has been commonplace now for nearly two decades. However, recent technological advances in communication systems including the Internet have enabled an explosion of offshoring.

4.6.1.3 Offshore Software Development

In pure offshoring, software development takes place in its entirety outside the country. There is little if any development done locally. Short visits or exchanges may take place to facilitate interenterprise interaction and training. The offshore resource takes the knowledge, training, and tools back to their home team, which enables other developers to come up the learning curve. Sometimes the local project or program manager will visit the offshore location to make sure of the following:

- All quality systems are in place.
- All infrastructure is as promised.
- Appropriate licensing for software and hardware systems is in place.
- Safeguards for maintaining and protecting confidential information are in place.
- Team is consistent per requirements of the vendor.

Having a good contract is another key requirement for a successful extraenterprise offshoring relationship. Gopal [6] provides a good description of software contracts for offshore development.

4.6.2 Onshore and Offshore Outsourcing Myths

The following are some of the widely held myths about offshore software development and developers. Lacity and Hirschheim [7] have explored many issues such as these in more detail.

4.6.2.1 Internal Staff Responsibility

Myth: Internal staff has failed if outsourcing has to be done.

Internal staff has to be more effective and efficient in their jobs if outsourcing has to succeed. Methodologies and policies for management and monitoring have to be thoroughly understood and practiced by internal staff to derive maximum benefits of outsourcing.

4.6.2.2 Saving Enterprise Money

Myth: Outsourcing and offshoring will always save the enterprise money.

Outsourcing and offshoring can actually cost more money if not planned and executed well. Project and development costs over a lifecycle of the project can become exorbitant if tight controls and management is not maintained. The outsourcer must also add SG&A expenses and profit to their cost before it becomes the cost to their enterprise customers. We will discuss a lot of these management issues and remedies in detail in this book.

4.6.2.3 Responsibility Shift

Myth: Responsibilities of the customer can be transferred to the outsourcer.

This is not true. The enterprise that has chosen to outsource continues to be the responsible party to its customer. The outsourcer is merely a third party that provides speed of execution and perhaps cost savings. There may be exceptions to this for cases such as call centers, business process outsourcing, and some large IT system contracts where the outsourcer takes over the customer communication and satisfaction responsibility.

4.6.2.4 Investment Requirement

> Myth: Outsourcing and offshoring can be accomplished with little investment.

As we discussed elsewhere, proper investment is required to make an outsourcing or offshoring effort successful for the enterprise. This investment may include providing better communication infrastructure, selecting a high quality outsourcer, and establishing appropriate controls in quality and deliverables.

4.6.2.5 Management Involvement

> Myth: Day-to-day management involvement is unnecessary when you outsource.

In our experience, close management supervision is required for successful outsourcing. Even though day-to-day work may be someone else's responsibility, each problem provides a unique learning experience to do things better and remedy it. This is possible by maintaining effective management controls and checkpoints on an ongoing basis.

4.6.2.6 Information Protection

> Myth: The outsourcer must know everything about my business to be most productive.

This is untrue. Enterprises must carefully balance sharing relevant information and giving away too much information. Most of the outsourcers work with several customers in each industry and the chances that they are working for one of your competitors is usually high. Care must be exercised in maintaining information confidentiality.

4.6.2.7 Information Sharing

> Myth: Enterprise information cannot be trusted with the outsourcer.

When the contract is being negotiated, include clauses to protect proprietary information. Several major software development countries now have copyright protection and intellectual property laws that are regularly enforced. Rights to software developed under the customer contract and rights to source code documentation should made explicit at the time of the contract. The outsourcer's physical security mechanisms may be evaluated and approved before engaging on a project.

4.6.2.8 Cheap Low-Skilled Labor

> Myth: Offshore development is just cheap access to low-skilled labor.

Offshore developers typically have high levels of skills and experience. Enterprises should insist that the outsourcer provide backgrounds of resources and should set up interviews. Most of the good outsourcing and offshoring companies have excellent skill sets and standards compliance.

4.6.2.9 Poor Working Conditions

> Myth: Offshore developers are paid little and work in bad conditions.

Throughout the world there is a strong demand for highly skilled software developers.

From a standards of living perspective, software developers are among the best paid and most successful people in most countries. For the outsourcer to attract and retain good resources and customers, working conditions and standards are generally good.

4.6.2.10 Old Equipment and Software Privacy

> Myth: Outsourcing companies have old equipment and rampant software piracy.

Most of the successful outsourcing companies have developed and invested in extensive hardware, software, and communication infrastructure because they have to cater to clients with multiple operating systems and development environment needs. Major software companies such as Microsoft, Oracle, BEA, and others enforce licensing and intellectual property rights internationally. The equipment and software in an outsourcer is usually good quality, current, and properly licensed.

4.7 SUMMARY

Global software development is a norm these days and a competitive edge for most major enterprises. An enterprise has several choices when it comes to pursuing global software development. It could pursue opening up development centers in different countries or may decide to outsource some or all of its software development. This chapter discusses in more detail all of these scenarios and provides pros and cons of each. Outsourcing and offshoring is discussed in more detail and most common myths are listed. It is important to note that depending on who is asked, one-half to two-thirds of Fortune 500 companies are outsourcing IT. Despite a large body of experience, there are sufficient details and complexities that if overlooked could lead to disastrous experiences. Management shares a tremendous responsibility to make the outsourcing and offshoring relationships successful and productive. In Section 4.4, we discussed specific items that the management can pursue. In Section 4.3, we covered technology that is enabling seamless information sharing, project sharing, source control, bug tracking, and secure communications between development and test teams. Success criteria for global software development are listed so that enterprises can measure their efforts objectively and apply improvements as appropriate. Some examples of successful outsourcing and offshoring efforts by global companies are listed with follow-up reading suggestions.

In the context of recent backlash against outsourcing, it is interesting to see how the U.S. and E.U. economies may benefit from outsourcing. The IT-enabled services market will be approximately $142 billion in 2009 according to McKinsey & Co. This is against the current cost of $532 billion for these services. The difference of $390 billion is the net savings the U.S. economy can expect from offshoring. The financial services market in the United States (i.e., banks, insurance, and financial services companies) have saved over $6 billion in the last four years by offshoring and added 125,000 new jobs in the United States helped by these savings in addition to approximately 15 to 20 percent of productivity gains.

REFERENCES

1. Sikka, V., ACTWare, an Engineering Analysis Application Framework and Shared Libraries, Intel Technical Memo, Santa Clara, November 1995.
2. Bartlett, C. and Ghoshal, S., *Managing Across Borders*, 2nd ed., Watertown, MA: Harvard Business School Press 2002.
3. Galbraith, J.R. and Galbraith, J.A., *Designing the Global Corporation*, 1st ed., San Francisco: Jossey-Bass, July 15, 2000.
4. Gupta, A.K. and Westney, E.D., Eds., *Smart Globalization: Designing Global Strategies, Creating Global Networks*, San Francisco: Jossey-Bass, 2003.
5. Hamel, G. and Prahalad, C.K., *Competing for the Future*, Watertown, MA: Harvard Business School Press; April 1996.
6. Gopal, A. and Krishnan, M.S., Offshore Software Development: An Empirical Analysis, *Management Science*, November 2002.
7. Lacity, M. and Hirschheim, R., *Information Systems Outsourcing: Myths, Metaphors and Realities*, New York: John Wiley & Sons, 1993.

5

SOFTWARE QUALITY AND TEST ROI

In the previous chapters, we reviewed the software development methodologies and contemporary software development. We presented the ROI models and the business case for maximizing software ROI. We also discussed how Applied ROI enhances the baseline ROI by methodologies, tools, techniques, and cosourcing. We presented the case for global software development and how to manage and measure it. In this chapter, we will take the specific tasks of SQA and testing and how to calculate ROI for testing, localization, and training.

5.1 HOW TO MINIMIZE RISK AND MAXIMIZE QUALITY

As has been said before, quality is never an accident. Improving quality does not automatically imply taking more time for deliverables and increased costs. It is possible to minimize risks in this marketplace while maximizing quality. We will view several techniques to help in this effort. Before we do that however, it is important to understand what myths are associated with software quality and testing.

5.1.1 Myths of Software Quality and Testing

5.1.1.1 Quality and Cost

Myth: High quality is expensive.

Achieving high quality of software is possible and does not cost too much. Studies have indicated that if software testing and inspection is incorporated into the software development process early on, it leads to significantly higher savings in cost of defects later. Figure 5.1 shows how

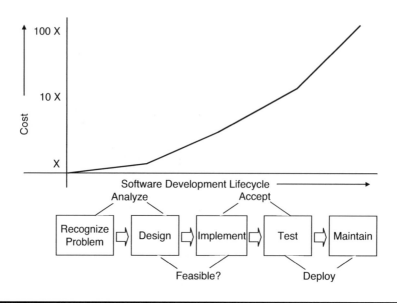

Figure 5.1   Escalating Cost of Fixing Defects

recognizing and fixing bugs late in the software development lifecycle has an escalation effect on costs.

5.1.1.2   Quality and Agile Programming

Myth: Agile programming results in poor quality.

Several techniques in the realm of Agile programming are disciplined about testing and writing good quality software contrary to popular belief. It is a myth that high quality requires a lengthy and expensive schedule, although faster cycle times must mean corners are being cut and quality is being sacrificed. For example, XP forces integration and unit testing at every iteration that results in good quality.

5.1.1.3   Software and Art

Myth: Software is an art form.

Software development is not an art and is certainly not magic. It can be carefully engineered and can be measured so that good quality software can be repeatedly produced.

5.1.1.4 CMM and Management

Myth: CMM is for management.

This could not be further from truth. Understanding and measuring the process of software development is for everyone, not just for management. Similarly, it is not good enough to reach CMM Level 2 or Level 3 and stop. More and more organizations are now achieving CMM Level 5 and it is not a pie in the sky. When all the developers and IT engineers in the enterprise understand that it is for everyone to contribute to improving process and quality, it is possible to achieve the highest levels of predictability and productivity in software development.

5.1.1.5 Wasted Time

Myth: Process methodologies take too much of my time.

Results of small process changes are readily visible and add to the momentum of improvement. Just like small amounts of regular exercise have significant health benefits, so does a small amount of time devoted regularly to understanding and improving process.

5.1.1.6 ROI and Quality

Myth: ROI is not affected by process and quality improvements.

It is definitely not cost prohibitive to achieve significant process improvements and every improvement in the process has a direct improvement on the cost savings and customer satisfaction for the enterprise. An enterprise's ability to compete effectively and implement change is greatly improved by improved quality and predictability of software. Customer satisfaction brings with it improved brand image and perception in the marketplace for the enterprise. All of these result in measurable and quantifiable ROI gains.

5.1.1.7 Shortcuts

Myth: Get certified without changing.

Although it may be possible to get certifications by doctoring documents and fooling CMM and ISO 9000 auditors, it is a great disservice to the enterprise that practices this. As we discussed earlier, quality improvements, good software development, and test processes are of significant benefit to the enterprise. These standards, models, and metrics are not to show, but to incorporate in the culture of the enterprise.

Development and testing groups attempting to maximize ROI need to first measure quality. Measuring the quality of software is not difficult and there are several good approaches, as we will describe below. Software QA and testing will lead to finding defects. Measuring defects is the first step to measuring quality of software. Risks of software are discussed in an excellent format in [1].

5.1.2 Software Inspection Techniques

A lot of software development still follows the model of "if you build it, they will come" and "if it isn't broken, don't fix it." Both the notions are incorrect; customers of the software are more demanding than ever for performance, reliability, and usability, and they have less patience toward software that is unwieldy, complex, and requires constant maintenance. Software should be constantly inspected to evaluate appropriateness and compactness. This will enable better performance, reliability, and maintainability. Software code that has been subjected to inspection enters QA and testing steps with higher quality and results in reduced resources for those stages. Let us examine the interrelationship of testing and inspection.

5.1.2.1 Testing and Inspection

Software testing is the final frontier in improving the overall quality of software. It is key to quality assurance, but it is a fairly expensive stage to detect defects as Figure 5.1 illustrates. There are several reasons for this escalation of costs.

- Test case generation and maintenance costs — generating and maintaining test cases takes effort and time. It also takes test engineers who have specialized skills and experience.
- Communication costs — the cost of communicating a defect back to the development team is high. It is both a time-consuming and resource-intensive task because different sets of people with different mindsets are involved.
- Testing never ends — full coverage of code is never achieved by testing and testing cannot uncover every defect. More testing resources and more testing improve the quality of software initially, but reaches a point of diminishing returns where more necessarily does not translate into better. There is a saying in the testing world that "testing is never finished, only abandoned."

■ Inspection helps testing — testing efficacy is improved with better quality software that is written to enable test case generation and repeatability. Inspection helps improve testing by introducing the opportunity of continuous improvement.

5.1.2.2 Manual Code Inspection

Traditionally, code inspection includes formal code review, with reviewers and contributors and structural program walk-throughs. This is an extremely manual, labor intensive technique that is tedious yet extremely useful for improving the quality of software. Volume of code and limits on time resources of participants generally limits code inspection and review to snippets that may or may not be picked by the developer. Code reviews generally should be independent reviews and structured and documented uniformly. However, too often, peers take the reviewer responsibility and try to find defects. Independent reviewers should ideally be trained inspectors who can identify defects and follow well-defined methodology to identify defects. Feedback on design, proper debugging style, and good software engineering practices can be shared among all the developers.

5.1.2.3 Automated Code Inspection

Limitations of manual code inspection are addressed by automated code inspection techniques. Several of these including sensitivities, human errors, and predispositions are frequently cited as addressed by automated code inspections. However, as we will see in more detail, this is not entirely true and the merits of each approach are unique and complimentary. Compiler-based lint tools and services from Gimpel Software, Programming Research, Reasoning, and Rational among others [2] can build the abstract syntax trees and enable structural analysis on them. Lint was an interesting program written by S.C. Johnson in the early 1970s for the C language and it was the first static code-validation tool. Defects in constructs of code, reliability, memory leaks, null pointers, arrays, and variable problems are some of those that can be found by automated code inspection. The major problem in this methodology is the large number of error messages generated, most of which are false positives that require significant developer time to parse and remove.

With global development and testing teams, different modules of the application can be inspected using automated and manual code inspection techniques and, when integrated, can again be inspected. Inspections should be performed after the feature complete stage of the code and before the testing is started. Code inspection teams need not be from inside the enterprise's software development organization. Outsourcing code inspection enables effective control on the quality of the software along with significant cost savings. Selection of the most appropriate outsourcing partner for this purpose is crucial [3,4].

5.1.3 Organizational Measures

5.1.3.1 Measure Defects to Improve Quality

We have discussed models of defect density metrics [5] earlier. These are simple models in which defect density is taken into account. Defect density refers to number of defects per thousand lines of code. This is a continuously measurable metric that should be made a part of the regular software testing and review process. Figure 5.1 describes how identifying and fixing defects early on in the software development lifecycle results in substantial savings in cost. Later in this section, we will discuss software inspection and measurement in more detail.

5.1.3.2 Obtain Organization Commitment

Management and all participant buy-in and commitment is crucial to starting the process of minimizing risk and maximizing ROI. Making sure that the entire organization from top executives to individual developers is committed to ROI, metrics to measure it, and steps to maximize it are necessary. New hires should be brought on with explicit understanding and commitment toward the same goals. The support and administrative staff should be committed to deliver their services concomitant with the ROI objectives. Sales and business development should project organization commitment to ROI process to customers and business partners.

5.1.3.3 Measure Organizational Success with ROI Goals

A written project plan should be created with explicit ROI goals laid out and milestone-based achievement highlighted. Successful achievers should be rewarded and so should the departments with winning strategies. Goals to aggressively achieve maximum ROI should be made the topmost priority and management should be with that vision at the forefront. Organizational adjustments must be made with the success of ROI goals in mind.

5.1.3.4 Use Key Performance Indicators

Key performance indicators (KPIs) around testing for organizational, functional, and ROI oriented performance are crucial. KPI represent how an organization defines and measures progress toward its goals. KPI should be quantifiable and appropriate to the role of the organization and its contribution. For example, if there is not a measure to establish how satisfied a customer is through survey or online feedback, then having a KPI of "have a more satisfied customer" for a help desk is not meaningful. It is important to first establish a good definition of KPI and then stay with the same definition over a period of time so that measurements can be refined and made accurate. Each KPI should have targets or goals that are in line with the organization's goals. Meeting KPI should be rewarded and the target updated to reflect better performance in the future.

5.1.3.5   Use Successive Rings of Applied ROI to Improve ROI

As the organization starts to use an appropriate software development and testing methodology and measures progress against it, it will be time to add test automation tools. Once test automation tools start to be used in an integrated fashion along with the manual testing and teams are working seamlessly, it will be time to add cosourcing. These successive levels are ways to expand on the Applied ROI rings that we have discussed before. As we mentioned before, it is possible to do one before the other, but this progression, which is equivalent to traversing outward on the applied ROI rings, is the most effective way to improving ROI. Organizational effectiveness improves with each step and it gets ready to move to the next ring. Later in this chapter, we discuss testing ROI with examples.

5.1.4   Continuous Software Testing

Traditional software testing models have focused on doing testing at the last stage of the software development lifecycle. These models are not useful for maximizing ROI and minimizing risk. As we have seen earlier, the cost of finding defects gets astronomically high by the time software development has progressed to testing. As Agile programming techniques, including XP suggest, testing should be a continuous process. Cross-functional teams should be involved in the software development and testing starting with the design phase. Let us look at what continuous software testing means in more detail.

5.1.4.1   Testing Is "Designed into" Software Development

Test team members should be involved in the project planning, requirements analysis, and design phase. A quality profile of the application should be generated based on what modules will require more testing and vice versa. A quality plan that is generated as a result should then be reviewed by a cross-functional team and approved. Following this, the test team members should prepare the test plan, test data, choose the automated test tools, and create test cases. The requirements document should be reviewed by test team members and evaluated for completeness, functional coverage, and accuracy. Unit testing and component testing should be made an early part of the coding effort. Successful development in newer environments including Web services, as we have discussed earlier, mandates early integration of testing in development.

5.1.4.2 Continuous Testing Stakeholders

Getting appropriate management buy-in is the most important first step in building momentum for continuous software testing. When the quality plan is created, it should be distributed to the senior management and approved. An outline of the business benefits, including how defect detection early on in software development lifecycle saves significant costs, should be highlighted. Prioritization of quality benefits and risks should be made available to all the stakeholders. Business groups including sales and marketing, business development, and customer support groups should be made participants of the quality plan. Regular review meetings should be held with the stakeholders through the duration of the project to enable key learnings and manage expectations of the development effort outcome. Risks, failure to achieve milestones, and successes should be communicated to all the stakeholders and suggestions should be sought from them for continuous improvement. This enables teams to develop and work effectively.

5.1.4.3 Business of Continuous Testing

Continuous testing involves cross-functional teams as we discussed earlier. This increases the need for effective coordination. Involvement of business groups and customer support groups as stakeholders increases the business oriented scrutiny. This additional scrutiny enables the evaluation of features and functions of the software in a better light resulting in cost savings. With the right level of resources, funding, communication, ownership, and teamwork, it becomes possible to maximize the benefits of early defect detection and increase software test ROI.

5.1.5 Metric versus Measure and a New International Standard

ISO is the developer of a new software measurement standard currently called "ISO/IEC 15939 — Information Technology — Software Engineering — Software Measurement Process." The intention is to identify the activities and tasks necessary to identify and apply software measurement for overall software project measurement.

There is no mention of the word "metric" in this standard, because it has been replaced by "measure." This is an interesting decision by the ISO Subcommittee on Software Engineering (SC/7) and meant to clearly indicate a drift away from much overused word "metric." There are distinct organizational and project measurement components covered by the standard as listed below.

5.1.5.1   Information Needs Evaluation

The first step is to identify what are the needs of the information and who will be the primary consumers of the information. The technical and management processes that will use the information will be identified. This will be followed by the development of an appropriate set of measures that are driven by the information need.

5.1.5.2   Measurement Process Resource Allocation

Identifying the resources required for making the measurement process successful is the next step. This includes human, machine, and financial resources. Resource allocation should be monitored throughout the process of measurement to make sure that it is adequate. If there are too many resources, they should be thinned out to bring them to appropriate levels. Similarly, if there is a scarcity of resources, they should be strengthened to become adequate.

5.1.5.3   Measurement Process Planning and Execution

The next step is to lay out a plan for measurement. This plan will take into account the resource availability, information needs, and timeline for completion. Measured data is then collected, stored, and followed through. Lack of data or holes in data collection methodology are compensated and reprocessed.

5.1.5.4   Measurement Process Evaluation, Data Capture, and Analysis

Data that is collected is then analyzed and interpreted. Reports are generated and analysis results are distributed to stakeholders. These stakeholders include management and development groups involved in coding as well as test design and quality assurance groups. The entire measurement process is evaluated and feedback on improvements and key learnings is generated.

5.1.5.5 Measurement Process Key Learnings and Communication

Key learnings generated from the evaluation process are communicated across review teams and formalized. This adds to the knowledge base about the measurement process.

ISO/IEC 15939 standard describes the organizational elements required to support a measurement process and it organizes measurement into four key activities:

1. Establish capability
2. Plan measurement
3. Perform the measurement process
4. Evaluate measurement

Measurement is defined in terms of a process and an information model with task breakdown for compliance with the standard. This standard will give a good set of guidelines for effective software measurement process.

5.2 SOFTWARE TESTING ROI

Let us begin with the costs of quality and testing and how to determine baseline ROI. We will discuss how cosourcing and automated test tools improve ROI. We will discuss several models with examples and cases to illustrate best mechanisms of Applied ROI.

5.2.1 Costs of Quality and Testing

Let us discuss the cost metrics for software development and quality that apply to software testing. It will be good to establish a KPI for each of these cost metrics. Some of these cost metrics are reviewed below.

5.2.1.1 Defects per 1000 Lines of Code

Most organizations have between 9 and 10 defects in every 1000 lines of code [6]. Some organizations have reported, as per a Verizon IT study listed earlier, reduction of defects by approximately 25 percent.

5.2.1.2 Fully Loaded Tester Cost

Most enterprises in the United States, the European Union, and Japan use this metric to include costs of salary, benefits, workers compensation, taxes for payroll and state disability fund, operational costs including computers, utilities, and office space. This is placed at between $10,000 and $15,000 per tester. These costs are sometimes substantially lower for outsourced locations where wages are less. A cosourcing model as we will discuss later where in-house SQA teams are supplemented by outsourced quality and testing can lead to best of both worlds.

5.2.1.3 Developer Time to Fix Defects

According to published studies [7,8], on average it takes about 6.3 hours for a developer to find and fix a defect. Usually, the average time spent fixing each bug is multiplied by the average number of bugs in a project to arrive at metrics for all the department's projects. Automated bug tracking tools, issue management processes, and good debugging tool sets reduce this time.

5.2.2 Applied ROI Considerations

As we have discussed in the chapters on software development, automated tools, methodologies, and processes are Applied ROI rings. These along with cosourcing, another ring of Applied ROI, contribute to improved software testing investment returns. Testing can be done manually and using tools can automate it. As we have discussed earlier, automated testing, if used correctly, increases ROI. As part of Applied ROI, it enables stretching the NBs while keeping NCs steady. We will discuss the pros and cons of manual and automated testing and different types of automated testing in more detail next, and follow that up with cosourcing discussion.

5.2.2.1 Manual versus Automated Testing

Since the dawn of software development, we all have debated the pros and cons of manual testing and automated testing. In this section, we will evaluate the features and benefits of each with the unique requirements of new computing systems and applications. Figure 5.2A shows how different types of testing are laid out between manual and automated testing categories. Notice that several testing types initially start as manual and become more automated as the project becomes more mature and the understanding of the project improves.

5.2.2.1.1 Manual Testing

Manual testing is when human resources perform testing after laying out a test plan and completing all aspects of testing. Validation and verification is also performed manually and the results are tabulated for review and

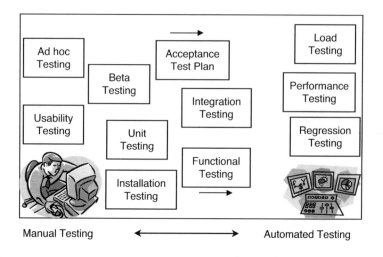

Figure 5.2A Testing Types Laid Out on Manual versus Automated Testing

improvements. Definition of tests to be performed, developing a quality plan, and creation of the test specifications cases are functions that have to be performed manually. Automation cannot be employed effectively for these steps. Key drivers for testing, whether automated or manual, are the requirements, specifications, and a well-defined quality and test plan. Without these, testing cannot be successful. Manual testing has a slower time per test run and less reliability due to the possibility of human errors and higher cost to repeat. However, manual testing is more flexible and has a lower cost to start, because the training requirements are few.

5.2.2.1.2 Advantages of Manual Testing

Ad hoc or exploratory testing is more easily defined and accomplished by manual testing. Testing when it is just starting out and interactivity and usability testing are best suited to manual testing. Natural language systems of modern computing systems and Web services are better handled at the current time with manual or semiautomated systems. In Chapter 7, we will explore a case study of wireless natural language systems and how a semiautomated system can effectively test the functionality. Testing at high level of semantics, graphical and picture driven systems, and knowledge-based systems are better suited to manual testing. Advantages of manual testing are listed below:

■ New bugs are more likely to be found in manual testing than automated testing and evolving product requirements can be easily handled.

- Repeatability of database driven, dynamic, real-time, multi-threaded systems is more likely.
- Rapid turnaround and lower cost in testing systems without predictable results and those that are hard to capture or define in test scripts.
- Confidence of completing the testing process is only achieved by manual testing. Automated testing by itself cannot complete a good quality plan.

5.2.2.1.3   Automated Testing

Automated testing is when software applications or programs are used to perform the task of testing and report generation. Human resources provide supervision, but all the testing and validation is completed in an automated way. Automated testing helps the test engineers focus on deeper manual testing and gets them out of basic repetitive tests. Automated testing has a faster time per test run and offers better repeat checking, redundancy, and reliability. However, automated testing does not offer easy flexibility of modifying and updating the test plan dynamically. It is easier to scale, but needs higher initial cost of investment due to increased training requirements on the test engineers. Given today's environment of faster time-to-market and quicker product cycles, automated testing offers more extensive testing as well as faster time to test completion. Costs of deployment, training, application licensing, and maintenance are higher in automated testing.

However, the automated unit or regression test suite is not a critical success factor for software development projects. Many systems have successfully deployed entirely using manual testing. Automated testing however improves the ability of testers to focus away from repetitive and arduous tasks. It allows them to trust the process to find problems if portions of code have changed in a patch release or if some bug has been accidentally introduced. Automated tests provide a level of reliability and dependability if they are integrated into the build script.

5.2.2.1.4   Advantages of Automated Testing

Automated testing works extremely well if the inputs and outputs are clearly defined and a test script has been prepared in advance. Regression tests including those of GUI, conformance testing (such as HTML validity, language validity), load, and performance testing are well suited to automated testing. Embedded systems, API testing, transactional performance testing, and boundary condition testing can be automated to great advantage. Portability and configuration testing for multiple environments is also an area that automated testing performs well on.

Advantages of automated testing include the following:

- Faster run times, coverage, and scalability
- Improved test documentation, record keeping, and consistency
- Less likelihood of human errors, omissions, and fatigue
- Cost effectiveness after initial setup and a few test runs are completed

It should be understood that automation requires commitment and appropriately trained resources. The scope and purpose of automation should be clearly defined in the quality plan document. Automation should be applied early and in small steps with measurement and a pause for reflection between each successful automation effort.

5.2.2.1.5   Recommended Strategy

There are situations in which automated testing simply does not work [9]. Examples being scenarios where requirements are unclear or the interface or environment is volatile. Examples are testing high level semantics and pervasive systems where automated testing fails. Manual testing should always be evaluated with the question: Can we identify a least common denominator process in manual testing so ROI can be increased? Being process-centric in QA and testing lets the process help increase efficiency of repeat jobs. The QA and testing roadmap discussed earlier and documentation generated from the test strategy and quality plan leads to effective control over the process of QA. This leads to reduction of resources (time and effort) and leads to cost savings. We believe automated testing is an effective Applied ROI component.

Application development methodologies approach testing in various ways. For instance, in XP, automated test development is a critical corollary of the standard application development process. In RAD/ASD direct testing by developers and users in the iterative cycles, including unit testing, may replace emphasis on automated testing. For large database applications, the ability to create test environments and test data sets can be limiting factors for both manual and automated testing.

The Test First design approach recommended by XP and the Zippered process by Crystal advocates reversal of commonly held separation of requirements, coding, and design stages. More test teams are required to participate in the architecture and design of the software application. Every function in the system would be tested and validated before reaching integration. Unit tests are written before writing the code. Unit testing also lends itself better to automation, besides improving overall quality and correctness of the code.

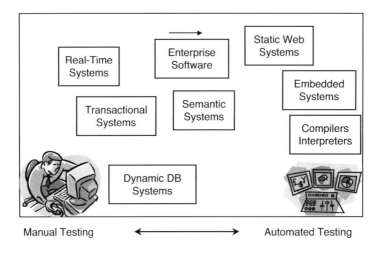

Figure 5.2B   Systems Suitable for Manual versus Automated Testing

The best bet is to proceed with a building blocks approach that uses a component test suite library and enables building larger complex tests using them as building blocks. This reduces resources required and enables quicker speeds in constituting test plans and testing. Defining an overall strategy and quality plan early on in the process, selecting the methodology and tools, and identifying proper candidates for automation are vital to testing success. A least common denominator approach should be pursued where planning, process, documentation, specification, test design, and results are common starting points for both manual and automated testing. Leveraging earlier experiences in both automated and manual testing increases ROI.

Figure 5.2B shows some of the software applications laid out on the manual and automated testing scale. Several systems including embedded, compilers, interpreters, and static Web systems can now be tested using a significant automation component. Others such as real-time systems and transactional systems with dynamic database components are still tested largely manually with little automation. Others including enterprise systems may start out manually, but as the understanding of the scripts for testing and system become better may be automated.

Figure 5.3 shows how security testing can be distributed among in-house and outsource and manual versus automated axes. Penetration testing is generally preferred done in-house and manually, but vulnerability scanning, including perimeter scanning can be automated and outsourced. Cosourcing can be applied to either case because, unlike pure outsourcing, internal resources are available.

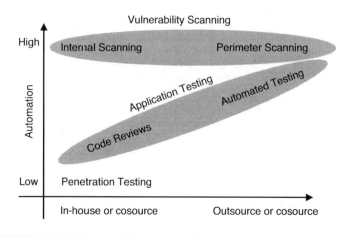

Figure 5.3 Typical Distribution of Security Testing

5.2.2.2 Automated Test Tools

A large number of automated test tools are currently available on the market. These include those for GUI testing including capture and play-back with remote testing capabilities, secure and nonsecure page testing, multiple user and data-set-based script generation, and testing among others. A newer generation of automated test tools has database support for both input data sets and storing outputs and results. Scheduling and the ability to run remotely as well as automated result comparison and report generation capabilities are available. After looking at over 15 automated test tools, we have put them in several broad categories as discussed in this section.

5.2.2.2.1 Test Design Tools

Test design tools are used for the following purposes:

- Generating a reasonably small set of test cases that include all pairings of each value of each of a set of parameters
- Increasing the effectiveness and efficiency of testing efforts by minimizing the number of tests required

Test design tools need to help a user decide what tests need to be executed. The overall philosophy behind these tools is to generate the minimum set of test case definitions necessary to detect a fault in the functional operation of the system under test.

5.2.2.2.2   GUI and Front End Testing Tools

The two major areas that should be tested using the GUI and Front End testing tools are XML/HTML (Hypertext Markup Language) syntax and broken links. The tools should be evaluated based on the criteria listed below:

- Technical and customer support provided by the vendor
- The current customer base of the vendor
- Ease of use of the product (e.g., scripting language used to write test scripts where applicable)
- Cost of the product under investigation
- Availability of the evaluation copy of the product to try before you buy

Designers and developers are encouraged to implement separation between GUI and application logic to enable ease of GUI-less testing. Automated testing tools operate much better in GUI-less testing situations.

5.2.2.2.3   Inline Test Tools

Unit tests or inline tests have become commonly used since the Agile approaches became popular. Every major programming language now supports unit tests. JUnit for Java programmers, CppUnit for C++, and similarly Visual Basic, Scheme, and C have unit tests. There are several good resources including [10,11] that describe inline testing in more details.

5.2.2.2.4   Functional, Regression, and Load Testing Tools

There are more than a dozen commercial vendors as well as free shareware sites that provide functional, regression, and load testing tools. One needs to select a tool based on the following criteria:

- Handling security issues and recording secure and nonsecure pages
- Running tests unattended and on off-site servers including production sites
- Easy to use user interface (UI) and compatibility with many different browsers
- Object-based smart testing — no rerecording if a button/text moves on a page
- Scripted runs with many different data sets — userid, registration, demographic data combinations
- No need for programming and enabling use of scripts

- Simulating large user sets with adequate database support
- Cost of the tool

Interested readers may obtain detailed documentation and evaluation of popular tools from the author. Evaluations are unbiased and kept current with updated tools and new vendors.

5.2.2.3 In-House, Outsource, or Cosource?

In this section, we will look at what drives the motivations of enterprises that have pursued outsourced software development and IT services.

From an enterprise customer perspective, a better application will not automatically translate to increased revenues. Having a large number of cheap trained labor is usually never enough reason for success in satisfying a customer. Enterprises that have succeeded in using outsourcing to their advantage have leveraged the clear and compelling reasons they had for using an outsourcer along with the checks and balances to manage it effectively.

5.2.2.3.1 Cosourcing

We believe that SQA and testing are suitable for leveraged outsourced offshore services as these provide easily measurable benefits and quantifiable ROI. Most IT and development organizations find it difficult to have adequate SQA resources and lab infrastructure and end up shipping substandard applications because of time-to-market pressures. In the current outsourced model followed by many companies, these companies cannot only easily get highly trained untainted SQA resources, but can also rent large SQA lab infrastructure for expanded quality testing at a fraction of the cost of doing it themselves. Leveraged outsourced services include the following in addition to the basic services of QA and testing:

- Better trained resources
- Better lab infrastructure
- Better quality results
- Faster scaling of resources for increased project load

We have seen in earlier chapters how outsourcing can be useful for software development. In this chapter, we will discuss the most appropriate model for testing that we will call the Cosourced Model. In the Cosourced Model, an outsourcing SQA team is not completely replacing the in-house SQA team. Instead, the outsourced SQA team is working as an extension

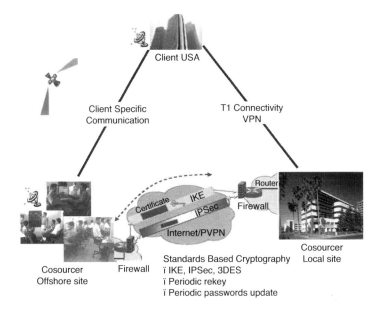

Client USA

Client Specific
Communication

T1 Connectivity
VPN

Router

Certificate IKE IPSec Firewall

Internet/PVPN

Cosourcer
Local site

Cosourcer
Offshore site

Firewall

Standards Based Cryptography
ï IKE, IPSec, 3DES
ï Periodic rekey
ï Periodic passwords update

Figure 5.4 Typical Cosourcing Infrastructure

of the in-house team with a key SQA manager on the in-house team maintaining full knowledge and control of the SQA tasks and project plan. Also, another model that has been reported to work is one of an Expert–Contributor or Mentor–Student model. The in-house team maintains a key expert and the outsourced SQA team provides one or more contributors. This model provides a round the clock operation where contributors work as extensions of the expert with that person's guidance and complete most of the work in an offshore location. The keyword in a successful Cosourcing Model is control. Figure 5.4 illustrates a typical infrastructure setup of a Cosourcing Model. The cosourcer, who would typically have an offshore site and an onshore presence, services clients in the European Union, the United States, or Japan. Secure high speed network connection between the various cosourcer sites allows uninterrupted communication and information flow.

We also believe that cosourcing strikes the best balance between saving costs and stemming job losses in the United States and the European Union. Weaker economy has forced several enterprises to look for cheap labor. This has resulted in several issues including job loss in the home country as well as potential flight of intellectual property. Cosourcing provides retention of proprietary capabilities of an enterprise and maintains key resources while maximizing the opportunity of using outside experts to save costs and enhance quality.

Whether all the SQA and testing resources are in-house, outsourced, or cosourced using the definition we have provided above, a frequently asked question in the minds of IT and development managers in a company is the following: What is the most ideal developer to tester ratio?

5.2.2.3.2 Developers to Testers Ratio for Cosourcing Model

A ratio emphasizes the wrong thing to the IT executives. Although it is most natural for IT executives to think in terms of headcount for planning purposes, there is no simple formula to determine: "If this project needs this many programmers, you need that many testers." The reasons to get headcount increased or get a larger budget are understandable, but this mindset sets the requestor up for failure.

If the project has a task backlog, adding testers will not necessarily help clear it [12,13]. The productivity, methods, processes, goals, and tasking issues cannot be addressed by adding warm bodies to testing the project. It is key to understand and flesh out the requirements and design in the beginning and revisit and update them throughout the project duration.

Those who are interested in reading more on this topic are directed to Microsoft and others [14–17]. As discussed above, hard ratios should never be taken at face value; the key to success in any project regardless of the ratio of developers to testers is well-defined requirements, APIs, peer reviews, and unit testing early in the project lifecycle.

5.2.3 Calculating Testing ROI

In the next section, we make certain assumptions about the ratios for illustrating the cost savings comparisons for a pure outsourcing and a cosourcing scenario. Pure outsourcing while it offers price advantages in offshoring to a country such as India, Russia, or China does not work as effectively as cosourcing where existing SQA and testing resources are supplemented by offshore teams. As Figure 5.5 suggests, the price point marked with a X, which is pure outsourcing, while being the cheapest is not as desirable from a successful project outcome point of view as the cosourcing scenario marked with a √. In the next section, we will illustrate the different scenarios with numbers to illustrate this point. We will see the dollar values that form the basis of Figure 5.5 in Table 5.1.

5.2.3.1 Tangible ROI Savings

This example involves an enterprise software application with significant amount of UI and e-commerce backend work involving database access

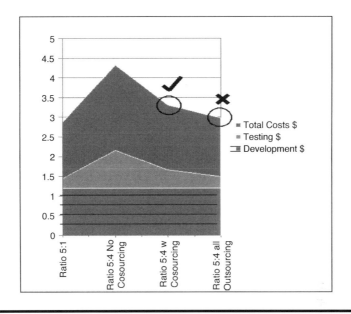

Figure 5.5 Cost Comparisons of In-House, Outsource, and Cosource

Table 5.1 Cost Comparison Matrix with Cosourcing Model

Money	Ratio 5:1	Ratio 5:4 No Cosourcing	Ratio 5:4 with Cosourcing	Ratio 5:4 All Outsourcing
Development	1.2	1.2	1.2	1.2
Testing	0.24	0.96	0.456	0.288
Total Costs	1.44	2.16	1.656	1.488

and multiple threads of business usage. The project duration is one year with the first major release happening in six months and subsequent releases happening on a quarterly basis. For the sake of simplicity, monthly cost per developer and tester is assumed to be $10,000.00. This cost includes salaries, benefits, and other expenses associated with full-time hire in the European Union or the United States.

This example focuses on the team size of SQA and testing and assumes a fixed development team size of ten developers. A key underlying assumption is that there is a good software engineering practice being followed by development teams including well-defined APIs, bug tracking systems, and source control systems as well as product requirements definitions and well-defined functional requirements. Also assumed are an offshore team with fully loaded costs of $3000 per tester. The fully loaded includes extra costs such as training and communication. The outsourcer bears the cost of employee benefits and other employment related expenses for the resource. For the one-year duration, the following numbers result (all values are in millions):

Ratio 5:4 — No Cosourcing for SQA Testing

10 developers @ $10,000 per month for 12 months:	$1.2m
8 testers @ $10,000 per month for 12 months:	$0.96m
Total Cost for 1 year project	$2.16m

Ratio 5:4 — With Cosourcing for SQA Testing

10 developers @ $10,000 per month for 12 months	$1.2m
2 testers locally @ $10,000 per month for 12 months	$0.24m
6 testers outsourced @ $3,000 per month for 12 months	$0.216m
Total Cost for 1 year project	$1.656m

ROI savings = $504,000

This simplistic model gives us a ROI savings of $504,000 for a one-year period. Table 5.1 shows a comparison matrix (all values in millions). As mentioned earlier, we do not recommend any developer to use tester ratio. In this case study, we are assuming if there are ten developers and two testers that the testing staff will be overwhelmed. A ratio of 5:4 with no cosourcing becomes expensive. On the other hand, if the two testers who started with the project are supplemented by six testers from an offshore company in a cosourced model, the chances of project success and delivering high quality applications on time is significantly increased. The outsourcing model where all testing staff is outsourced is not effective because SQA and testing is a communication-oriented activity. With newer trends in software development including emphasis on Web services, SQA and testing are becoming more intertwined with early development. Consequently, it is more effective to retain some in-house SQA resources and supplement them with cosourced offshore SQA and test resources.

5.2.3.2 Intangible ROI Savings

In addition to the direct benefits of cosourcing, there are several intangible benefits as discussed below:

- Proven methodologies — established cosourcing QA and test companies have streamlined operations and test practices. Documentation, test plan templates, methodologies, and processes of a good cosourcing partner can help QA managers effectively plan, manage, and deliver results.

■ Resource strengths — most good cosourcing QA and test companies have highly trained and enthusiastic engineers who are familiar with a gamut of tools and technologies. This provides significant resource strength and team motivation required for the success of projects.

■ Faster time-to-market — cosourcing enables 24/7 test and QA cycles and reduces the time required for conceptualization to the final product. Ramping up of a large pool of resources becomes possible.

5.2.3.3 *Refining the Cost Savings Model*

Further refinements to the cost model presented above are possible. The following outlines some of those refinements. For the purposes of simplification, we have used $10,000 per month or $120,000 per year as the fully loaded cost of hiring a tester in the United States or the European Union. Fully loaded includes the taxes, benefits, insurance, and other human resource costs. Similarly, we used $3,000 per month or $36,000 per year as the cost of hiring an offshore tester. These numbers are only approximations. Table 5.2 illustrates more detailed costs for hiring a tester in a metropolitan center such as San Francisco Bay area.

Table 5.2 compares hiring one employee locally versus offshore. It is for representative purposes only and attempts to capture the details of costing for both in-house and offshore models. Testing requirements, geographical locations, team compositions, vendors, and several other factors change costs, and readers are encouraged to use these only as a guideline and analyze their own requirements carefully. The case studies in Chapter 7 further elaborate on software testing ROI.

5.3 LOCALIZATION AND INTERNATIONALIZATION ROI

According to IDC, in 2001, 48 percent of worldwide software revenues were realized outside North America. Localization and internationalization are processes by which enterprises adapt their applications for the targeted international market and realize increased revenues and adoption rates. Increasing revenue, reducing the cost of training, improved adoption, better market capture, increased customer loyalty, and other strategic factors are the reasons enterprises adopt localization. Localization is usually the last step in software development and is interrelated with testing phases for the application. Localization is also unavoidable for many enterprises given the current markets and global competition.

Table 5.2 Refining the Cost Model

In-House Cost Refinement	Total per Year	Offshore Costs Refinement
Senior QA Engineer Yearly Salary	$65,000–$85,000	$36,000–$48,000
Training costs: $1,500 per session, 3 sessions per year	$4,500	$3000
Office space: $3.00/sq. ft./month (150 sq. ft. per person)	$5,400	
Office security cost	$5,000	
Human resource benefits: 20 percent of salary	$13,000–$17,000	
Operating costs per employee	$17,000	$3000
Initial hiring costs	$1,500	$1,000
Hardware costs	$3,300	
Software costs: basic operating system and third-party applications such as virus check, office productivity, Internet applications	$2,800	
HR and IT Support	$12,000	
Total	$129,500–$153,500	$43,000–$55,000

We discuss localization and internationalization in the context of quality and testing, because quality needs to be built into the localized product from the beginning. The effort of localization and internationalization that comes near the end of the development cycle will be smoother that way. SQA activities that need to be integrated with the localization and internationalization in mind are listed below:

- Language-related
- Supportability-related
- Capability-related
- GUI-related
- Technology-related

Language-related SQA activities focus on translation, vocabulary, terminology, consistency and stylistic elements, and accuracy. Subtle local linguistic elements can have significant impact on acceptability of the product. Supportability includes training the staff that is selling or supporting the product. If SQA guidelines are incorporated during building the product, supportability of localized and internationalized versions is more effective and cost friendly. Proper review and editing stages are required as well. Capability-related SQA involves making sure that validation and verification mechanisms are in place to ensure desired behavior. All the functionality should work and interoperability of the product should be tested. Conventions followed in different countries regarding menu layouts, privacy notices, legal notices, and database generated messages that may get displayed to the users are covered in the GUI-related SQA and testing. Although the software application should follow the appropriate practices of the localization language and country, it should not lose its ease of use features. Technology-related SQA includes Unicode testing and data source testing. Memory, code, and hyperlink testing as well as keyboard mapping, language, and character mapping should be tested and approved. We will see in our case study in Chapter 7 that a variety of automated and manual testing techniques can be used for this purpose.

5.3.1 Factors for ROI Calculation

Many factors influence ROI calculation of localization effort. Some of these are quantifiable and others are not. We will use factors that are quantifiable in calculating a simple localization ROI model. Those that are not easily measured include factors such as brand name recognition, customer satisfaction, competitive pressures, and costs related to cultural differences of localization-related employees and countries where the product will be sold. In addition, there are financial measures such as currency fluctuations, foreign stock and market fluctuations, import and export regulations, and political environment that are difficult to measure and are outside the scope of the current discussion. Let us look at the quantifiable factors of localization ROI calculation.

5.3.1.1 Cost of Localization

When we estimate cost of localization, we will need to include additional resources with expertise in country-specific language and culture skills. These may be development and test resources. The alternative is to get a quote from an outsourcer who has experience working on localization projects. This cost will be in addition to the cost of originally developing the software application by the enterprise.

The majority of localization will involve language-related translation and interface work. In addition, documentation, marketing, support, and help desks will need to be involved. A variety of tools and techniques are becoming available these days to help in localization including localization

Table 5.3 Calculating Cost of Localization

Type of Source	Multiplier	Comment
Language	0.7	Some languages such as Chinese, Spanish, and Korean may cost less than German, Japanese, and French due to resource and ancillary costs in latter countries.
Code base	0.8	This is a multiplier for lines of code.
Collateral (user's guide, marketing material, help text, others)	0.3	Use this multiplier with number of words in the collateral material.
User interface	0.5	Use this multiplier with number of words in user interface.

support by major operating systems and testing tools in multiple languages. Costs of the tools will be dependent on the size of the application, its user base (whether engineering and technical or end user), its market size, and competitors. Competition, market size, and time-to-market factors can increase the time pressure on completion and may require additional resources and costs.

When dealing with outsourcers for localization, it is important to understand their business and revenue models. This will help you understand how they will charge for their service and how discounts can be arranged. Understanding and analyzing the proposal completely is required for good budgeting estimates. There are some consulting companies who provide help in selecting appropriate localization outsourcers.

To calculate cost of localization, consider the following major source factors (see Table 5.3):

■ Language to localize in
■ Code base
■ Help text, user's guide, programmer's guide, and marketing collateral
■ User interface

Localization costs for languages vary, for instance, Chinese, Spanish, and Korean generally cost less than Japanese, German, and French. A factor of 0.7 applied to the former is generally used as an overall multiplier. Remember that all calculations and formulae presented here are simply guidelines. Actual costs could vary considerably and readers are encouraged to do their own calculations.

Cost of Localization = $(0.8 × Lines in Code base + 0.3 × Words in collateral material + 0.5 × User Interface)

Help desk, ongoing maintenance, and support staff costs are extra.

In other words, if there are 50,000 lines in code base and 60,000 words in collateral material and 2000 words in UI, then the cost of localization will approximately be $40,000 + $18,000 + $1,000 = $59,000 per language for Japanese, German, and French. For Chinese, Spanish, and Korean, this number is approximately 0.7 x $59,000 = $41,300.

5.3.1.2   Cost of Internationalization

The intent to internationalize a software application should be established upfront and the code base should incorporate features to enable it. This minimizes costs of internationalization. Separation of application logic from data and user interfaces (also referred to as model, view, and control) when done correctly can help internationalization efforts. Character encoding such as Unicode is now standard in major operating systems and is a key facilitator for internationalization. Significant manual programming and rewriting and testing effort can be avoided if a good separation is maintained between the layers mentioned above, and interfaces are kept clean and separate with well-defined functionality.

The bulk of investment required in internationalizing software that is not well designed is spent on manual programming effort and testing effort. This generally requires experts familiar with conventions and languages of the intended region. These costs can run quite high to the tune of cost of software developed. Additional time required to internationalize also results in lost time-to-market and potential opening to competitor products. Extreme care must be maintained in source control and backward propagation of changes. Preferably, a single version of the application software should be made available that caters to both domestic and international markets. Source code branching, versioning, and maintenance can become significant cost sinks if internationalization is not managed properly.

5.3.1.3   Revenue from Localization

Most probably with the localization effort, the sales and top line revenue of the product will increase. Market research, customer surveys, and projected sales targets can facilitate the sales impact calculation. Calculating the revenue from the localized product is generally difficult because sometimes both the English language and localized product may be selling. Management is encouraged to work closely with field sales to get the accurate split of the revenues and historical performance metrics. In the absence of accurate sales data, estimates or forecasts may be used effectively.

5.3.1.4 Nonquantifiable Factors

As we mentioned earlier, in addition to factors that can be measured, there are several nonquantifiable, but extremely valuable effects of localization and internationalization. Let us look at these in more detail.

5.3.1.4.1 Brand Name Recognition

As localization of the application gets completed, enterprise starts to advertise and market its application to the local market. This will build brand name and a relatively hard to quantify equity for the target customers in that market. This also offers an advantage over competitive offerings from other enterprises that may not be localized yet. Good localization enables successful differentiation from competitive applications.

5.3.1.4.2 Customer Satisfaction

The more the marketing collateral, UI, help, and documentation are in the target customers' local language, the better the customer satisfaction with the application. Customer satisfaction results in good word of mouth and peer to peer marketing, which has an explosive effect on customer acquisition.

5.3.1.4.3 Cultural Differences among Employees

People from different parts of the world are different, and cultural differences figure among those enterprises that intend to localize their applications in a particular country. However, as we discussed earlier, growing knowledge and use of English and widespread communication and information mediums including Internet, telephone, and television have facilitated bridging this cultural divide and it is relatively easier to manage these days.

5.3.2 Calculating ROI of Localization

As we defined in Chapter 3, ROI = (Net Benefits/Net Costs) * 100. Let us take a simple model of software localization and calculate the NBs as follows.

5.3.2.1 Net Benefit

A major CRM company wanted to localize its software for the Asia Pacific market. This included Unicode support and localized versions of its application. When they were selling the U.S.-based version as a nonlocalized product, its annual revenue was $1,000,000. Now when the software is ready to be sold as a localized product, its revenue increased and after taking out the cost of revenue we see that the NB is $2,000,000.

5.3.2.2 Net Cost

Assume that the original cost of software development was $500,000. Additional localization effort required was equal to $250,000. This gives us the NC of $750,000.

5.3.2.3 Baseline ROI

Using our ROI formula described above, we get an ROI of 267 percent. This is a simple, yet powerful illustration of how software localization has an impact on ROI. This simple ROI calculation can be augmented with time estimates and leveraging the past investments in similar efforts. On an average, companies are spending approximately 2 percent of their annual revenue for purposes of localization. However, if the ROI is 267 percent, then it is worth the costs and, combined with good marketing efforts and a driven team for major markets, software enterprises can gain significant benefits from localization and internationalization.

5.3.3 Applied ROI Considerations

Leveraging returns on the cost of localization and internationalization over multiple application lifecycles is possible. We will discuss in this section how using a building blocks approach to localization can be useful. Several translation programs are now available that can remember the original translations and apply them again when it is appropriate. Automation of testing localized product is also possible now with many tools available from major test vendors. This facilitates reuse of test cases and past work in localization. In addition, many outsourcing destinations now offer low cost translation and localization resources that can be used to augment expert resources in the destination country. These have been known to offer nearly 50 percent reduction in costs associated with localization. In general, localization and internationalization efforts are more expensive in the first pass but become cheaper and more effective with subsequent efforts. Over a period of time, with the use of automated tools and outsourcing, localization returns can be increased. Before, during, or after budgeting exercises for localization, one question inevitably arises. How do I reduce localization costs? Earlier we briefly mentioned ways to stretch returns on localization investment. Let us look at them in more detail.

5.3.3.1 Reduce Costs

Reducing costs of localization can be achieved by trimming complexity in different aspects of the program. This includes eliminating excessive documentation, reducing complexity of formatting and help text, and using the building blocks approach to leverage multiple applications as discussed earlier. Translations should be reused as much as possible to reduce the costly human translator involvement and increase consistency for readers. Identifying and localizing only the marketing collateral necessary and required for a specific country also reduces costs significantly. Some programmer's guides and reference guides need not be translated if there is not a substantial developer community in the target country working on the localized application. Online help should be localized to help international users as opposed to flooding them with large and difficult to use paper material.

5.3.3.2 Understand Target Market

Time is well spent if analysis of intended target market for localization and internationalization is done in advance. This helps determine who the users are who need the translation most and prioritizes localization rollout. This also helps focus on the most profitable markets. Effort spent on localization for languages that the product is not going to be sold into or accepted in significant quantities is not wise. Knowing the competition and whether or not their products are localized are important considerations for understanding the target market. Moving away from popular localization languages to those that may provide lower hanging fruits and increased market share and competitive advantage may be a good strategy. Examples of some of the newly developing markets include Latin America (Spanish and Portuguese with variations for individual countries) and Asia (Chinese and Korean).

5.3.3.3 Use Automation

Localization projects can be significantly expedited if automated tools are used. The implement, build, and test cycle is repeated several times for each language. If automated tools are used for building and testing, a good amount of time can be saved. Separation of model, view, and control or data, interface, and logic helps improve flexibility of the code and localization can proceed quickly. Reducing the amount of formatting and the details in documents allows attaching automated translation and reusing human translation effectively. Avoid investing in unproven automation tools. The investment in understanding them and making them work may prove to be prohibitive. Semiautomated processes such as reusing interface elements, test cases, test scripts, measurement, and reporting techniques can all contribute in improving speed and accuracy of localization projects.

5.3.3.4   Use Effective Process and Methodology

Investments in improving the process and methodology of localization lead to significant cost savings and repeatability for multiple language implementations. In addition to cost improvements, intangible benefits that can be realized may better competitive positioning, improve customer satisfaction, increase market share, and increase ROI. All the elements of SQA for localization that we discussed earlier combined with effective project management, conflict resolution, and build and version management are parts of localization process. As we discussed earlier, integrating localization and internationalization requirements in product design and architecture planning stage is required for effective process and methodology. Including the feedback of the target audience and making the development teams interact with customers helps reduce revisits and reworks later.

5.3.3.5   Use Cosourcing

There are many specialized companies who have built localization expertise and can help in such projects. Several offer good quality and significant cost savings when compared to hiring these resources in-house. We refer to cosourcing as retaining one or two stakeholders in-house and using an outsourcer to provide other resources. It is important to understand the process and billing methods followed by the localization vendor. Sometimes they offer discounts for repeat works and building blocks for multiple languages as we discussed earlier. Discuss SLAs and how the vendor will respond to change requests and support calls. Ask them about their process and methodology of reuse and localization. Find out how they handle version control, language dependence, byte code, testing, development, and inspection. Provide them with up-to-date documentation and collateral including marketing and users' and programming guides. Understand how the internationalized version will be integrated back into the development group's version control and build system. Discuss the requirements, user feedback, project scope, and management issues upfront and agree on deliverables and schedules. Understand how conflict management, issue management, and problem resolution works and the escalation paths for dealing with difficult people.

5.3.4 Localization and Internationalization ROI Summary

We have so far discussed how localization and internationalization can be accomplished effectively with cost controls and predictability. We discussed how ROI could be calculated after estimating the costs and benefits of each. It is important to understand that when budgetary pressures are high, management can be tempted to reduce the resources for localization effort and that can be counterproductive. Significant effort can be spent on rework related to implement, build, and test cycles when language-specific versions are readied. This can have an adverse impact on time-to-market, competitive positioning, quality, and customer satisfaction.

Sacrificing quality has a negative impact on the enterprise's brand and consequently on profitability. It is advisable to focus and narrow down the number of localization versions with criteria that we discussed. Improving the process and methodology of localization helps improve reliability and predictability of the software applications performance. It also helps manage deliverables and change management from an outsourcer. We recommend that cosourcing be pursued with stakeholders maintained in-house to help manage and achieve cost benefits. We also discussed several Applied ROI considerations where the initial investment in localization and internationalization can be enhanced and improved for different language implementations of the application. Through the case of a large enterprise CRM company, we discussed how the costs, benefits, and ROI of localization can be calculated. We also discussed how it is important to build internationalization requirements at the time of application design and planning. We discussed how SQA can be applied to localization.

5.4 SOFTWARE TRAINING ROI

New projects, software applications, technology initiatives, and capital investments warrant incredible amounts of scrutiny and ROI analysis. Most CIOs and IT and development managers have followed rigorous cost benefit analysis procedures for these investments. Software training by contrast has never received similar levels of scrutiny and investigation. It has always been assumed to be the right thing to do and help employee morale. It has always been associated with improving customer satisfaction and improved product quality due to improved employee skills. Software training however has not been effectively measured or analyzed.

On an average, training costs an employer about $2000 according to Gartner. In the United States alone there are approximately 10 million IT professionals. This puts the size of the training market at more than $20 billion. As the training industry has become more mature, enterprises are no longer assuming that training is good enough. They are beginning to ask is this specific training the best value for the money? Motherhood and apple pie reasoning that training makes employees happy or helps retention is being critically evaluated and quantified. Training is being viewed as investment in resources just like capital equipment or new IT initiatives. It is being analyzed and cost benefit ratios are being calculated to determine relevance and returns on the training dollar. Questions such as how much training is enough and how do we extend our training dollars are being asked.

5.4.1 Why Training Needs ROI

Lack of adequate training has usually been given as the reason for loss of productivity and worker confidence, which leads to turnover. This practice has several flaws. Training needs to be measured and continuous analysis should be undertaken to determine its efficiency and effectiveness. Simply shifting the reason to training is not enough. Several people believe that measuring training is possible by having a classroom feedback form. Again, that is not an adequate way to measure return on training investment dollars. ROI analysis for training is not difficult and does not involve complex economic theory or mathematics. It is simply an analysis of NBs to NCs as we have seen earlier. However, it should be understood that ROI analysis is not one-size-fits-all. Merely copying other companies and applying their results will not be successful. ROI analysis should be done after thorough understanding of the strengths, weaknesses, and business environment for one's own company. ROI analysis will also be only useful in situations where the training program is of strategic and operational importance and is being done for a long lifecycle project or initiative. Short term, short lifecycle projects with little or no impact on the business value may not require a detailed ROI analysis. It is usually a judgment call upon the management to engage ROI analysis for a particular training initiative. We will see in this chapter first the reasons why training needs ROI and later how to calculate training ROI.

5.4.1.1 ROI Gives Valuable Insights into Training

Effectiveness of training, as we mentioned earlier, is not only achieved through feedback sheets. Its effects should be measured when the resources who received the training are applying it in their projects. In addition, successful training increases employee morale and provides employees with tools to respond to customer needs thus increasing customer satisfaction. All of these are factors for improvement of the business value of the enterprise. ROI of training may be useful to gain the following additional insights:

- Trade off between hiring new employees and training them in specialized skills or hiring consultants who are trained in those skills already
- Trade off between hiring employees with fewer skills and training them versus hiring more experienced and expensive employees
- Redeploying internal resources after proper training to new tasks and responsibilities thus preventing new hiring and saving costs

5.4.1.2 Training Provides Business Value

As we have seen in earlier chapters, any activity that provides business value should be evaluated in the context of ROI analysis. Because training is intended to help an enterprise increase the value of its human assets, it has direct impact on both top-line (revenue) and bottom-line (costs) of the enterprise. This means that it should be treated as equal to other activities that have similar impact, for example, capital investments, new IT initiatives, application software, and hiring resources among others. Once the metrics and benchmarks of evaluating training through ROI analysis are set up, it will become easier to compare with other activities in the enterprise. This will improve cost center predictability and forecasting.

5.4.1.3 Training Consumes Resources

In the economic conditions of the present days, enterprises are justifying every dollar spent. Activities that require resources are being evaluated and measured. Before investments are readied, ROI and cost benefit analyses are conducted. Contracting and training are usually the first two departments that are "zero base budgeted." Resources are cut and budgets evaporate. If ROI analysis is done correctly, it becomes easier to convince the management not to reduce training budgets drastically. The potential of negative impact on productivity, customer satisfaction, and employee morale among other things can be better quantified and presented.

5.4.1.4 Older Models of Training Are Becoming Obsolete

According to the American Society for Training and Development (ASTD) 2003 whitepaper on Human Capital Challenge (2003), three broad trends are emerging that enterprises need to be aware of:

- Rate of growth of the labor pool is slowing, resulting in 2.3 million jobs remaining unfilled in 2004 and 4.6 million in 2008. This is resulting in more employers reaching out to larger groups of resources and then training them to meet the job requirements.
- Median age of a worker has increased from 32.9 years in 1990 to 35.3 in 2000 and the fastest growing age group is the 45- to 54-year-olds. This is resulting in enterprises gearing up to continually train its older employees with new skill sets due to shortages in hiring younger talent.
- Globalization trends are increasing the diversity in the population of the workforce. According to the U.S. Census Bureau, Asian-, Pacific Islander-, Hispanic-, and African-Americans will be the fastest growing population groups in the United States. This is increasing the employer-sponsored programs to have diverse teams working together effectively as well as improving the skill sets of teams with diverse race, educational, and cultural backgrounds.
- Budgets are tighter for enterprises and the need for training is growing, so the training programs need to be more efficient and effective.

5.4.1.5 Selecting the Best Training Method is Important

The ASTD survey found that even though the companies placed a lot of importance on training, only about 60 percent predicted that their budgets would increase. This increases the importance of continuous improvement and selection of most appropriate training method. These days, effective training is available by traditional methods such as classroom training as well as by newer opportunities such as distance learning, self-study, and online training methods. Using the appropriate training method based on the ROI analysis and budget is important to get the best value for the money.

5.4.2 Factors for Measuring Training

It has been said before that answers are only as good as the questions that are asked. The measurement of training ROI will be as good as the criteria and input data that forms part of the analysis. With this in mind, let us look at various factors that should be accounted for when measuring training ROI.

5.4.2.1 During Training Factors

Whether training is in class or online, enrollment is a good indicator of the interest. Below, we identify all the enrollment factors:

■ Attendance number — during the training session, the number of participants is the attendance number. This usually indicates the business need of the training and whether the format of training makes sense.

■ Timeliness of training attendees — another upfront factor is whether the participants for training are on time if it is in-class training. For online or distance training, this translates to Web logs of when the participant entered the Web site and reviewed the material or participated in online forums such as instant message or chat or e-mail.

■ Timeliness of training completion — it is important to deliver training during a given period of time. Sometimes this is related to requirements of a project deadline. How effectively and timely the training was will usually govern how useful and applicable it was.

■ Response on feedback sheet — most training includes some type of feedback from the participants. In-class training may have this as a sheet distributed to the participants during or at the end of the training. Online training may have this as an online form to complete. Response on the feedback sheet is a good indicator of the training style of the instructor, format of the training, venue of the training if it is in-class training, performance of the Web site and ease of use if it is online training, and quality and appropriateness of the material handed out during the training. It also provides good feedback on the duration of the training and timeliness from the perspective of the participants. Suggestions for improvement should form a key part of the feedback sheet and these suggestions should be incorporated in future training sessions.

5.4.2.2 Post-Training Factors

Once the training has been delivered, several other factors can be measured. These are listed below:

■ Cost of training — several different types of costs are involved with training. These include direct costs such as the cost of instructor, travel expenses, venue costs (if in-class training), Web site design and development costs (if online training), and collateral preparation costs and such. Indirect costs would be maintaining a training Web site, training staff and salaries, ongoing costs of printing and updates to training announcements, and cost of participant in terms of the work they did not do during the training and such.

- Revenue of training — earning training revenue is not only limited to external training providers and consultants. Internal business units also operate on the basis of cost centers and the training department usually charges the participants' business units for the training. This would factor into the ROI calculations.
- Network effect of training — in-class training generally tends to involve participants from different groups, perspectives, and backgrounds. Formal and informal interaction and contacts made during training usually result in a positive network effect where different groups understand and appreciate each other, problems are discussed, and solutions and learnings of one group can be used by another. Distance learning and online learning may also have the same effect by e-mail address sharing, work groups, chat groups, and free participant interaction sessions.
- Analyzing the training — improvement in skills and new concepts learned result in impact on participants work when they return back to their jobs. Instant learning feedback can be measured by a quiz or an exam at the conclusion of the training. Often, this is not the practice because the objective of the training is to enable long-term growth and improvement. This can also be measured in the form of application of lessons learned during training and sometimes through interaction with colleagues and exchanges. Long-term effects of training could be measured in the form of productivity gains such as successful software written, bugs reduced, less turnover of employees, and several others. Other such factors are reduced customer complaints, number of units sold, and number of calls made to customers or others as appropriate. A regularly used approach in pharmaceutical drug trials could be applied where a control or placebo group that had no training is compared over a period of time to the group that underwent training. Results could be measured in this way.

5.4.3   Calculating Training ROI

Calculating training ROI involves measuring the business impact of the during-training factors and post-training factors discussed earlier. The business impact is the financial value of the change due to training as measured. We have discussed training ROI computation in this book because training has to be an integral part of any enterprise's software strategy. Training measurements are an ongoing process and, as part of the software strategy, they should be isolated and evaluated independent of other influencing factors.

Table 5.4   Net Costs for Training

Administrative Costs	Marketing Costs	Participant Costs
Curriculum development	Promotion and advertising costs (external or internal)	Instructors: fees, expenses, supplies, travel, support
Training planning and external consultant hiring	Collateral development and printing	Trainees: loss of work, travel, food, lodging
General and administrative	External advertising agency and training agency hiring	Productivity loss
Registration fees, licenses, and regulatory approvals	Evaluation and fine-tuning training through surveys	
Facilities, training venue, supplies, equipment	Analysis and ROI computation	

Economic benefits derived by a training program over a given period of time and costs involved in running the training program are two key measurements used for calculating ROI. Remember our definition of ROI in terms of NBs and NCs as we have considered earlier in the book. With that, let us look at the costs.

5.4.3.1   Net Costs

NCs (Table 5.4) will be the sum of several different types of costs as we have outlined earlier in this section. Let us look at these costs in more detail.

5.4.3.1.1   Administrative Costs

Setting up the training program will involve development of the curriculum, training planners, Web site design (if online training), and general and administrative costs and purchases. If any external planning and training program implementation consultants are used, this is where those costs are factored in. Administrative costs will include registration fees, any licenses required to be obtained as part of training, and any regulatory approvals such as fire marshal review of the premises. Another key administrative cost element is the cost of renting or using the training venue. This will include projector, conference room, writing material, equipment, food, and other items.

5.4.3.1.2 Marketing Costs

This involves promotions and collateral material development, any costs of hiring external advertising or training marketing agencies, and focus groups. Effective marketing ensures the right level of training participation with direct impact on the benefit of the training. Marketing costs will also involve evaluating and fine-tuning both the training message and the feedback gathered from it. Conducting online and in-class surveys and collating the results is part of this marketing costs. We will group the analysis and ROI computation costs into the marketing costs of training as well.

5.4.3.1.3 Participant Costs

Training is not complete without the instructor and trainees. These two groups are the biggest costs associated with training. Instructor-led training offers unique advantages of one-to-one learning and interaction opportunity with an expert in the area. Even if training is being provided online or through self-study courses, the instructor cost is what it took someone to develop the training. Costs of the instructors can be calculated by taking into account the fees charged by the instructor, number of hours in the training, time spent by the instructor outside of the classroom for evaluation, preparation, grading or answering questions, and miscellaneous expenses for travel, food, and lodging.

The other major participant cost is the trainee cost. The time that the trainee is away from their normal day-to-day work is part of the trainee cost. In addition, travel, lodging, food, training material, and other miscellaneous costs could be involved. In addition to these tangible costs, there are also intangible costs to the business such as productivity loss for the duration of the training. This could be in the form of new business or new products or customer complaints handled or other added business value. Intangible costs should be added to the cost of training just like we will add intangible benefits to the training benefits in the next section.

5.4.3.2 Net Benefits

Measuring benefits of training is a difficult task and should be carefully planned and executed. As we have mentioned earlier, benefits of training are not quantifiable by feedback forms filled out at the class or online

Table 5.5   Benefits of Training

Bottom-Line Benefits	Top-Line Benefits
Savings of labor (overtime or payroll)	Productivity increase
Faster completion and improved cycle times	Customer retention and satisfaction due to improved employee customer relationship
Lower hiring and job loss expenses because of increased employee satisfaction	Additional revenue through customer upgrade, better help desk and support
Lower maintenance and repair costs	Better product ideas and increased market share
Potential reduction in force opportunity	Newer customer acquisition

and trainee comments. It is not even measurable just by doing an exam or quiz at the end of training session. The biggest benefits of training are derived by improvements in business functions of the trainees and key learnings that are incorporated in day-to-day life for improved productivity. In the next sections, we will look at each benefit of training in more detail (Table 5.5).

5.4.3.2.1   Top-Line Benefits

Top-line benefits include increase in revenue directly or indirectly as a result of training. This includes productivity increases of employees through improved processes, reuse, methodologies, or skill sets. Productivity increases may also be derived from increased employee morale and motivation. As we mentioned earlier, network effect of training enables problem solving knowledge to get distributed among employees of different departments who communicate with each other after the training is completed. This in turn further increases productivity and decreases downtime. Customer satisfaction is a direct benefit from this and improved customer satisfaction leads to better customer retention and better word of mouth. Having customers that will provide a reference for a company helps bring in more customers, which results in increase of revenue. Intangible top-line benefits also include innovation and better product ideas, improved confidence and success rate with customer conversion, and better support in help desk and technical staff.

5.4.3.2.2 Bottom-Line Benefits

Bottom-line benefits are savings that are a direct result of training. Sometimes, if employees who have received training have improved productivity, they can complete work faster. This leads to savings of labor (such as overtime or employee payroll). In addition, it may enable reduction in duplication of effort, streamlining an operation and completing it faster, detecting bugs faster and completing projects ahead of schedule, fewer bugs and less time fixing bugs, and better access to problem solving information. All of these are examples of bottom-line benefits. If reduction in force is a result and the number of jobs is reduced, those are also cost benefits of training. Notice that redeployment or taking on more challenging problems are not mechanisms to realize or capture bottom-line benefits of training.

Cost savings also include improved customer reach-out cycle times, support staff efficiency increase, lower maintenance and repair costs, lower hiring and job related expenses, and potentially less job loss and employee attrition.

5.4.3.3 Baseline ROI

Before the enterprise invests in training, we can evaluate the projected ROI based on the NBs and NCs described earlier. The timeline of when the training is going to commence and when the results will be measured becomes important for budgeting and management buy-in. In addition, it may be worthwhile to use these ROI numbers for making a business case. We will follow the definition of baseline ROI as outlined earlier by us.

$$ROI = (Net\ Benefits/Net\ Costs) * 100$$

5.4.3.4 Case

Let us take a case of a support desk in a major bank. This bank has just added the ability to do online banking transactions to its customers. The customers have lots of questions and there is a dedicated team of 50 support specialists who currently provide support and answer questions regarding online banking. The bank has determined that the support team needs to be trained for online banking or 7 new people will need to be hired. The training will take 80 hours. The salaries of support staff currently are $23 per hour and it will take 50 x 80 x 23 total cost for training = $92,000. Other costs including training, collateral, software, and instructor will cost $62,000 and so a total cost for training the existing support staff will be $154,000. Hiring 7 new people with expertise in the online banking arena would have cost for duration of one year $245,000. This gives an ROI of 59 percent. Well worth the training investment over a benefit period of one year. However, it should be noted that it is indeed possible for the employees to be given too much training that is wasteful and inappropriate or overkill. In scenarios like that, the training investment becomes counterproductive and it is possible to register a negative ROI. Employee or staff dissatisfaction, productivity loss, and potential job switch may also result.

A thorough analysis of ROI will need several details based on both NBs and NCs. We will see how certain newer training methodologies that are effective are lending themselves to saving costs and collectively helping improve Applied ROI. The next section discusses Applied ROI considerations in more details. The CIO, IT manager, or development manager can use the services of external consultants or internal resources to do the ROI analysis and use the data generated to determine business value. Decision making for both current and future training projects is enhanced by the information collection and analysis during ROI analysis.

5.4.4 Applied ROI Considerations

We have discussed the concept of Applied ROI in earlier chapters. Techniques, tools, methodologies, new technologies, and outsourcing are all factors that contribute to enhancing the baseline ROI calculations. NBs are improved or costs are further reduced and the same investment can go a longer way in realizing business value. Applied ROI for training is being driven by new training delivery techniques and technology as well as outsourcing collateral material generation and distance and online learning. People have also referred to these techniques as e-learning or blended learning. The World Wide Web and Internet are enabling some of these learning approaches. Traditional methods of in-class training and instructor-led training are being supplemented and in some cases replaced by these new techniques. Again the technology is becoming an enabler of cost savings and Applied ROI just as in software development.

5.4.4.1 Online Training

E-learning, Web-based training, and online training are synonymous with cost savings today when used in conjunction with traditional training programs. Several companies including SAP, General Electric, Microsoft, and others have implemented distance learning initiatives that use the Internet along with well-developed and customizable training programs. The online training marketplace is expected to grow to $15 billion in the next two years. Usually online learning systems lose the interpersonal and people-to-people interaction, but cost savings are enormous, and they should be used in blended models just like cosourcing as we discussed earlier.

Applied ROI is improved because the savings are in the form of saved employee productivity time, customer travel and living expenses time, training facility and collateral costs, instructor costs, and administration costs. Benefits of the online learning also include repeatability, because coursework once generated can be offered as many times on the Web as required. There is no limit to the number of participants and, unlike instructor-led courses, scheduling and availability logistics are eliminated. Employees are also sometimes able to absorb and digest more material in online training than in face-to-face interactions due to a more relaxed setting of online training such as home. Online training reduces the need for travel so participants are not away from their families. The mental and physical well-being of the employees who are not away from home for long periods of time and not spending time on the airplanes and hotels helps morale and improves job productivity.

5.4.4.2 Outsourcing Collateral and Marketing

As more organizations are approaching ways to reduce costs of training, other factors are also playing a role. Outsourcing collateral generation and marketing are two of them. Documentation generation, printing, and publishing costs are sometimes significantly less when produced outside the enterprise and sometimes even in a different country. There are several countries including Canada, Ireland, and India that offer cheaper alternatives to producing training collateral for enterprises located in the United States. Marketing for training that includes content generation, advertising, telemarketing, direct mailings, and promotions are effectively done from offshore. The recent trends to BPO has demonstrated huge savings that many large enterprises including American Express, General Electric, Amazon.com, Intel, and others are realizing by outsourcing some of these BPO opportunities.

Using the NCs and NBs itemization that we had presented earlier, we will see how a training organization can realize Applied ROI benefits that extend the baseline ROI. Table 5.6 describes detailed Applied ROI in the Training Model with sample data.

5.4.5 Training ROI Summary

Measuring, calculating, and analyzing ROI of training is an extremely powerful tool. It does not provide solutions to all the issues and problems, yet embarking on the ROI analysis provides much needed accountability

Table 5.6 Applied ROI in Training

	Baseline ROI	Applied ROI	Comments for Applied ROI
Duration of training	80 hrs	80 hrs	May require less hours
Estimated number of participants	50	50	
Period over which benefits are calculated	12 months	12 months	12 months
Costs			
Administrative Costs			
Development of training	$10,900	$19,930	Slightly higher due to design and development costs
General and administrative	$17,700	$4,500	Less regulatory, licensing requirements
Registration fees	$25,000	$25,000	
Training venue and facilities	$60,500	$5,000	No travel required because of extensive use of online
Marketing Costs			
Collateral and materials	$15,500	$5,000	Outsourced
Evaluation and surveys	$995	$2,900	More analysis because more data collected
External advertising and consulting	$4,500	$4,500	
Promotion	$8,700	$1,700	Outsourced
Participants Costs			
Instructors, fees, preparation, and expenses	$62,000	$15,000	Remote training development
Loss of productivity	$100,000	$100,000	
Students	$92,000	$92,000	

Table 5.6   Applied ROI in Training (continued)

	Baseline ROI	Applied ROI	Comments for Applied ROI
Travel, hotel, and meals	$50,000	$0	
Total Cost	$447,795	$275,530	
Benefits			
Top-Line Benefits			
Productivity increases	$305,000	$305,000	
Customer retention and satisfaction	$140,000	$140,000	*
Additional revenue through customer upgrades and new customer acquisition	$70,000	$70,000	**
Better product ideas, shorter development times, increased market share	$125,000	$125,000	
Bottom-Line Benefits			
Savings of labor (overtime or payroll)	$90,000	$90,000	
Lower maintenance and repair costs	$54,000	$54,000	
Lower hiring and job loss expenses	$55,000	$55,000	***
Reduction in force	$0	$0	
Total benefits	$839,000	$839,000	
ROI	87%	204%	
Payback period	6.4 months	4 months	

* Assuming 20 percent annual customer churn
** 10 percent increase from each customer profitability
*** 15 percent employee churn rate

and process improvements. Training is the least understood and measured enterprise activity and should be aligned with the business objectives of the enterprise. CIOs and IT and development managers can use the learnings from training ROI analysis to help improve methodology, free up resources, make business cases, and align activities that satisfy overall strategy.

In today's times, it is important to keep in mind the benefits of online learning, outsourcing, and other methods of improving ROI beyond baseline. We have called that Applied ROI, and it is an effective tool to keep up the employee skill set and morale while improving customer satisfaction. Investment in training should be made with proper analysis and supporting measurements. That ensures that this powerful human capital enhancement tool is used for continuous improvement of the enterprise.

5.5   SUMMARY

In this chapter, we have presented the business case for outsourced testing and ROI for testing, localization, and training. In Section 5.1, we discussed the myths of software quality and testing and how to counter them. We emphasize that software quality is a shared responsibility and the time investment in process methodologies is a good one. In this section on maximizing ROI while minimizing risk, we discussed metrics, organizational measures, inspection techniques, defect measurements, and continuous software testing. In Section 5.2, we discussed software testing ROI. We discussed automated testing versus manual testing and, in many ways, the frontiers of automation in software are there right now. In five years or so, we will be looking at programming with the same perspective with similar tools for automatic code generation. In this section, we compared in-house, outsource, and offshore models. We discussed cosourcing models where in-house efforts are reinforced with outsourcing. In Section 5.3 and Section 5.4, we presented the ROI numbers and calculations for software localization and training. We have also presented the reasons behind investment in training and how to measure efficacy of training investment. We discussed how applied ROI improves the investment returns for each of these scenarios.

REFERENCES

1. Jones, T.C., *Assessment and Control of Software Risks*, 1st ed., Upper Saddle River, NJ: Prentice Hall, February 1994.
2. Aho, A., Sethi, R., and Ullman, J., *Compilers, Principles, Techniques and Tools*, Boston: Addison Wesley, 1988.
3. Grady, R.B., *Successful Software Process Improvement*, Upper Saddle River, NJ: Prentice Hall, 1997.

4. Humphrey, W.S., *Managing the Software Process*, Boston: Addison Wesley, 1989.
5. Kan, S., *Metrics and Models in Software Quality Engineering*, Boston: Addison Wesley, 1995.
6. Piestasanta, A.M., A Strategy for Software Process Improvement, *Ninth Annual Pacific Northwest Software Quality Conference*, Portland, OR, October 7–8, 1991.
7. Boehm, B.W., *Software Engineering Economics*, Upper Saddle River, NJ: Prentice Hall, 1981.
8. Grady, R.B., *Practical Software Metrics for Project Management and Process Improvement*, Upper Saddle River, NJ: Prentice Hall, 1992.
9. Khemka, A. and Sikka, V., Comparisons between Automated and Manual Testing. *SRI's Quality Week Conference 2002*, San Francisco.
10. Beck, K., *Test-Driven Development*. 1st ed., Boston: Addison Wesley, November 8, 2002.
11. Fowler, M., *Patterns of Enterprise Application Architecture*, 1st ed., Boston: Addison Wesley, November 5, 2002.
12. Kaner, C. et al., Managing the Proportion of Testers to (other) Developers, *Pacific Northwest Software Quality Conference,* October 2001.
13. Iberle, K. and Bartlett, S., Estimating Tester to Developer Ratios (or Not). Pacific Northwest Software Quality Conference, 2001.
14. Cusamano, M.A. and Selby, R.W., *Microsoft Secrets*, New York: Simon and Schuster, 1995.
15. Rothman, J., It Depends: Deciding on the Correct Ratio of Developers to Testers, http://www.jrothman.com/papers/ItDepends.html, Rothman Consulting Group, Inc., 2000.
16. Software Program Manager's Network, Best Practices, 1999, www.spmn.com.
17. McConnell, S., *Rapid Development*, Redmond, WA: Microsoft Press, 1996.

6

HOW DO YOU IMPLEMENT GLOBAL SOFTWARE DEVELOPMENT AND TESTING

This chapter presents how to execute globalization and outsourcing. It presents strategies to successfully leverage the cost benefits of outsourcing while improving quality. It builds and elaborates on the Global Software Development and Testing model, quality practices, product readiness, and automated test tools. It presents checklists and best practices to select, train, and manage outsourcers and measure results of outcome. This chapter presents the development and quality infrastructure and discusses how reducing costs of development and testing can maximize software ROI while improving quality.

6.1 THE GLOBAL SOFTWARE DEVELOPMENT AND TESTING MODEL

Recent downward market trends, waning revenues, and emphasis on the bottom-line have prompted a resurgence in the trend of outsourcing. Nearly half of Fortune 500 companies are using outsourced services, whether they are business process management, customer service, software development, transcription, or SQA and testing. All the top 20 ISVs now have software development and SQA labs in countries such as India, Ireland, China, and Israel among several others. Figure 6.1 describes how a quality and cost matrix compares different countries. The trend lines indicate which way a particular country is growing in this matrix. For example, some countries have government-introduced programs that are improving quality. Yet others have excellent quality and are relatively stationary on this matrix such as Israel and Ireland. Others such as India

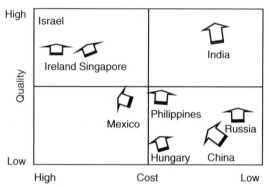

Source: McKinsey & Co. and author's research.
Quality depends on resource availability, capability
maturity model (Software Engineering Institute),
and cultural fit.
Labor costs include taxes, markups, risks, and insurance.
Trend arrows are based on author's research.

Figure 6.1   Cost and Quality Comparison for Outsourcing Destinations

are unique because they offer excellent quality with low costs, although
more recently, software development in India is becoming more expensive.

According to IDC, the global information systems outsourcing market
is expected to pass $72 billion by 2003. Gartner recently forecast that
more than 80 percent of multinationals will use IT outsourcing to save
money, overcome skills shortages, or increase flexibility. Gartner's research
indicates that 200 of the Fortune 500 companies used offshore application
outsourcing [1] in the year 2000. Meta Group, in 2002, recommends,
"Global 2000 organizations should rigorously evaluate offshore outsourcing
possibilities for IT and related services and projects for possible inclusion
in their overall portfolio of sourcing options." During the economic downturn of the past 12 months, efforts by Global 2000 organizations to reduce
IT costs have added a counterrecessionary impetus to the long-term trend
toward increased use of offshore outsourcing service providers.

If you outsource a project to a third-party company, you also outsource
the day-to-day project management responsibilities. However, your company still needs to have a level of involvement to validate that the project
is going well and that the outsourcer will deliver within your expectations.
This requires the outsourcer to provide meaningful and proactive feedback
on the status of the project. It also requires you to be comfortable with
the overall processes that the vendor is using to manage the project. Let
us discuss the overview of software development and quality strategies
to establish a framework by which readers can plan and execute an
effective outsourcing relationship.

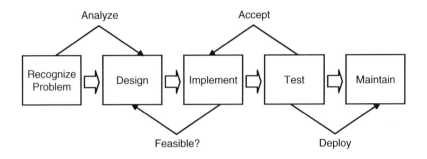

Figure 6.2   Classic Software Development Lifecycle

Classical software systems can be divided into five phases. These five phases that are collectively referred to as software development lifecycle are detailed below. The author uses the classical development model to elucidate different stages of development and QA testing overlaps. Agile methods including XP, RAD/ASD, Crystal, SCRUM, and others discussed earlier repeat the software development lifecycle in several iterative phases. Each iteration encompasses all the phases of the software development lifecycle defined below.

6.1.1   Software Development Lifecycle

The software development lifecycle has five phases as shown in Figure 6.2.

6.1.1.1   Recognize Problem

The idea of developing a new system occurs to the user when he recognizes that he has a problem in the way that he currently carries out his business or when he identifies an opportunity to improve his business.

6.1.1.2   Analyze

This involves business system analysis and specification. It includes feature discussions as well as cost, benefits, and resource requirements. The output is a design based on specification.

6.1.1.3   Design

Program flowcharts file layouts and data descriptions: everything but code are developed. The design phase also includes physical configuration and discussions on feasibility.

6.1.1.4   Implement

The implement phase develops what was created during design into code. Implementation is updated if testing determines acceptance criteria are not met.

6.1.1.5   Test

Separate parts of the system are tested followed by integration testing. For more details refer to the QA and testing roadmap described later. Structured techniques emphasize the meshing of testing phase as much as possible with implementation so that system quality is built in.

6.1.1.6   Maintain

The end product of successful acceptance testing is deployment. Following that, the software system is maintained and upgraded if necessary.

6.1.2   QA and Testing Roadmap

Laid out on the software development lifecycle is a typical roadmap for QA and testing of software. In the table below, we discuss what the importance of each of these steps is and how missing any of these steps may lead to cost overruns and reduction in product quality and readiness. Of special interest here is to note that in Agile software development methodology, the system architect and design roles are critical for success. It is not possible to rapidly and iteratively QA, test, and debug applications if the design is flawed. In such cases, each fix usually breaks some other part of the system and in scenarios like that the resulting product has unpredictable behavior. The disciplined approach of XP and some other Agile Methodologies and their emphasis on testing as an ongoing process helps enormously. Figure 6.3 shows the QA and testing roadmap laid out on the software development lifecycle. Table 6.1 presents details of QA and testing roadmap.

Having discussed the QA and testing roadmap, let us turn our attention to product readiness and deployment infrastructure. The discussion we present will be generalized and the user is encouraged to adapt and modify it to their specific situations.

6.2   PRODUCT READINESS AND DEPLOYMENT INFRASTRUCTURE

Quality assurance and testing go hand-in-hand with product readiness. This section discusses how product readiness is a necessary condition for

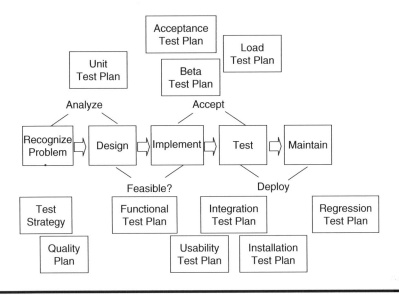

Figure 6.3   QA and Test Roadmap Laid Out on Software Development Lifecycle

production worthiness, not a sufficient one. The notion of readiness needs to be seen along two distinct dimensions:

1. Is the product ready to go live? This has largely to do with features and quality.
2. Is the deployment environment ready to receive the product in a scalable, secure, and supportable manner? The considerations for deployment, although related to the product, constitute a different level of review.

Presented in this section are checklists under the two dimensions of readiness. Successful quality and test reviews should cover the readiness items. This becomes especially critical in an outsourced quality and test environment.

6.2.1   Product Readiness

We are simply stating the FLURPS framework for declaring product readiness. Users are encouraged to review the different components of the product readiness discussed below. Table 6.2 presents a checklist for all the product readiness elements.

6.2.1.1   Functionality/Features

Is the product feature complete as defined in a requirements document or statement? This is a good time to revisit the product requirements

Table 6.1 Details of QA and Testing Roadmap

Roadmap Item	Value (of Implementing)	Risk Factor (of Not Implementing)
Test strategy	Organization of testing Strategic choices Best possible use of resources and time Important basis for a structured approach to testing Manageable test process	Without a documented test strategy, parties may have: – Different understandings of levels of testing to be conducted – Focus or objectives of testing – Disagreement over what was to be achieved during all levels of tests
Quality plan	Set out specific quality objectives Practices Resources Relevant sequence of activities	Without a documented quality plan: Quality efforts such as requirements validation, user document verification, stress testing, etc, may remain unidentified and not addressed during tests
Unit test plans	Individually test components of software Determine when unit testing is completed	Unit testing may not be conducted consistently or at all Discovery of defects is delayed until later
Functional test plans	Describe testing of single or multiple functions When testing of functions is ready to begin and when the testing is complete	Comprehensive functional testing may be overlooked and not completed Test case selection and execution may not be based on specification
Acceptance test plans	Determine whether a system satisfies defined user criteria Final opportunity for users to identify deficiencies by means of documented test cases or scenarios	No opportunity to test software in a systematic way Serious conflict and deficiencies after the system is in production

Beta test plans	Ensure that operational testing at a site is successfully completed No testing by the software developers, so higher likelihood of finding defects	Exploratory, *ad hoc* testing by users, not trained testers No planned scenarios and tests of important functions
Usability test plans	Ease with which users can learn and use a product	Deliver software first and then bandage usability characteristics in
Integration test plans	Expose faults in the interfaces Test interaction between integrated components	All interfaces may not be identified and tested
Performance, stress, and load test plans	Evaluate a system or component at or beyond the limits of its specified requirements	Users are the first to encounter poor performance, time-outs, lost data, and outages System brought down and out of production while problems related to system capacity are corrected
Installation test plans	Ensure that all users can install and begin using the system	May miss testing key steps that new users will encounter
Regression test plans	Retesting major, minor, and patch releases for backward compatibility of results Ensure that faults have not been introduced or uncovered as a result of the changes made	Unreliable behavior and outputs of the system System function has regressed since changes were made What works before has stopped working and compatibility issues emerge
Testing standards and policies	Organization's official position or rules for testing Base for testing documentation Support the need for consistency from release to release and project to project.	Documentation may not meet user needs Inconsistent applications of Test Roadmap items Test plans not completed before testing has to begin Product quality and readiness deterioration

Table 6.2   Product Readiness Checklist

Product Readiness	Status
Functionality/Features	
Localization	
Usability	
Reliability	
Performance	
Supportability	
Data migration issues	

document (assuming there is one), or else, one should at least review the proposed functionality being released.

6.2.1.2   Localization

Are text items like UI field names, help text, error messages, etc., hard-coded or are they coming from separate files and catalogs? This may not be a high priority. Support for the native byte and Unicode should be evaluated.

6.2.1.3   Usability

The main question here would be: Has the product been through formal usability testing? This will tell things about the placement of supportive text, the positioning of information and banners, labels on buttons and tabs, etc.

6.2.1.4   Reliability

Reliability encapsulates quality and robustness. In the ideal case, the following need to be stated as part of the readiness checklist:

- Regression testing coverage — functionality covered, error cases covered, or path coverage (through a real path flow analyzer). Refer to Quality Road Map presented earlier.
- Continuous operations — what is the maximum number of continuous hours this service has been up for? This is a good way to catch memory leaks.

- Crash-n-burn — at some point, one needs to incorporate severe failure testing, e.g., reboot the system in the middle of a service signup, validation action, or transaction and watch it recover. In any case, at least the service should come back up nicely. If it has left strange values behind from a previous instance, subsequent recovery instances may be impacted.
- Stress testing — subject the system to heavy concurrent loads and state the maximum concurrency tested. Refer to Quality Road Map presented earlier.
- Boundary conditions and limits — part of robustness includes testing for limits and boundary conditions.

6.2.1.5   Performance

Need to do at least the basic performance measurements of throughput and response times under controlled conditions. At any rate, the product release should be accompanied, at least internally, by a performance announcement.

6.2.1.6   Supportability

The author has always maintained that support comes from people, but supportability comes from the product itself. One needs to ask the following questions:

- Does the product have configurable trace levels that will help debugging?
- Does the product have any configurable breakpoints that will help debugging?
- Does the product have version stamps in the binary so we can uniquely identify the release?

6.2.1.7   Data Migration Issues

The migration issue has to do with the ability to easily modify the schema for persistent data without causing long downtime periods when the database for the current installation is being migrated to the new future schema.

6.2.2   Deployment Readiness

As stated previously, product readiness is a necessary condition for production worthiness, not a sufficient one. Here is a quick list of deployment considerations.

Table 6.3   Deployment Readiness Checklist

Deployment Readiness	Status
Sizing	
Deployment reviews done?	
Support infrastructure in place?	

6.2.2.1   Sizing

Has formal exercise for sizing been done? The goal here is to be able to confidently make a statement regarding the maximum load the environment can handle? By the way, sizing should ideally be done with fault-resilience in mind if the service guarantees fault-resilience.

6.2.2.2   Deployment Reviews Done?

At least two formal reviews should be done for the deployment environment — a complete topology review that allows participants to understand and agree (or not) with the final deployment view and a security review of the entire environment.

6.2.2.3   Support Infrastructure in Place?

One should document at least the basic support process. This need not be elaborate at all — just a few slides that track the end-to-end flow of a user call. This process of support should be reviewed and documented.

There are other minor deployment checklist items, but the above are the big ones. Table 6.3 presents the deployment readiness checklist.

6.2.3   Development and Deployment Infrastructure

This section outlines a suggested infrastructure required to support quality software release and support. The infrastructure defined here is a typical setup; an actual implementation in a software development or an IT enterprise will vary based on the enterprise's needs, resources, and market conditions. This section is not about the software development lifecycle described earlier.

To produce quality software, a development or IT enterprise must deploy appropriate tools at all stages of the software development and deployment lifecycle. These tools are for the purpose of developing, analyzing, and managing development and deployment across the enterprise. The ability to instill predictability in the software development lifecycle empowers diverse groups that are part of the process and helps improve quality. Requirements definition, source control, version control, release process, bug tracking, remote management, and change control are all important steps in making sure a quality software application is released to customers. The entire software development infrastructure can be expressed as define, develop, build, release, deploy, and maintain phases. In the next few sections, we will discuss these six phases in more detail.

6.2.3.1 Define

All applications start from the first step of definition. Business groups determine requirements in conjunction with customers or focus groups and write product requirement definitions (PRD) or management requirement definitions (MRD). This requirement definition phase may also discuss functional requirements. The versions of requirement definitions are also source controlled for adequate tracking purposes. Requirement definitions are blue prints or templates on which software application development will be based.

6.2.3.2 Develop

This phase requires development environments, as we have discussed before, and a version control system. Development machines should be separated from a build machine where the latest working versions of source are deployed. Version control system keeps track of all updates to software components and is linked back to the source for generating a complete build at a given time. Software applications have different builds in deployment for different platforms and customer environments. Simultaneously, software developers are continually working on versions to improve features and fix bugs. Version control enables the ability to reproduce and patch a previous version of software without interrupting continuous development on the current version. Figure 6.4 describes a typical top-level process.

6.2.3.3 Build

Build machines should have a complete development environment in a clean state so that object code that is produced upon compilation is reproducible. The typical development environment would contain the operating system, appropriate language development environment including compilers, linkers, any required software and libraries, and appropriate drivers. The intention in keeping the build machine separate and controlled

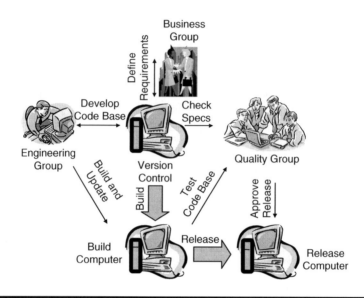

Figure 6.4   Software Development and Deployment Process

is to make sure that at a later time it is possible to create a final object code from a given version of source code. Most software development enterprises and IT departments build the latest software version on a regular basis that may even be daily or twice daily at a given time. This is done to ensure that all have the latest version for testing and, if there are any problems, they are found at the earliest. Sometimes there can be two build computers — one for internal development group to update and develop and the other for the development group to make available to the QA group to test.

6.2.3.4   Release

Object code from the build computer is regularly pushed to release computers where QA groups test them. QA groups may also be given the release on a media format such as compact disk (CD) or floppy disk. QA groups have inspectors and testers to validate, error check, test, and document the bug fixes or feature enhancements that have been completed recently. They employ a test environment for testing purposes. The comprehensiveness of the test environment is determined by the enterprise's management, but should account for various platforms, operating systems, and other deployment conditions at the customer's company. Figure 6.5 describes a typical test environment. Defects, inconsistencies, or improvements that the QA group identifies are reported in a defect tracking system,

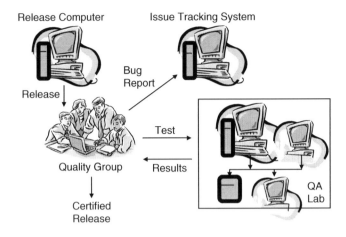

Figure 6.5   QA and Test Environment

also known as a bug tracking system. Current generation of bug tracking systems enable multiple global teams to work simultaneously on testing. Bugs and defects discovered are reported back to the engineering groups for fixing. A review team consisting of business, engineering, and quality team members verifies, approves, and monitors the bug fixing process. The QA group approves a release for production after certification.

6.2.3.5   Deploy

Software released for production deployment can be installed by the customer or by the enterprise providing the software application. There are three potential scenarios for deployment:

1. Shrink wrap
2. Human wrap
3. Services

6.2.3.5.1   Shrink Wrap

Smaller software applications are delivered to the customer in media or downloadable form. The media could be CDs or floppy disks from which the customer can deploy the application themselves. Similarly, the software can be downloaded to the customer's computer and the customer installs the software application by running an installation script. This is popularly referred to as shrink wrap because of the thin transparent plastic wrapping covering the software package.

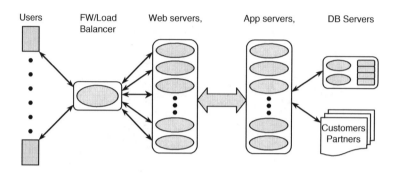

Figure 6.6   Services Model Deployment

6.2.3.5.2   Human Wrap

Professional service organization of the enterprise may be used to help the customer deploy larger and more complex software applications. This is particularly true with situations where integration with legacy systems is to be performed. The customer deploying a new software application may also use third-party system integrators or consulting organizations holding special skills in the applications.

6.2.3.5.3   Services

Another deployment model that has gained strength recently is the Services Model. In this model, the enterprise building the application or a third party may provide the computing and related infrastructure to the customer on "rent." In this model shown in Figure 6.6, the data center of the enterprise hosts the application and the customer accesses it via private network or Internet. Adding or deleting more computing or application resources is easier and because the enterprise that built the application also has expertise in it, maintenance costs could be lower.

On-demand computing, utility computing, adaptive computing, and grid computing [2] are names of emerging technologies that some refer to as the Services Model where instead of renting the infrastructure including computers and network, customers can rent applications and computing power. This model is becoming possible due in part to the potential held by Web services of ubiquitous availability, scalability, and low integration cost.

A release cycle is considered completed with the production software deployed as shown in Figure 6.7. Services Models have strict requirements and SLAs regarding downtime and service interruptions. There may be additional stages in those cases to testing and staging servers before deployment.

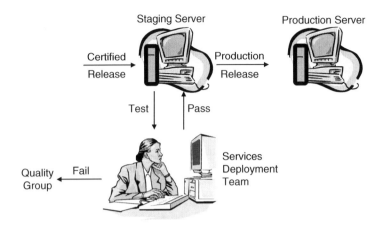

Figure 6.7   Release Cycle Completion

6.2.3.6   Maintain

Software applications that are deployed on a customer site enter maintenance phase as shown in Figure 6.8. This is when a support team helps the customer with any application problems related to deployment. Support levels are maintained with escalation between levels for bugs found and problems encountered. A trouble ticket system is used to keep track of customer reported bugs and a link to call centers and help desks is maintained in real-time. Tracking and managing customer reported issues are assigned a priority and if the first level support is not able to solve it, the issue is usually passed to the QA and test group. Support and help desk are generally separate from QA and test groups. The QA and test groups then enter the bug into the defect tracking system of the engineering team. The review team will then assign priorities and times to fix the bug and patch release to the customer. In large software enterprises, a separate maintenance group may be responsible for small patches to the deployed software application in response to customer reported bugs. Major releases and version releases are the responsibilities of the engineering teams and the patch release fixes have to find their way back into them. Proper controls, guidelines, and interfaces need to be in place for effective handling of this.

6.2.3.7   Resource Requirements

Software development, deployment, and quality require commitment from management for both people and system resources. As we have seen so

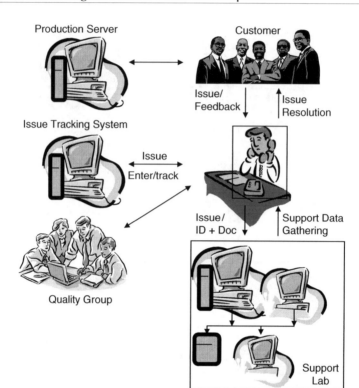

Figure 6.8   Maintenance Environment

Table 6.4   People Resources for Groups in Enterprise

Business group → product marketing, product manager, and sometimes sales
Engineering group → software development and documentation team
Quality group → SQA and test engineers, localization engineers
Deployment group → operations, production, and release engineering
Support group → support team, help desk, ASP, or hosting group
Product maintenance group → maintenance and customer training

far in this book, software systems are complex and in order to maximize ROI, identification and better use of these resources is key.

6.2.3.7.1   People Resources

For each of the steps that we described earlier, the people and resource requirements are listed in Table 6.4.

Table 6.5   Listing of Resources for Software Development and Deployment

Version control system
Build computer(s)
Release computer(s)
QA, testing, and localization lab
Defect tracking system
Trouble ticket system

6.2.3.7.2   Hardware Resources

Software development teams need workstations, servers, development and productivity tools, file and mail servers, network servers, and firewalls. In addition, software development and deployment needs the resources listed in Table 6.5.

For services solutions, staging and production computers are also needed. In addition, larger and more complex software systems will need separate support labs, help desk and call center systems, and maintenance labs.

We have discussed earlier how several companies are outsourcing software development or QA and testing or both. We have also discussed how using global software development can increase Applied ROI significantly. In the next section, we will discuss how to select and manage outsourcers.

6.3   SELECTING AND MANAGING THE OUTSOURCER

Outsourcing usually hands over the ongoing project management responsibilities to the outside company. However, the enterprise still needs to have a level of involvement to determine that the project is going well and that the outsourcer will deliver within budget and time expectations. This requires the outsourcer to provide meaningful and proactive updates on the status of the project. It also requires the IT and development manager to be comfortable with the overall processes that the outsourcer is using to manage the project.

This checklist assumes outsourcing an IT development or QA and test project. This checklist will not work for BPO service. For instance, if you are outsourcing your ongoing help desk, call center, or payroll services, this checklist will not be applicable.

Table 6.6 Project Definition Checklist

	Item	*Check*
1	Has a project definition (or similar document) for the outsourcer been created?	
2	Is the project scope defined, including a description of every milestone and deliverable?	
3	Are out of scope items and project expectations defined?	
4	Is the budget to bring in the outsourcer committed?	
5	Has the management bought in and appropriate stakeholders lined up?	
6	Have deadlines been identified and do they accommodate learning curve and ramp up times?	
7	Have the training needs as deliverables been addressed?	
8	Has a comprehensive project plan for the outsourcer been created?	
9	Is documentation and localization going to be part of outsourcer's scope?	
10	Is the type and number of outsourcing resources required clear?	
11	Does the company have a clearly defined role in managing risks, contingencies, and plan project adjustments?	

6.3.1 Selecting the Outsourcer

6.3.1.1 Project Definition

Table 6.6 presents a detailed project definition checklist for selecting the outsourcer.

6.3.1.2 Interview

Now that we have identified the project definition, we are ready to interview the potential outsourcer. Table 6.7 lists the interview checklist.

6.3.1.3 Addressing Language, Culture, and Time Barriers

In the global connected world of today, we are constantly interacting with people of different cultures, in different time zones, and with different languages. Table 6.8 lists addressing language, culture, and time barriers.

Table 6.7   Interview Checklist

	Item	Check
12	Find out what the financials are: – Find out if they are profitable and how long have they been in business. – Be prepared to request financial statements under nondisclosure agreement.	
13	Ask for customer references: – Request at least five customer references. – Request existing customer references, not past ones.	
14	Ask to interview engineers who will work on the project: – Conduct interview personally and request absence of any coordinators or middlemen. – Evaluate whether communication and experience is consistent and up to requirements. – Ask to be provided with copies of any U.S. certifications and diplomas. – Evaluate how good the phone, communication, and meeting infrastructure is. – Understand from the outsourced engineers what process they follow to keep in sync with local development or QA teams. – Gauge engineers' understanding of confidentiality, security, licensing, and copyrights.	
15	Understand the outsourcer security infrastructure: – Find out if secure remote access capability exists. – Find out what is done to handle intrasite and intersite failures. – Find out if physical asset locking capability exists.	
16	Understand the outsource power infrastructure: – Find out if they have battery backup and surge protectors. – Find out about the duration and frequency of power failures. – Find out if there are backup power generators if there is a prolonged power failure.	
17	Does the outsourcer have a continuous improvement and quality system in place?	

6.3.1.4   Statement of Work and Formal Contract

The assumption for the checklist is that a Statement of Work (SOW) was created, along with a formal contract. If this important planning document is not prepared and formally approved, the information in the next section, Managing the Outsourcer, needs to be a part of the contract. However, discussion of the legal terms of the formal contract is outside the scope

Table 6.8   Addressing Barriers

	Item	*Check*
18	Most countries other than the United States, the United Kingdom, Canada, and Australia are nonnative English speakers. Although one may find people with good English skills, they may not match accent and spoken English requirements.	
19	Consider that other countries may have different work habits, hours, and cultures including different national holidays.	
20	Be aware that the best productivity is achieved when the time difference is used for round the clock operations by leveraging work sequencing.	
21	Be prepared to ask the outsourcer for a small regular common overlapping work time when team members can teleconference or chat over the Internet to resolve any issues that require one-on-one meeting. Without that, logistics of arranging a meeting can be time-consuming.	
22	Make sure that the stakeholders and management are aware that sometimes interaction with the outsourcer will take place from home during nonworking hours. This will be to resolve unforeseen issues or problems and to accommodate time differences.	

of this document. Readers can find a good outsourcing contract discussion in the November 2002 *Management Science* reference cited in Chapter 5. Table 6.9 presents a checklist for formal contract and SOW-related activities.

6.3.2   Managing the Outsourcer

This section picks up when the project has already been defined and the outsourcer has been chosen. However, reviewing this checklist in advance provides better understanding of the overall process of outsourcing and may help in selection. The checklist in this section addresses three basic things:

1. Feedback on updating upfront agreements as the project progresses and interim deliverables are validated and accepted.
2. The project is on track and any deviations or overruns from the plan are manageable.
3. The project is going to conclude as planned and it will be a win-win situation for both the company and the outsourcer.

Table 6.9   Formal Contract

	Item	*Check*
23	Was a Statement of Work created?	
24	Is there clear ownership of different parts of Statement of Work?	
25	Is there a formal contract that spells out the expectations of both parties? – Specific items covered include, deliverables, deadlines, payment schedule, validation, and verification, etc.	
26	Does the formal contract describe a process for amending the agreement in the future?	
27	Does the formal contract cover the outsourcer of failing to meet deadline or quality expectations?	
28	Is the payment schedule clear?	
29	Are privacy, security, and confidentiality statements included in the formal contract?	
30	Are appropriate code ownership and property rights included in the contract?	
31	Has the contract been prepared, reviewed, and approved by your legal staff?	
32	Has the contract been formally signed by all appropriate parties?	

This checklist contains the basic criteria to look for. Individual situations may vary and this list should be supplemented with items that are specific to the project and the contract with the outsourcer. If the outsourcer makes any agreements or commitments, they should be added to this checklist so that they can be monitored throughout the duration of the project.

Any items that have not been checked or that have been answered "no" should be evaluated and explained. Usually this is a sign of impending trouble in deliverables and the project. Readers are encouraged to address these items with the outsourcer, get explanations, and remedy the situation before it becomes worse.

6.3.2.1   Methods and Systems

Table 6.10 defines the appropriate processes one should have in place to derive maximum returns from outsourcing.

Table 6.10 Methods and Systems

	Item	Check
33	Is a bug tracking system used? – Provide outsourcer with accounts, appropriate secure remote access, and walkthrough with guidelines for use. – Note: some outsourcers will provide a bug tracking system, it may be worthwhile to ask.	
34	Are the issue reporting procedures established? – This should include procedures, ability to notify after the issue is fixed, verification, validation, and issue disposition guidelines.	
35	Are the release procedures for the software prepared? – Be prepared to provide the latest release of software through a download site. – Initially and at least after every significant release send a physical CD with software to the outsourcer. – Provide appropriate database setup, configuration parameters, and database administrator notes. – Provide sample data and test files along with information on creating a new database as well as migrating existing database. – Provide shutdown, startup procedures. – Provide operating system special configuration instructions, Internet browser restrictions, versions, application server configuration, and any special runtime requirements.	
36	Be prepared to provide the outsourcer with market requirements documents, functional specifications, product design specifications, product user documentation, installation instructions, release notes, and any other pertinent documentation for the release.	
37	Be prepared to walk through the installation with outsourcer personnel (only needed initially and whenever significant changes are done to installation procedure).	
38	Create e-mail accounts for the outsourcer with authorized secure access.	

6.3.2.2 Goals and Tasking

Checklist for goals and tasking in managing the outsourcer is presented in Table 6.11.

Table 6.11 Goals and Tasking

	Item	*Check*
39	Define goals at a functional level (e.g., "Exhaustive Task Test for e-mail task").	
40	Prepare to submit sets of goals and functional test assignments to the outsourcer.	
41	Ask the outsourcer to write detailed test specifications and write the test programs. Identify any special test bed setup or testing requirements.	
42	Specify a first approximation deadline for each set of goals.	
43	Have the outsourcer review the necessary work and propose an adjustment to the deadline as appropriate. Agree with the outsourcer about the deadline to make it a deliverable goal.	
44	Provide general guidelines for writing a test specification along with examples of test specifications and copies of existing test programs if available. This will help in consistency and accuracy of results.	
45	Establish guidelines and format on status reporting from the outsourcer.	
46	Determine what frequency of status updates would be required for the project. Is it weekly by e-mail or daily by phone and is it more frequent during release crunch?	

6.3.3   Release Candidate Certification Guidelines

6.3.3.1   Release Guidelines

Table 6.12 presents the checklist for release guidelines.

6.3.3.2   During the Project

Table 6.13 presents the checklist for during the project.

6.3.3.3   End of the Project

Table 6.14 presents the checklist for the end of the project.

The project should be marked as completed and moved to maintenance and support mode. Any questions that have been answered "no" should be pursued and explained.

Table 6.12   Guidelines

	Item	Check
47	Set up a mechanism to provide the outsourcer with upcoming releases and timeframes.	
48	Get a commitment that outsourcer personnel will provide daily, weekly, and monthly updates on status tracking.	
49	Set up regular meetings with outsourcer personnel to iterate through testing results, issue reports, and testing coverage.	
50	Based on gap analysis, outsourcer will create more tests, do regressions, or performance/load tests as appropriate.	
51	Make sure the outsourcer is prepared to provide certification indicating release candidate is ready and all test cases generated by them have been run successfully.	

6.4   METHODOLOGIES AND MEASUREMENT

As mentioned earlier, we spent time discussing the best practices and key guidelines with several CTOs, directors of SQA, VP engineering colleagues, and customers. Based on that discussion, we gathered the best practices and key guidelines that work effectively in outsourcing projects. The best practices we are identifying here fit with each other like cells in a honeycomb. They are interdependent and each one is critical for the success of the entire outsourcing structure to stay and work together. There are three columns of best practices and guidelines — in-house SQA, productive experience and costs, and timeliness of the deliverables.

6.4.1   Three Columns of Best Practices and Guidelines

Figure 6.9 shows the best practices and key guidelines honeycomb.

6.4.1.1   In-House SQA

The first is the strength and composition of in-house SQA, types of testing desired, and whether it is important to adhere to standards bodies and models such as SEI's CMM and ISO's ISO 9001 or Software ISO 14000.

6.4.1.2   Productive Experience

The second column deals with how to make the experience productive through better interteam interaction, including communication channels,

Table 6.13   During the Project

	Item	Check
52	Update the project plan and milestones based on the outsourcer performance.	
53	Is the outsourcer following procedures articulated by it earlier for all of the following? – Managing delays or early completion. – Quality of deliverables. – Reporting and update procedures. – Managing issues, scope, and risk.	
54	Get an accurate measure of project progress from the vendor.	
55	Does in-house team report successful ongoing communications and issue resolution with the outsourcer?	
56	Is management stakeholder supportive and approving the changes to the scope and schedule updates?	
57	Are project management tools, methods, and systems being faithfully and accurately followed?	
58	Are the in-house resources at the right level to support the outsourcer?	
59	Does the outsourcer have the right level of resources to support the project needs?	
60	Is the status of deliverables and milestones consistent with those specified in the Statement of Work?	
61	Is the project expected to complete on time?	
62	Does management stakeholder formally approve all the milestones and deliverables remaining?	
63	Should the Statement of Work or the formal contract be updated to reflect any changes in the deliverables or milestones?	
64	If milestone-based payments are due, has the outsourcer delivered consistent to the plan?	
65	Make sure that the payments are promptly disbursed to the outsourcer if they are due as per the plan.	

language and culture issues, and interviewing the prospective outsourcer team members.

Table 6.14   End of the Project

	Item	Check
66	Is the Statement of Work completely satisfied with the deliverables and milestones achieved in the project?	
67	Does in-house team formally accept all deliverables?	
68	Has management stakeholder approved the deliverables?	
69	Have documentation and training needs been met?	
70	Has there been any change in resource composition at the outsourcer? This gives a data point to revisit if the change in resources led to delayed execution of deliverables and milestones.	
71	Are all past due payments for interim deliverables complete?	
72	Remove all outsourcer File Transfer Protocol (FTP), e-mail, and login accounts.	
73	Verify that outsourcer will remove or archive all instances of proprietary code, documentation, and material after project completion.	
74	Determine maintenance and ongoing outsourcer involvement if any.	
75	Get ready to sign off on the completed contract and pay final installment of monies.	

6.4.1.3   Costs and Timelines

The third column is the cost considerations and outsourcing destinations including the location (near shore, offshore) and company (large, medium, small).

In the next section, we detail out how people that we talked to summarized their experiences of working with outsourcers.

6.4.2   Best Practices Criteria Details

6.4.2.1   Productive Experience

Most of the colleagues believed that pure outsourcing models did not work as intended. They had no proximity with the SQA team and closed loop interaction. They felt that outsourced SQA work resulted in the following common feedback:

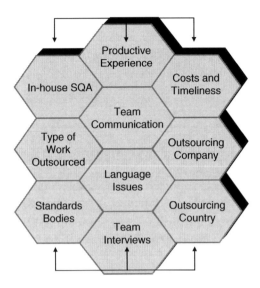

Figure 6.9   Best Practices and Key Guidelines Honeycomb

- Outsourcer did not understand our product.
- Outsourcer did not find a lot of bugs they should have found.
- Outsourcer did not understand what they were supposed to do.
- Outsourcer did not get good reporting.

Several had more pleasant experiences if they had internal SQA managers interacting and controlling the outsourcing team. This is what we have referred to as the Cosourcing Model in earlier chapters.

6.4.2.2   Costs and Timeliness

Responses on this ranged from some successful and well-managed projects and product deliverables resulting in cost savings to unhappy campers who shipped products that did not work and spent more than planned. Another key aspect that emerged was that cost should never be the only consideration when outsourcing SQA. The cost of not doing SQA or doing poor SQA would be increased exponentially if a product were released with bugs that prevent users from using it.

6.4.2.3   Outsourcing Companies

Most of those surveyed preferred to keep the names of the companies they worked with anonymous. All of the colleagues believed that asking the companies for current customer references and checking with them for satisfaction worked well. Several outsourced SQA and test companies maintain a satisfaction percentage metric of their customers through established interviews and questionnaires. It is a good idea to ask the outsourcing provider for a report on this metric.

6.4.2.4 Outsourcing Country

Most respondents had worked with Indian outsourcing vendors. Most cited proficiency in English and quality of work from Indian companies as better than other outsourcing countries. Some cited experience working with Indian companies that maintained strong management presence in America as well as SQA labs in India as better suited to their working style. A few did not enjoy working with outsourcers from any other country.

6.4.2.5 Hurdles for Team Communication

All agreed that the time difference in team communication could become a hurdle in productivity if the outsourcing company with a good methodology and process did not address it. It was observed also that addressing the time difference issue with good process led to better handling of tighter build or regression schedules as release dates came closer. Most of the colleagues observed the following cycle to be effective in proactively handling the time difference to an advantage:

1. Developers deposited the latest build and release in the source control at night before leaving for the day.
2. The SQA and test experts in the outsourcing company would run the test cases and generate reports on the release and upload the bug tracking system for the developers.
3. Developers would review the bugs and test result reports and work on fixing the bugs.

This cycle reportedly worked effectively with outsourcing SQA and test companies in India that were 12.5 hours ahead in time.

Some outsourcing companies reportedly worked in multiple shifts to accommodate overlaps with the developers in the United States for conferencing and one-on-one communication.

6.4.2.6 Language Issues

People reported issues with accented English from outsourcing companies and the fact that Americans are not trained to talk at ESL (English as

Second Language) speeds. Both of these issues were addressed by companies that used outsourcing through Internet Relay Chat and teleconferencing that involved people from the outsourcing companies who were in the United States. It helped to work with outsourcing companies that maintained offices and key executives and management in the United States.

6.4.2.7 Types of Testing Outsourced

Most of the companies that have used outsourcing reported trying functional, unit, white box, and black box testing.

6.4.2.8 Replace SQA Department?

All of the companies that have worked with outsourcing SQA and test providers reported working with them as extensions of their existing SQA departments. That was the model that worked best for them. Some companies who once had SQA departments reportedly replaced them with an outsourced company. Often the outsourcing company in the beginning acted as overflow for SQA departments who were overloaded. Sometimes outsourcing SQA and test experts were brought in where the customers never had SQA and used the outsourcing company to help them transition into having their own SQA team.

6.4.2.9 Required Backgrounds of SQA and Testing People

Most companies and colleagues we talked to wanted SQA and testing people with computer science and software backgrounds. However, they sometimes lamented that SQA outsourcing companies gave them people with limited or no technical or programming backgrounds. Companies also warned against accepting at face value claims by the outsourcing company that they had "UNIX experts" or "Windows experts." Most recommended finding out if the SQA and test people had certifications by Sun or Microsoft or some other U.S.-based training and certification organization.

An important factor in each successful outsourcing partnership was that having a SQA manager who was already familiar with the product and company-testing practices should be leading the offshore team (i.e., onsite at the remote location).

6.4.2.10 Standards Bodies

All companies and colleagues reported that standards bodies provided a documentation model. However even though using standards was useful as a filtering criterion, it was not a guaranteed success criterion. In their opinions, certifications and standards did not ensure that the outsourcing project would be productive and successful.

Based on this distillation of experiences, we start to develop a checklist for what to expect from an outsourcer. This checklist covers dual purposes: it helps manage expectations from both sides and streamline selection and execution of a successful outsourcer relationship.

6.4.3   Experiences of Outsourcing

A summary of experiences of outsourcing derived from the discussions and interviews presented earlier is listed in Table 6.15.

Table 6.15   Summary of Experiences

Summary of Experience	Evaluation	Comments
Productive experience	Yes	Mostly
Costs and timeliness	Yes	
Outsourcing company	Pick company with good financials	Profitability and management team
Outsourcing country	India	85 percent of all outsourcing done there
Hurdles to team communication	Language	
Language issues	Existing and prescreening should be employed	
Types of testing outsourced	Black box, functional, load, and stress	
Replace in-house SQA?	No	Supplement in-house SQA using cosourcing
Required background for testers	Do thorough interviews, do not go by statements of vendors	
Standards bodies	Only moderately useful	

6.5   SUMMARY OF CHAPTER

Let us turn the art of outsourcing, which some IT managers will liken to sorcery, into science. This chapter discusses strategies to evaluate and execute in companies that readers may be picking for software development, SQA, test, and verification. We have distilled the evaluation criteria over several years of outsourcing experience to provide unique visibility and perspective on outsourcing. Specific experiences of dealing with communication, time zone, and cultural differences are discussed. Background requirements of people who work on SQA and testing as well as the types of testing outsourcing lends itself best to are identified. Discussions range from whether outsourcing QA and testing was a productive experience for companies to whether or not the promise of cost savings was fulfilled.

In this chapter, we started out with a discussion of product and deployment readiness criteria and a quality roadmap. In Section 6.3, we provided valuable checklists that address selecting and managing outsourcers. We presented a software support and quality infrastructure that enables readers to understand the layout of different components of software development. We discussed various deployment strategies including grid or on-demand computing. In Section 6.4, we followed that up with discussion on best practices and key guidelines that we got from talking to several CTOs and IT and development managers, directors of SQA, and VP engineering colleagues and customers. The final sections were devoted to discussions on what models work best and how to select and manage cosourced projects.

In the next chapter, we will discuss case studies involving global software development and testing. The author has worked for several years in outsourcing both development and test projects and has gained experience managing the entire process. The case studies will demonstrate how successful global and publicly traded companies (names withheld to maintain confidentiality) have employed global teams including third-party offshore vendor partnerships. Results are excellent if the appropriate management steps, as we have discussed throughout the book, are taken and expectations are effectively managed.

REFERENCES

1. Terdiman, R., Offshore Outsourcing Is Mainstream for Fortune 500 Enterprises, Gartner Research, September 7, 2001.
2. Open Grid Services Architecture and Globus Alliance, http://www.globus.org/ogsa/.

7

CASE STUDIES

.

7.1 ANATOMY OF OUR CASE STUDIES

7.1.1 Introduction

Readers who have read the whole book to this point will be conceptually ready to pursue global software development and testing. However, being ready in concept is not really the same thing as actually doing it. Even though we have presented several small cases throughout the book, we will present in this chapter two actual cases in more detail. The first case is one where, due to product and technical complexity, automation cannot be done easily and outsourcing coupled with better tools works. The other case is where just a small component that is highly repetitive, yet important, but also orthogonal to the main product is tested offshore.

All the cases are real. We do not reveal the source of each case, nor do we identify the people or companies involved, but every case described in this chapter solves a key problem. The time duration over which work on these cases was monitored and compiled is approximately two years. These case studies strengthen the author's belief that it is possible to globalize development and testing steps for diverse types of projects, but needs careful planning and execution. Also, it is difficult to fit the experience of outsourcing in a single formula — whether good or bad — and individual situations may vary considerably.

7.1.2 Sources

The case studies in this chapter are derived from a few sources.

- A software quality company that outsources such projects
- An enterprise CRM market leader that is publicly traded on NAS-DAQ

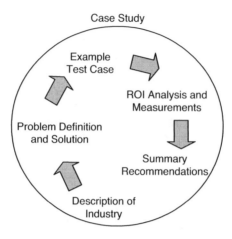

Figure 7.1 Anatomy of Our Case Studies

- A global wireless software provider that develops natural language systems
- Author's visits and interactions with these and other companies
- Questions, answers, and discussions on public news groups including quality, W3C, and others

We will present each of the case studies with details as described in the attached illustration, anatomy of the case studies (Figure 7.1). First, we will talk about a project using that type of system. Next, we will give a sample test specification for that case and finally we will follow-up by ROI analysis and measurements for the case along with conclusions.

The case studies covered in this chapter are listed below.

- Developing and testing natural language systems for mobile devices — in this case, we discuss how development of a test tool becomes important to semiautomate testing. Semiautomated testing along with cosourcing results in considerable Applied ROI savings for a major multinational natural language interface infrastructure company.
- Global testing of enterprise grade CRM software — in this case study, we illustrate how it is possible for development teams located in the United States, Canada, and India and testing teams located in the United States and two centers in India including one extraenterprise offshore partner to gain significant Applied ROI benefits. The software developed and tested is for mature enterprise class product versions of a publicly listed CRM Company in use by about 2000 customers.

7.2 CASE 1: DEVELOPING AND TESTING NATURAL LANGUAGE SYSTEMS FOR MOBILE DEVICES

7.2.1 Natural Language System Profile

In this case study, we discuss how to test products and online services providing self-service search, navigation, and natural language interfaces. Examples of companies providing natural language interfaces from mobile devices are iPhrase™, NativeMinds, Dejima, Ask Jeeves®, and major search engines such as Google™ and AltaVista®. Some of these sites provide an ability to interact using easy question phrases. This enables people to interact naturally with technology just as they would with another person. Such sites facilitate access to information; carry out transactions including transactions through wireless networks using e-mail (desktop or wireless), PDAs, or phones; and for various platforms including Palm™, BlackBerry®, and Microsoft Pocket PC. Most of these products and services are embedded in mission critical CRM applications of Fortune 500 companies or enterprises.

This case study focuses on functional and regression testing of e-mail and wireless Web interfaces of such natural language applications. We describe two test tools that help automate such testing — one for test case and query generation and another for automating the tests and test queries. Specific examples using XML interfaces and actual code are presented.

7.2.2 Case Introduction

7.2.2.1 E-Mail Interface

Using the e-mail interface, from an e-mail client, a user can send e-mail (PC Email Client or Eudora® or BlackBerry e-mail client) asking for some information. The underlying service processes the information and generates the e-mail sending the results to the user. All functionality is accessed using e-mail.

7.2.2.2 Wireless Web Interface

In the wireless Web interface, users open the browser software on their PDAs (e.g., BlackBerry, Palm, Pocket PC compatible device) and point the browser for service. The user may now interact with the application by completing the Search Request field. The underlying service processes the information and displays matching results for user query.

7.2.3 Technical Overview

Agent-based architecture enables end users to access information, carry out transactions, and control devices directly through intuitive words or phrases, thereby saving time and avoiding frustration. The basis of the technology is an engineering methodology that breaks up complex software into a community of simpler, collaborating, message-driven components known as agents.

7.2.3.1 Agents

Agents are independent software entities that interact with each other by exchanging messages in an agent communication language. Each agent has its own areas of expertise, which it shares with other agents as needed.

7.2.3.2 Networks of Agents

Networks of agents are organized to address a given target domain. Because no single agent has the ability to solve the entire problem, they attack it as a group, sometimes competing, often cooperating, but always moving forward collectively toward a solution. The approach is noncentralized, yet modular. Agent subgroups are specialized in different aspects of the problem and work in parallel on pending tasks. Ambiguities may arise and are resolved by other agents or through a dialog with the user.

7.2.4 Supported Platforms

Deployment of this wireless natural language application would be supported on the following platforms.

7.2.4.1 E-Mail Clients

- Wireless e-mail clients:
  - BlackBerry
  - Palm
- Desktop e-mail clients:
  - MS Outlook®
  - MS Outlook Express
  - Eudora
  - Netscape Communicator
  - Lotus Notes®
  - Web e-mail clients (Yahoo!®, Hotmail®, etc.)

7.2.4.2 Browsers for Wireless Handheld Devices

As of the press date, the current generation of wireless handheld device browsers includes:

- Handspring Blazer (Palm OS)
- EudoraWeb Browser (Palm OS)
- AvantGo® Browser (Palm OS)
- GoAmerica Browser (RIM OS)
- MS Internet Explorer (Windows CE OS)

7.2.5   Problem Definition and Solution

Manual functional and regression testing of products and online services providing self-service search, navigation, and natural language interfaces is a tedious process. One needs to automate testing efforts as the scope of such systems is wide and manual testing difficult [1–3].

The wireless Web can be accessed through a standard browser. The display will be, in this case, formatted for a PDA browser's small form factor and limited graphics, but still functional from a standard Web browser. Thus, testing can be done from any standard Web browser with simulated PDA browser functionality. E-mail interfaces can similarly be tested with the tool in the same manner as the Web interface, but needs some additional information such as <username> and <password>. This credential information is used to log into multiple systems, including the e-mail server. The test results generated will be the same as for the Web interface.

The outsourcer had developed customized tools, which were used to ease testing efforts and improve overall productivity. These tools can also be used for testing natural language database query systems [4]. This case study will describe the testing requirements and how the outsourcer used customized tools for testing e-mail and wireless Web interface in an automated and semiautomated fashion. These customized tools are developed in Java and Compaq's Web Language hereinafter abbreviated to WebL [5]. In the next sections, we will describe the Query Builder tool that is written Java and TestRunner tool that is written in WebL.

7.2.5.1   Functional Testing

Functional testing is geared to functional requirements of the application to make sure the application is sound enough from a functional point of view. Normally in functional testing, the testers do testing for each feature by referring to the functional requirements document of an application. Using Query Builder tool, as we will describe in more detail later, the tester can create XML test cases with validation for correctness of results. Depending on the validations mentioned in the XML test case file for expected results, tests will pass or fail. Each WebL TestRunner tool run generates a directory full of reports, detailing whether the cases succeeded or failed, and showing screen dumps of the session from each test. In

Table 7.1 Natural Language Interface Testing Scenarios and System Responses

Testing Scenario	System Response
"Show me movie theaters in Sunnyvale, CA."	List of theatres in Sunnyvale, CA.
"Where is Oracle?"	Location, directions, and phone information for Oracle.
"Show me sales, cash, profit, and stock price for Cisco and AOL."	Tabulated financial information on requested companies.
"Do you carry Nokia 1100 mobile phone?"	"Yes, we carry it in silver, red, and green and there is a $50 off promotion going on."
"What is a good IRA if I am 33 and may withdraw funds before I am 59?"	"Friendly Bank's Roth IRA is the most appropriate one for you, here are more details."

addition, reports generated will display percentage of tests passed. By analyzing failed test cases, the tester can submit bugs in the bug tracking system. For functional testing of natural interaction applications, this type of automation plays an important role for catching bugs. As in natural interaction, the user interacts with the application in their own words and this varies from person to person. Thus, in manual testing there is a chance of missing some combinations for query, which will cover bugs.

The tester can build a regression test suite using the Query Builder tool. As and when a new build is ready after fixes or modifications of the software or its environment, this regression testing suite can be run using TestRunner tool described later. By analyzing the generated report, percentage of test passed, the testers will be sure of whether the existing features are working along with the newly added ones.

7.2.6   Test Case Example

Table 7.1 describes a typical set of queries to the system and expected responses. These examples form the basis of building test cases and expected outputs as discussed later.

7.2.7   Testing Tools Used

7.2.7.1   WebLOAD 4.51

WebLOAD is a testing tool for testing the scalability, functionality, and performance of Web-based applications — both Internet and intranet. It can measure the performance of an application under variable load conditions. Testers are encouraged to use WebLOAD to test how well their Web site will perform under real-world conditions by combining performance, load, and functional tests or by running them individually. WebLOAD supports Hypertext Transfer Protocol (HTTP) 1.0 and 1.1, including cookies, proxies, Secure Sockets Layer (SSL), client certificates, authentications, persistent connections, and chunked transfer coding. Web-LOAD generates load by creating virtual clients that emulate network traffic. JavaScript test scripts (called agendas) are created to instruct those virtual clients what to do. When WebLOAD runs the test, it gathers results at per client, per transaction, and per instance level from the computers that are generating the load. WebLOAD can also gather information from the application server's performance monitor. Results are available for display iteratively. WebLOAD displays the results in graphs and tables in real-time and exports the results when the test is finished. For Wireless Application, WebLOAD Tool is used for Load Testing on Web sites.

7.2.7.2 Query Builder Tool

For testing natural interaction systems, manual designing of XML test cases is cumbersome. Because a single query can be formatted in a number of different ways, the testers have to consider automating XML test case file creation. Using a requirements document, the testers have to decide scope for testing and have to design a matrix for test case creation. The first step is to design general forms for query: for example, "show me movie theaters in <city name>" can be formatted in a number of different ways:

- Show me theaters in <city name>
- Display theaters in city of <city name>
- List theaters in <city name> city
- Find cinema hall in <city name> city
- Get cinema halls in city of <city name>

So here are general forms for words used:

```
[Show] = show, display, get, report, find, list
[Theater] = Theater, cinema hall
```

Depending on the scope of an application, it becomes difficult to manually create such XML test cases for a particular testing feature. There is a possibility of missing some combinations. So here an in-house Java program had to be developed to generate XML test cases along with validation for correctness of data that will pass or fail tests depending on

Table 7.2   A Simple Query Format

General Form of Query:	Examples of Query:
[Show] [Theaters] in {city} Synonyms: [Show] = show, display, get, list, report, find [Theater] = theaters, cinema+halls	Display theaters in city XYZ. Show me theaters in XYZ. List theaters in XYZ city. Find cinema hall in XYZ city. Cinema halls in city XYZ.

the expected result. This program takes input as a general form matrix with synonyms and covers almost all combinations for the query. Once the tester is sure that one form is working for different queries — show, display, get, report, find, list — and all are giving expected results, then the tester can concentrate on another form combination by eliminating all synonyms for show. This reduces the size of test cases and the test suite will be optimum.

Java source code for generating XML test case files is available from the author upon request. This program can be altered according to the feature under test for regression and functional testing. Table 7.2 shows a simple model of a program for a simple query format.

Using the Query Builder tool, the testers can semiautomate testing efforts. The testers have to decide on the basic format for natural interaction and synonyms. Once the tester is ready with this, they can modify the program according to their requirements and generate XML test case files. When testing scope is wide, this reduces manual efforts significantly.

7.2.7.3   TestRunner Tool

WebL has built-in support for common Web protocols like HTTP and FTP with cookies and popular data types like HTML and XML. WebL can easily fill in Web-based forms and navigate between pages. It is implemented as a stand-alone application that fetches and processes Web pages according to programmed scripts. Two of the language's unique features are service combinators and markup algebra. Service combinators are an exception-handling mechanism that makes computations on the Web more reliable. Markup algebra provides a way to extract information from and manipulate Web pages.

7.2.7.4   Searching Functions

There are several ways in which piece sets, using markup algebra, can be created:

- Searching for markup elements by explicitly naming interesting elements
- Searching for character patterns that match a regular expression
- Searching for text segments
- Searching for stylized sequences of markup patterns
- Searching for segments delimited by explicitly named markup elements (e.g., paragraph extraction)

For these tools, the input is XML file of cases. Essentially the tool loads an XML file that defines "cases": sets of input commands (e.g., filling in a form, clicking a link) and test validations, which will pass or fail the test according to expected results mentioned. Each run generates a directory full of reports, detailing whether the cases succeeded or failed, and showing screen dumps of the session from each test. Also, the report generated will display percentage of tests passed. By analyzing the report generated, the tester can submit bugs in a bug tracking system.

If the tester needs to perform more complex tests, then these can be implemented using the test definitions described in the previous section using external validation scripts written in a language such as WebL. If the Validation Script element has a filename, this file will be dynamically loaded and run.

```
<ValidationScript>Test1</ValidationScript>
```

7.2.8   Output Results from Testing Tool

Here are examples of test reports generated by Query Builder tool. When running Query Builder tool on a test definition file, an output directory is created. This directory contains:

- A copy of the test script that was run.
- A log file (testlog.htm) containing results for all cases defined in the test file.
- A report (report.htm) containing a summary of results by functional point.
- Saved HTML files for each case run during the test. These files are altered to contain a header and footer bar that provides details about the tests run on that page.

7.2.8.1   Log File

The log file contains a list of all the inputs and whether they passed or failed. Links are included for each case to the saved HTML page associated with the case. Table 7.3 describes a typical log file for this case.

Table 7.3   Log File with Pass/Fail Status of Tests

Feature Under Test	Case Name	P/F
Theaters by city	Show theaters in city xyz.	Passed
Theaters by city	Show me movie theaters in Sunnyvale, CA.	Passed
Health service by city	Show dental clinic in xyz city.	Passed
Health service by city	Where I can buy individual health insurance?	Passed
Company by location	Where is CISCO, San Jose?	Passed
Business information by company	Show me stock price for Intel.	Passed
Business information by company	Show me last quarter sale of Cisco.	Passed
Shopping centers by city	List shopping malls in San Jose.	Passed
Shopping centers by city	Show me location of JCPenney in San Jose.	Failed

Table 7.4   Report File with Pass Percentages and Input Numbers

Feature Under Test	Percent Passed	Input per Feature
Theaters by city	100	3
Health service by city	68	3
Company by location	100	2
Business information by company	100	2
Shopping centers by city	34	3

7.2.8.2   Report File

The report file contains a summary of all cases, grouped by feature under test. Table 7.4 shows a report file.

7.2.9   Bug Tracking System Tools

We will now discuss the bug tracking system used for this particular test case. It is important to note that this is not an endorsement of any

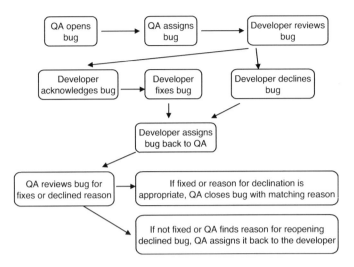

Figure 7.2   Lifecycle of a Bug

commercial product. The company whose tool is mentioned here is one of several offering comparable products.

7.2.9.1   Rational ClearQuest

Rational ClearQuest® is a Web-based system. It includes the information regarding issues. An issue is represented with an identification number, description, progress status, work description, and other dynamic properties. At all times throughout its history, an issue is always assigned to an owner, which can be a team member, a team group, or a group folder. The system tracks the entire history of an issue from its creation to closure by recording all changes of its ownership, work description, progress status, and other issue properties. The tester starts by entering the new bug into bug tracking system and tracks until the closure of this issue, which involves the complete lifecycle of a bug.

7.2.9.2   Bug Lifecycle

Figure 7.2 shows the lifecycle of a bug and its journey from QA to development and back.

With reference to above illustration, the testing and QA team does following activities:

- Opens new bug.
- Assigns bug.

- Reviews bug for fixes or declined reason.
- If fixed or reason for declination is appropriate, the testing and QA team closes bug with matching reason.
- If not fixed or testing and QA team finds reason for reopening the declined bug, it is assigned back to the developer.

7.2.10 Return on Investment

ROI is defined in the *Dictionary of Modern Economics* as:

> A general concept referring to Earnings from the Investment of Capital, where the earnings are expressed as a proportion of the outlay.

As we discussed earlier, the equation for calculating the percentage of ROI is:

$$ROI = (Net\ Benefits/Net\ Costs) * 100$$

NBs can be either direct, in terms of incremental revenue generated, productivity gained, or expense saved or indirect, from the redeployment of resources to tasks that the organization would alternatively have had to hire new and like resources to perform. NCs include recruiting, salaries, benefits, software licensing, and general and administrative overheads. The ROI for each project is compared with the NCs on a yearly basis. ROI analysis means that where expected benefits and costs are realized within the same year of implementation of the project, the project is more likely to proceed. Sometimes ROI is a number (Net Benefits/Net Costs).

ROI is high, using cosourcing, in which an outsourcing SQA team is not completely replacing the in-house SQA team. Instead, the outsourced SQA team is working as an extension of the in-house team with a key SQA manager on the in-house team maintaining full knowledge and control of the SQA tasks and project plan.

The above statement is summarized in the two tables below. Assumption is a testing and QA team size of five.

7.2.10.1 No Cosourcing for SQA Testing

Table 7.5 shows the average cost of testers in the United States with no cosourcing.

7.2.10.2 Cosourcing for SQA Testing

As we saw earlier, Applied ROI involves not just automation, but also improved methodology and process to enable doing some of the work

Table 7.5 Average Cost of Testers in the United States with No Cosourcing

Location	No. of Testers	$ per Month per tester fully loaded	$ per Year
United States	05	10,000	600,000

Table 7.6 Cosourced Resources between the United States and India

Location	No. of Testers	$ per Month	$ per Year
India	04	5,000	60,000
United States	01	10,000	120,000
		Total	184,000

Total ROI (%) per Year = Net Benefit/Net Cost * 100
= (600,000 – 184,000)/184,000 * 100
= 226.09

from a high quality and cost-effective destination. For this particular case study, the cosourcing location was in India and four test engineers were located there along with one team leader and stakeholder located in the United States (see Table 7.6).

7.2.11 Conclusion

Applications providing selfservice search, virtual customer representatives, and natural language interactions are more complex to test. Users may interact with the applications in various ways and the interaction varies significantly between individual users. Users can query applications in their own words using email interfaces or using PDAs with a wireless Web interface and the applications return matching results.

Benefits of automated programs that lead to applied ROI savings discussed in this case are listed below:

- Query Builder tool (used for creation of XML test cases) reduces manual efforts required for creation of XML test cases. It can also semiautomate building of regression test suites.
- XML test cases created by Query Builder have wide coverage for each feature, something that is impossible to do manually.
- The combination of Query Builder tool and TestRunner tool is best suited for functional or regression testing of Webbased natural interaction applications.

- WebL is well suited for automation of tasks on the Web because of its builtin support for common Web protocols like HTTP (including cookie support) and FTP and popular data types like HTML and XML.

We see that using cosourcing leads to a significant ROI savings and cost advantages in the wireless mobile case study we have presented above. This case study was based on an actual project delivered to a multinational wireless mobile software company.

7.3 CASE 2: GLOBAL TESTING OF ENTERPRISE CRM MARKET LEADER

7.3.1 CRM Company Profile

This case study is based around managing and testing enterprise class (100 megabyte releases) multiyear, multiversion licensed CRM solution. A large publicly traded CRM company that delivers this software and these services for companies and business units in the revenue range of $100 million to $3 billion was involved in this case. The CRM Company has more than 2000 customers and is a significant player in its industry.

7.3.2 Case Introduction

CRM Company's MarketingDiva is an enterprise-class software application that allows marketing professionals to automate efforts using e-mail, Web, and fax. Using a process flow interface, marketers can design, implement, and evaluate marketing initiatives. The Campaign Portal operates with the MarketingDiva application to offer automated marketing functionality via a Web browser interface.

CRM Company's products can manage and display documents in multiple languages based on the translated content. The correct translation is displayed based on the preferred language information that the sales or marketing staff have collected about their contacts and stored in the CRM Company base profile. Additionally, certain localization aspects, such as appropriate number formats are controlled through their contact's correlating country information.

CRM Company products currently can work with and provide documents using languages based on the Unicode 3.0 character set. This means that CRM Company users should be able to create and launch truly multilingual global campaigns. Contacts should be able to receive and reply to CRM Company documents in their native encoding. In this case study, we will present a brief overview of Unicode for users who are not familiar with it. Those users who are already familiar with Unicode can skip this section. Discussion of Unicode establishes the role of this character-encoding scheme in internationalization of software applications.

7.3.3 Technical Overview of Unicode

7.3.3.1 What Is Unicode?

The Unicode Standard is the universal character-encoding scheme for written characters and text. It defines a consistent way of encoding multilingual text that enables the exchange of text data internationally and creates the foundation for global software.

Unicode provides a unique number for every character, no matter what the platform, no matter what the program, no matter what the language. Although modeled on the American Standard Code for Information Interchange (ASCII) character set, the Unicode Standard goes far beyond ASCII's limited ability to encode only the upper- and lowercase letters A through Z. It provides the capacity to encode all characters used for the written languages of the world: more than 1 million characters can be encoded.

7.3.3.2 Unicode and ISO/IEC 10646

The Unicode Standard is closely aligned with the international standard ISO/IEC 10646 (also known as the Universal Character Set, or UCS, for short). Close cooperation and formal liaison between the committees has ensured that all additions to either standard are coordinated and kept in sync, so that the two standards maintain exactly the same character repertoire and encoding.

Version 3.0 of the Unicode Standard is code-for-code identical to ISO/IEC 10646-1:2000. This code-for-code identity is true for all encoded characters in the two standards, including the East Asian (Han) ideographic characters. Subsequent versions of the Unicode Standard track additional parts and amendments to ISO/IEC 10646.

The Unicode encoding forms correspond exactly to forms of use and transformation formats also defined in ISO/IEC 10646. UCS Transformation Format 8 (UTF-8) and UTF-16 are defined in annexes to ISO/IEC 10646-1:2000. And UTF-32 corresponds to the four-octet form UCS-4 of 10646.

7.3.3.3 Encoding Forms

Character encoding standards define not only the identity of each character and its numeric value or code point, but also how this value is represented in bits. Unicode maps code points to characters, but does not actually specify how the data will be represented in memory, in a database, or on a Web page. This is where the actual encoding of Unicode data comes into play.

The Unicode Standard defines three encoding forms that allow the same data to be transmitted in a byte-, word-, or double word-oriented format (i.e., in 8, 16, or 32 bits per code unit). All three encoding forms encode the same common character repertoire and can be efficiently transformed into one another without loss of data. The Unicode Consortium fully endorses the use of any of these encoding forms as a conformant way of implementing the Unicode Standard.

UTF-8 is popular for HTML and similar protocols. UTF-8 is a way of transforming all Unicode characters into a variable length encoding of bytes. It has the advantages that the Unicode characters corresponding to the familiar ASCII set have the same byte values as ASCII and that Unicode characters transformed into UTF-8 can be used with much existing software without extensive software rewrites. Many ASCII and other byte-oriented systems that require 8-bit encoding (such as mail servers) must span a vast array of computers that use different encoding, different byte orders, and different languages. UTF-8 is an encoding scheme that is designed to treat Unicode data in a way that is independent of the byte ordering on the computer.

UTF-16 is popular in many environments that need to balance efficient access to characters with economical use of storage. It is reasonably compact and all the heavily used characters fit into a single 16-bit code unit and all other characters are accessible via pairs of 16-bit code units. UTF-16 is the primary Unicode encoding used by Microsoft Windows 2000.

UTF-32 is popular where memory space is no concern, but fixed width, single code unit access to characters is desired. Each Unicode character is encoded in a single 32-bit code unit when using UTF-32. All three encoding forms need at most 4 bytes (or 32 bits) of data for each character.

UCS-2 is the main Unicode encoding used by Microsoft Windows NT® 4.0, Microsoft SQL Server version 7.0, and Microsoft SQL Server 2000. UCS-2 is a strict subset of UTF-16. The only difference between these two is that UCS-2 is surrogate neutral. It treats surrogate characters as two separate characters.

7.3.4 Supported Platforms

MarketingDiva would be supported on the platforms listed in this section:

- Operating system platform support:
  – Windows 2000 (Professional and Server)
  – Solaris™ 8
  – Windows 2003

- Marketing client operating systems:
  - Windows 2000
  - Windows XP
  - Windows 2003
- Database server platform support:
  - Oracle9i
  - SQL Server 2000
- Web browser support:
  - Microsoft Internet Explorer 5.5 and 6.0
  - Netscape 4.x and 6.x
- E-mail clients support:
  - Outlook
  - Lotus Notes
  - Yahoo!
  - Hotmail
  - America Online

7.3.5 Problem Definition and Solution

The global development facilities of the CRM Company included sites in the United States, Canada, and India. The testing was done at sites in the United States and two locations in India, one of which was an offshore partner company. The total number of offshore engineers working for CRM Company software quality and testing was 8, so an average of 64 hours of work done would be reported daily. Build release size was approximately 100 megabytes, as mentioned earlier, and a new release would be downloaded from the CRM Company server located in the United States on a daily basis. The global testing effort was conducted on both the Microsoft Windows and Sun Solaris platforms. The Solaris machines were located at CRM Company office in the United States. So, to perform testing on Solaris, a high speed Internet connection was used.

The builds were generally downloaded at off-peak hours to accommodate the daytime use of the servers. Specialized tools to maintain continuity of downloads including Download Accelerator were used.

E-mail, Internet-enabled instant messaging, and Internet-based voice chat and meeting tools were used to communicate between developers and testers when bugs had to be verified or reproduced. Communication with the offshore partner was direct: enabling developer and tester communication to their counterparts at global offices. Bug fixes would generally take two to three days and depended on severity and priority of the bugs.

7.3.6 Test Case Example

The table below refers to testing scenarios and system responses. These form the building blocks of the test case example.

Table 7.7 Testing Scenarios for Test Case

Testing Scenario	System Response
Enter all contact data in Japanese and English using IME.	Should save all records in database and also display them correctly when retrieved.
Launch the campaign containing all documents resources in Japanese and English.	Should be able to launch the campaign successfully.
Import/export data from single-byte/Unicode database.	Should import/export contact data from/to both single-byte and double-byte databases.
Create a CRM Company user in Japanese and English.	Should create users in both languages.
View the reports containing Unicode data.	Reports should display Unicode data successfully.
Install the MarketingDiva product into U.S. platforms as well as Japanese platforms.	Should install successfully.
Upgrade the previous release to MarketingDiva.	Should be seamlessly upgradeable to MarketingDiva with Unicode support.
Install any language blueprint into MarketingDiva.	Should be able to install blueprint in a Unicode enabled MarketingDiva system provided targeted database has support for languages used in the blueprint.
Exchange Unicode data with Pivotal® Content Management System (CMS) in the native encoding of the CMS.	Should be able to exchange Unicode data with Pivotal CMS in the native encoding of the CMS.

7.3.6.1 Testing Scenario and System Response

Table 7.7 lists testing scenarios for this test case.

7.3.7 Verification and Validation Testing Strategies

7.3.7.1 Verification Strategies

Verification is a human examination or review of the work product. There are various types of reviews like inspection, walkthroughs, and technical reviews. The CRM Company product team did verification at different phases as follows:

- Verifying requirements — in this phase, inspection of PRD is done.
- Verifying the functional design — in this phase, inspection of functional design documents is done.

Following this inspection process, the outputs given to CRM Company are listed below:

- Inspection summary/report
- Data on error types

7.3.7.2 Validation Strategies

Validation is the process of evaluating a system or component during or at the end of the development process to determine whether or not it satisfies specified requirements.

Validation activities can be divided into the following:

- Low level testing:
  - Unit testing
  - Integration testing
- High level testing:
  - Functional testing
  - System testing
  - Sanity testing
  - Regression testing
  - Acceptance testing
  - Stress testing
  - Usability testing
  - Security testing

7.3.7.3 Sequence of Testing

For CRM Company, the testing and QA team did "High Level Validation Type" of testing. The following types of testing were done in sequence when a new version of CRM Company product was released.

- Sanity testing — typically, an initial testing effort to determine if a new CRM Company software version was performing well enough to accept it for a major testing effort.

■ Regression testing — retesting after fixes or modifications of the CRM Company software or its environment. It was sometimes difficult to determine how much retesting was needed, especially near the end of the development cycle. There were certain automated testing tools like WebLoad and WinRunner™ 7.0 that were useful for this type of testing. Regression test plan was followed for regression testing.

■ Acceptance testing — acceptance testing is defined as final testing based on specifications of the end user or customer or based on use by end users or customers over some limited period of time. In this testing, certain basic functional programs were validated. Acceptance test plan was followed for acceptance testing.

■ Stress testing — in this type of testing, CRM Company product was tested under unusually heavy loads, heavy repetition of certain actions or inputs, input of large numerical values and large complex queries to a database system. Stress test plan was followed for stress testing.

■ Security testing — security testing typically shows how well the system protects against unauthorized internal or external access and willful damage, etc. For CRM Company, we followed a security test plan in which various privileges of users were defined.

7.3.8 Testing Tools Used

7.3.8.1 *Automated Tools: WebLOAD 4.51*

WebLOAD is a testing tool for testing the scalability, functionality, and performance of Web-based applications — both Internet and intranet. It can measure the performance of applications under varying load conditions. WebLOAD is used to test Web site performance under real-world conditions by combining performance, load, and functional tests or by running them individually. WebLOAD generates load by creating virtual clients that emulate network traffic. The testers create JavaScript test scripts (called agendas) that instruct those virtual clients about what to do. When WebLOAD runs the test, it gathers results at a per client, per transaction, and per instance level from the computers that are generating the load. WebLOAD can also gather information from the application server's performance monitor. Testers can view the results displayed in graphs and tables in real-time and can save and export the results when the test is finished. For CRM Company, WebLOAD was extensively used for load testing on Web sites.

7.3.8.2 Manual Tools: Microsoft Project 2000

The offshore test and QA team uses this tool. Status versus plan and progress of the project was tracked for the CRM Company product.

7.3.9 Bug Tracking System Tools

7.3.9.1 DevTrack

DevTrack conceptualizes the defect and project tracking process with a Lifecycle Model. An issue is represented with an ID, description, progress status, work description, and other dynamic properties. At all times throughout its history, an issue is always assigned to an owner, which can be a team member, a team group, or a group folder. DevTrack tracks the entire history of an issue from its creation to closure by recording all changes of its ownership, work description, progress status, and other issue properties. The offshore partner was involved in the complete lifecycle of a bug: from entering the new bug into DevTrack to the closure of the issue.

7.3.9.2 RD System

RD System is a Web-based system that includes the information of test cases, issues, project, products, employees, and reports. An issue is represented with an ID, description, progress status, work description, and other dynamic properties. At all times throughout its history, an issue was always assigned to an owner, which can be a team member, a team group, or a group leader. RD System tracked the entire history of an issue from its creation to closure by recording all changes of its ownership, work description, progress status, and other issue properties. The offshore partner's role was involved in the complete lifecycle of the bug: from entering the new bug into RD System to the closure of the issue.

With the reference to Figure 7.2 that shows the lifecycle of a bug, the offshore partner did the following activities:

- Opens new bug.
- Assigns bug.
- Reviews bug for fixes or declined reason.
- If fixed or reason for declination is appropriate, the offshore partner closes bug with matching reason.
- If not fixed or the offshore partner found reason for reopening declined bug, the offshore partner assigned it back to the developer.

7.3.10 Remote Communication Tools Used

Tools used for communication between the offshore partner and CRM Company are listed below:

- Outlook Express 6.0 — this is used for e-mail transactions between the offshore partner and pivotal teams.
- VPN — VPN is used to access the resources of CRM Company. For example, the QA test plan, bug tracking system, and VNC (VNCViewer) to connect to Solaris machine. With the help of this connection, the offshore vendor was able to enter into the corporate intranet.
- VNC (Virtual Network Computing) and pcAnywhere® — these tools were sometimes used to control and develop or test on a remote machine located in the United States.

7.3.10.1 Three Testing Sites

As we have discussed before, the CRM Company project QA testing was going on in the United States and Bangalore, India. The offshore vendor was located in Pune, India and so there were three sites where the testing of the product was taking place. The offshore vendor and internal team in India were in the same time zone and reported the daily update status to CRM Company office using remote communication tools discussed earlier.

The offshore vendor performed the following steps:

1. Offshore vendor team in Pune, India office connects using high Internet to its server located in the United States. A VPN connection is used to connect.
2. Remote control of the dedicated server in the United States is maintained including scheduled downtimes, remote restarting, new software loading, etc.
3. Connect using VPN to access the servers (both Solaris and Windows 2000) located in CRM Company office.
4. Connect the CRM Company client to access the CRM Company servers. Also, VNC is used to perform some database actions and to view some log files.

7.3.11 ROI

ROI, as we defined earlier, can be expressed in the equation form as a ratio of NBs to NCs.

Table 7.8 Cost without Cosourcing

Location	No. of Testers	$ per Month Fully Loaded Costs per Tester	$ per Year
United States	08	10,000	960,000

The equation for calculating the percentage of ROI is:

$$ROI = (Net\ Benefits/Net\ Costs) * 100$$

NBs can be either direct, in terms of incremental revenue generated, productivity gained, or expense saved, or indirect, from the redeployment of resources to tasks that the organization would alternatively have had to hire new and like resources to perform. NCs include recruiting, salaries, benefits, software licensing, and general and administrative overheads. The ROI for each project is compared with the NCs on a yearly basis. ROI analysis means that where expected benefits and costs are realized within the same year of implementation of the project, the project is more likely to proceed. Sometimes ROI is a number (Net Benefits/Net Costs).

ROI for CRM Company's project was fairly high, as the offshore vendor provided cosourcing. As we discussed earlier, in cosourcing unlike pure outsourcing, the SQA team is not completely replacing the in-house SQA team. Instead, the outsourced SQA team is working as an extension of the in-house team with a key SQA manager on the in-house team maintaining full knowledge and control of the SQA tasks and project plan.

The above statement can be justified in mathematical terms as follows.

7.3.11.1 No Cosourcing for SQA Testing

Table 7.8 lists the cost without cosourcing.

7.3.11.2 Cosourcing for SQA Testing

Table 7.9 lists the cost with cosourcing.

7.3.12 Case Summary

This case described and demonstrated that it is possible to maintain multiple global development and test sites including utilizing an outside quality vendor in a remote offshore location. CRM Company has created several major products in the marketplace and is still the leader in its

Table 7.9 Cost with Cosourcing

Location	No. of Testers	$ per Month Fully Loaded Costs All Testers	$ per Year
India	8	8,000	96,000
United States	01	10,000	120,000
		Total	216,000
Total ROI (%) per Year = Net Benefit/Net Cost * 100 = (960,000 − 216,000)/216,000 * 100 = 344.44.			

category. We have withheld the name of the company to protect confidentiality. The offshore partner offered competitive services with the help of latest communication and sharing technologies.

7.4 BOOK SUMMARY

Quality encompasses looking at the software application as a whole that is bigger than the sum of its parts. Good software engineering practices such as separation of business rules from data and UI as well as change management should be applied to the entire application and not just its components. Testing, performance gathering, and flow of the system should be evaluated at the complete application level for best quality. Diverse teams should be integrated into the workflow through careful planning and enhanced communication. Outsourcing and other approaches can be used to enhance the quality while preserving costs and business value. We spend a lot of time in this book on quality practices and testing to improve the ROI of software.

Engineering managers and IT leaders today have to perform QA and testing on today's demanding software systems while keeping costs low. Prevalent data indicates that outsourcing or best shore QA and testing can help reduce costs while maintaining quality. The majority of enterprises to date have outsourced for cost savings, but that trend is now shifting more toward quality and productivity. Overall process savings of 35 to 70 percent are not unheard of and that has been an attractive recipe for companies to outsource. Outsourcing has also enabled a focus on processes and this has led to improved productivity and quality of service and execution. Improvement on business functions and strategic areas is a gradual but longer term effect. More recently, several groups have been concerned about the erosion of organizational efficacy and loss of competitiveness. It is highly unlikely that key strategic areas get outsourced if a company has followed a good strategy and plan of outsourcing. If only cost is used as a driving force for outsourcing, then there is an increased risk of that happening. Innovation could be hurt and market credibility of that company would be adversely affected. Thoughtful and carefully managed outsourcing and cosourcing can actually lead to competitiveness and profitability by allowing more effective execution of noncore, nonstrategic areas.

Even though about 75 percent of all outsourcing work being conducted these days is going to India, we will see that several other countries are emerging in the next few years. The Philippines has established competitive call center services and accounting outsourcing. China is growing into providing good infrastructure and resources for data entry and maintenance functions in addition to it being a market leader for outsourced manufacturing. Eastern Europe has highly educated people, a strong technical base, and low costs in addition to proximity with the rest of Europe. Canada and Mexico have near shore facilities including English language skills, an educated labor force, and service capabilities that are lower risk. Over the next few years, however, India will continue to reign supreme because of its large English speaking labor pool, growing domestic market, breadth and depth of technical talent, favorable government stance, and democratic institutions.

IT services outsourcing, while still a leader in the volume of outsourcing, will be overtaken by BPO services in the near future. Software development and testing, call center, help desk, and basic accounting are current favorites for outsourcing. Payroll processing, banking, finance, insurance services, credit cards, and investment outsourcing will receive a boost in the next few years. Several governance models for global teams are possible and in this book we have discussed a few of those models including captive centers and offshore partnerships.

Throughout this book, we introduced quality practices and how reducing costs of testing can maximize software ROI by improving quality. We examined how SQA and testing can be suitable for leveraged outsourced offshore services as it provides easily measurable benefits and quantifiable ROI. Most IT and ISV organizations find it difficult to have adequate SQA resources and lab infrastructure and end up shipping substandard products under time-to-market pressures. In the current outsourced model followed by many companies, not only can these companies easily get highly trained untainted SQA resources, but also rent large SQA lab infrastructures for expanded quality testing at a fraction of the cost of doing it themselves. We discussed how best to leverage the Cosourced Model for maximum profitability while keeping costs in check. We presented models to compare the ROI on in-house, outsourced, and cosourced SQA teams. We have discussed strategies to evaluate and execute in companies that the user may be picking for outsourced development, SQA, and test and verification. We have shared the evaluation criteria distilled over several years of outsourcing experience. Specific experiences of dealing with communication, time zone, and cultural differences were presented. Background requirements of people who work on SQA and testing as well as the types of testing that outsourcing best lends itself to were identified. We presented whether outsourcing QA and testing had been a productive experience for companies and whether or not the promise of cost savings was fulfilled. We presented the models, processes, and QA standards that make outsourcing experience the most effective for CIOs, business executives, and information systems professionals.

REFERENCES

1. Rosario, S. and Robinson, H., Applying Models in Your Testing Process, *Information and Software Technology*, Vol. 42, No. 12, September 1, 2000.
2. Aissi, S., Test Vector Generation: Current Status and Future Trends. *Software Quality Professional*, Vol. 4, No. 2, March 2002.
3. Cooke, D. et al., Languages for the Specification of Software. *Journal of Systems Software*, Vol. 32, Pp. 269–308, 1996.
4. Zarate, A. et al. A Portable Natural Language Interface for Diverse Databases Using Ontologies. Computational Linguistics and Intelligent Text Processing, *Lecture Notes in Computer Science,* Vol. 2588, Pp. 494–505, New York: Springer-Verlag, 2003.
5. Kistler, T., WebL — A Programming Language for the Web, *Information and Computer Science,* University of California — Irvine, Hannes Marais: DIGITAL Systems Research Center, Palo Alto, CA.

Appendix A

THE QUALITY ASSURANCE
AND TESTING PROCESS

This section describes the steps involved in the QA and testing process. We start out by showing the stages of QA and testing as a subset of overall development cycle. Then we zoom into each of these stages and show the process details within planning, inspection, testing, and certification. Finally, we present what to look for in an outsourcing vendor.

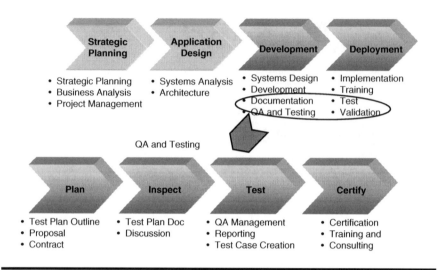

Figure A.1   QA and Testing Process Stages Overview

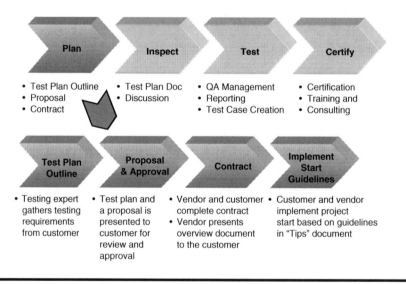

Figure A.2   QA and Testing Process Stages Details — Planning

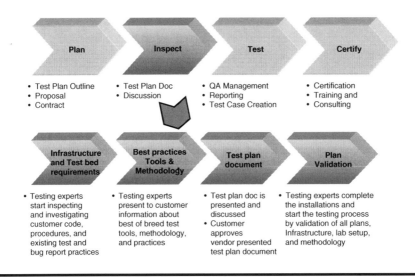

Figure A.3 QA and Testing Process Stages Details — Inspection

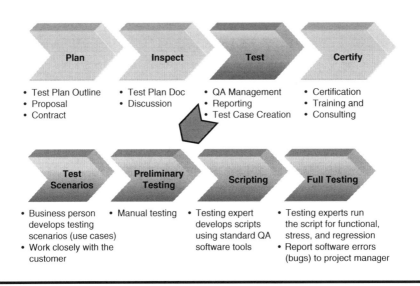

Figure A.4 QA and Testing Process Stages Details — Testing

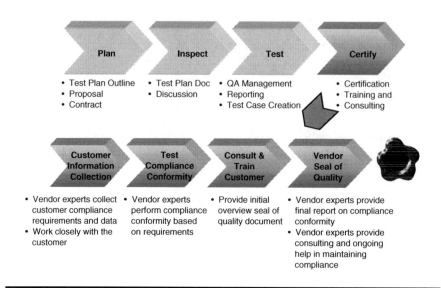

Figure A.5   QA and Testing Process Stages Details — Certification

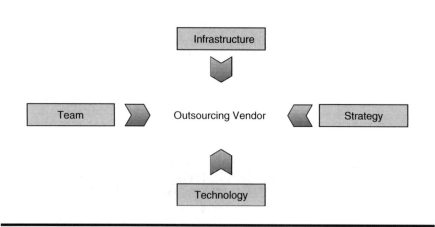

Figure A.6   What to Look for in an Outsourcing Vendor

INDEX

A

Agile development, future of, 29–30
  agile economy, 29
  application examples, 30
  strategic capability, 29
Agile methodology, 12–24
  advanced software development, 15–17
  crystal family, 22–23
  dynamic systems development model, 22
  eXtreme programming, 13–15
  feature driven development, 18–19
  highlights, 12
  lean software development, 19–22
  rational unified process, 23
  SCRUM, 17–18
  unified modeling language, 23
Agile programming, quality and, 134
Agile themes, 10–12
  business systems, unpredictability, 11
  design, 11
  developers, 12
  implement, review, iterate, 11–12
Anti-Americanism, in global software
        development, testing, 122
Application trends, 30–33
  agile application integration, 32
  application integration opportunity,
        31–32
  management responsibilities, 32–33
  platforms, evolving, 31
  software reuse, 32
Approval regimes, with global software
        development, testing, 124–125
Automated code inspection, 137–138

Automated testing, 145
  advantages of, 145–146
Automated test tools, 148–150
Automation, 162–163

B

Baseline ROI, 84–91
  definition of ROI, 85
Benefits of ROI, 66–69
  best practices, 68–69
  business value, 67
  data collection, 69
  metrics, 67–68
  reality, 68
Best practices, 68–69
Brand equity, quantification difficulty, 102
Brand name recognition, 160
Browsers for wireless handheld devices,
        216–217
Bug lifecycle, 223–224
Bug tracking system tools, 222–224, 233–234
Business model, 81–82
Business value capture using ROI, 70–71
  continuous improvement, 71
  decisions, 70
  opportunities, 70
  portfolio, management, 70–71
  strategy, 70

C

Capability maturity models, 48–50, 94–96
  defined, 49, 95

initial, 49, 95
managed, 49, 95
managed through numbers, 49–50
optimizing, 50, 95
repeatable, 95
Case studies, 213–238
Certification
    in quality assurance, testing process, 242
    release candidate, guidelines, 203–204
Changing role of information technology,
        60–63
    global software development, test
            opportunity, 61–62
    governments, role of, 63
    human factors, 63
    IT-enabled, business process
            outsourcing, differences, 63
    outsourcing, offshoring, 62–63
    software development skills as
            commodity, 62
    technical training, availability of, 61–62
    world as software consumer, 62
Cleanroom methodology, 6–8
    boxes, 7
    starting assumptions, 6–7
    steps, 7–8
    verification, testing in, 8
Common standards, with global software
        development, testing, 114
Competitive pressures, quantification
        difficulty, 102–103
Complexity of software, 39–78
    assumptions, 72–73
    best practices, 68–69
    business value, 67, 70–71
    capability maturity model, 47
    capability maturity model integrated,
            48–50
    change management, 52
    changing role of information technology,
            60–63
    configuration management, 51
    continuous improvement, 71
    continuous quality improvement, 47
    control objectives for information
            technology, 53–54
    data, unsubstantiated, supporting
            evidence, 76
    data collection, 69
    defect classification, prevention models,
            48

diverse, platforms, 42
domain expertise, lack of, 75
evolutionary approach to product line,
        58
expertise, 65
gains, overestimating, 76
governments, role of, 63
human factors, 63
implementing product line, 59–60
inaccurate assumptions, 75
incident management, 52
information technology infrastructure
        library, 50–53
investments, 73
IT-enabled, business process
        outsourcing, differences, 63
J2EE, 45
J2SE, 45
Java platforms, 45
Linux, 46
locations, development, diverse, 40–41
market trends, diversity and, 42–60
maximizing software ROI, 63–76
measurements, 74
metrics, 67–68
Microsoft platforms, 44–45
mistakes with ROI, 74–76
mobile operating system, 46
mobile platforms, 46
multifaceted nature of contemporary
        software development, 39–42
nonapplication of product lines, 58
not calculating ROI, 64–66
numbers, over-reliance on, 72
old care, computers analogy, 39–41
open source platforms, 45–46
other's data, use of, 66
outsourcing, offshoring, 62–63
performance objectives, 71–72
portfolio, management, 70–71
product line development, reuse model,
        48
product line model, 55–60
release management, 53
revolutionary approach to product line,
        59
risk, cost profile, missing, 75–76
ROI, positive, 65–66
ROI analysis, preparation, 71–74
security, configuration, 51
service desk management, 52–53

Six Sigma quality model, 47–48
software development, proliferation of, 44–46
software development skills as commodity, 62
software inspection process, 48
software maturity models, proliferation of, 47–60
software process models, 47–48
stakeholder buy-in, 73–74
statistical process control, 48
strategic vision, missing, 74
strategy, 70
teams, development, diverse, 41–42
technical training, availability of, 61–62
timelines, 71
timing, incorrect, 75
waiting until later, 65
wasteful number crunching, 64
world as software consumer, 62
Component-based software architecture, with global software development, testing, 114
Components of ROI, 85–88
discount rate, internal rate of return, 86–87
factor, 86
net benefit, 86
net cost, 86
net present value, 87–88
payback period, 87
percentage, 86
Continuous improvement, 71
Continuous software testing, 139–140
Contract, outsourcer, 199–201
Control objectives for information technology, 53–54
COBIT characteristics, 54–55
COBIT components, 55–56
Cosourcing, 92, 150–152, 163–164
developers to testers ratio for, 152
Cost, quality and, 133–134
Cost of ownership
calculating, 93–94
calculating total cost of ownership, 93–94
ROI, 93–94
steps to calculate total cost of ownership, 94
total, ROI, 93–94
Cultural currents, with global software development, testing, 121–122

Cultural differences among employees, 160
Customers
priority of, 82–83
satisfaction, 160

D

Data, unsubstantiated, supporting evidence, 76
Data collection, 69, 88–90
mythical 1000 percent ROI, 88–89
sales force automation application, 89–90
timeframes of ROI, 88
Data migration issues, product readiness and, 189
Defects per 1000 lines of code, 142
Definition of ROI, 85
Deliverables, financial view of, 84
Deployment readiness, 189–190
deployment reviews, 190
sizing, 190
support infrastructure, 190
Deployment reviews, 190
Developer time to fix defects, 143
DevTrack, 233
Discount rate, internal rate of return, 86–87
Distributed code management, test tools, with global software development, testing, 114
Distributed development, reliability through, with global software development, testing, 110–111
Diverse, platforms, 42
Domain expertise, lack of, 75

E

Easy to upgrade services, future developments, 33
Enterprise CRM market leader, global testing, case study, 226–236
Enterprise money, saving, with global software development, testing, 127
Evolutionary predictions, 28–34
agile application integration, 32
agile development, future of, 29–30
agile economy, 29
agile services, 33
application examples, 30

application integration opportunity,
31–32
application trends, 30–33
easy to upgrade services, 33
loosely coupled scaleable services, 33–34
management responsibilities, 32–33
platform independent services, 34
platforms, evolving, 31
self-aware services, 33
software reuse, 32
strategic capability, 29
Web services development, future of,
33–34
write once use anywhere, 33
Extraenterprise, with global software
development, testing, onshore,
offshore, 109
EXtreme programming ROI, 99–100

F

Front end testing tools, 149
Fully loaded tester cost, 142

G

Gains, overestimating, 76
Global software development
anti-Americanism, 122
approval regimes, 124–125
benefits, 109–111
business issues, 124–125
cautions, 120–125
common standards, 114
communication tools, 112–114
component-based software architecture,
114
cost savings, 110
cultural currents, 121–122
define, execute, measure to plan,
116–117
deployment infrastructure, 184–197
distributed code management, test tools,
114
distributed development, reliability
through, 110–111
enterprise money, saving, 127
extraenterprise, onshore, offshore, 109
global software development, test, 62
implementation, 181–212
information protection, 128

information sharing, 129
infrastructure, services, varying, 122–123
internal staff responsibility, 127
intraenterprise, onshore, offshore,
108–109
investment requirement, 128
language barriers, 123–124
low-skilled labor, cost of, 129
management involvement, 128
management responsibilities, 117–118
measurement, 204–210
methodologies, 204–210
model, 181–184
offshoring, 126–127
onshore, offshore outsourcing myths,
127–130
outsourcer, selecting, managing, 197–204
outsourcing, 125–127
peaks, valleys in demand, 111
personal strategies, 118–120
political issues, 124
poor working conditions, 129
privacy, software, 129–130
product readiness, 184–197
project management tools, 111–112
proximity, software consumers,
marketplaces, 110
reciprocity, investment laws, 124
remote conferencing, 113
responsibility shift, 127–128
scenarios, 108–109
seamless, secure networks, 114–115
software development skills as
commodity, 62
success criteria for, 115–120
talent pool, diversified, 109–110
taxation laws, 125
technical training, availability of, 61–62
technology, as global enabler, 111–115
testing, 62, 107–132
test opportunity, 61–62
twenty-four-hour software development
cycle, 109
world as software consumer, 62

H

Hardware resources, 197
History, software development, 1–38
agile development, future of, 29–30
agile methodologies, 12–24

agile themes, 10–12
application trends, 30–33
classic methodologies, 2–10
cleanroom, 6–8
evolutionary predictions, 28–34
evolving methodologies, 10–28
future, Web services development, 33–34
incremental, 3–4
model driven architecture, 24–26
object-oriented, 8–10
prototyping, 6
spiral, 4–5
waterfall, 2–3
Web services development, 26
Human wrap, 194

I

Incremental methodology, 3–4
Information protection, with global software development, testing, 128
Information sharing, with global software development, testing, 129
Information technology infrastructure library, 50–53
change management, 52
configuration management, 51
incident management, 52
IT security, configuration, 51
release management, 53
service desk management, 52–53
Infrastructure, services, varying, with global software development, testing, 122–123
Inline test tools, 149
Intangible ROI savings, 154–155
Interfaces neutral to technology, 84
Internal rate of return, 86–87
Internal staff responsibility, with global software development, testing, 127
Internationalization, 155–164
cost of, 159
Intraenterprise, onshore, offshore, 108–109
Investments, 73
requirement of, with global software development, testing, 128
ISO 9001, 96–97
ISO/IEC 10646, unicode and, 227

J

Java platforms, 45
J2EE, 45
J2SE, 45

K

Key performance indicators, 138–139

L

Language barriers, with global software development, testing, 123–124
Lifecycle, software development, 183–184
analyzing, 183
designing, 183
implementation, 184
maintaining, 184
recognizing problem, 183
testing, 184
Load testing tools, 149–150
Localization, 155–164
baseline ROI, 161
calculating ROI of, 160–161
cost of, 157–159
net benefit, 161
net cost, 161
product readiness and, 188
revenue from, 159–160
Loosely coupled scaleable services, future developments, 33–34
Low-skilled labor, cost of, with global software development, testing, 129

M

Management involvement, with global software development, testing, 128
Management responsibilities, with global software development, testing, 117–118
Manual code inspection, 137
Manual testing, 143–144
advantages of, 144–145
Manual *versus* automated testing, 143–148
Marketing, outsourcing, 175–177
Market share, quantification difficulty, brand equity, 102

Market trends, diversity and, 42–60
  capability maturity model, 47
  capability maturity model integrated,
    48–50
  change management, 52
  configuration management, 51
  continuous quality improvement, 47
  control objectives for information
    technology, 53–54
  defect classification, prevention models,
    48
  deployment environments, proliferation
    of, 44–46
  evolutionary approach to product line,
    58
  implementing product line, 59–60
  incident management, 52
  information technology infrastructure
    library, 50–53
  IT security, configuration, 51
  J2EE, 45
  J2SE, 45
  Java platforms, 45
  Linux, 46
  Microsoft platforms, 44–45
  mobile operating system, 46
  mobile platforms, 46
  nonapplication of product lines, 58
  open source platforms, 45–46
  product line development, reuse model,
    48
  product line model, 55–60
  release management, 53
  revolutionary approach to product line,
    59
  service desk management, 52–53
  Six Sigma quality model, 47–48
  software development, proliferation of,
    44–46
  software inspection process, 48
  software maturity models, proliferation
    of, 47–60
  software process models, 47–48
  statistical process control, 48
Maximizing software ROI, 63–76
  assumptions, 72–73
  benefits of ROI, 66–69
  best practices, 68–69
  business value, 67, 70–71
  continuous improvement, 71

data, unsubstantiated, supporting
    evidence, 76
  data collection, 69
  decisions, 70
  domain expertise, lack of, 75
  expertise, 65
  gains, overestimating, 76
  inaccurate assumptions, 75
  investments, 73
  measurements, 74
  metrics, 67–68
  mistakes with ROI, 74–76
  not calculating ROI, 64–66
  numbers, over-reliance on, 72
  opportunities, 70
  other's data, use of, 66
  performance objectives, 71–72
  portfolio, management, 70–71
  reality, 68
  risk, cost profile, missing, 75–76
  ROI analysis, preparation, 71–74
  stakeholder buy-in, 73–74
  strategic vision, missing, 74
  strategy, 70
  timelines, 71
  timing, incorrect, 75
  waiting until later, 65
  wasteful number crunching, 64
Measurement process, 74
  evaluation, data capture, 141
  planning, execution, 141
Methodologies
  advanced software development, 15–17
  agile, 10–24
  classic, 2–10
  cleanroom, 6–8
  crystal family, 22–23
  dynamic systems development model, 22
  evolving, 10–28
  eXtreme programming, 13–15
  feature driven development, 18–19
  highlights, 12
  incremental, 3–4
  lean software development, 19–22
  model driven architecture, 24–26
  object-oriented, 8–10
  prototyping, 6
  rational unified process, 23
  SCRUM, 17–18
  spiral, 4–5
  unified modeling language, 23

waterfall, 2–3
Web services development, 26–28
Metrics, 67–68
Microsoft platforms, 44–45
Microsoft Project 2000, 233
Mistakes with ROI, 74–76
    assumptions, inaccurate, 75
    data, unsubstantiated, supporting
        evidence, 76
    domain expertise, lack of, 75
    gains, overestimating, 76
    risk, cost profile, missing, 75–76
    strategic vision, missing, 74
    timing, incorrect, 75
Mobile devices, natural language systems,
        case study, 215–226
Mobile platforms, 46
    mobile operating system, 46
Model driven architecture, 24–26
    enhanced return on investment, 25–26
    improved communication, 25
    independence from platforms, 25
    interoperability between platforms, 25
    portability, 25
Multifaceted nature of contemporary
        software development, 39–42

N

Natural language system profile, case study,
        215
Net benefit, 86
Net cost, 86
Net present value, 87–88
Not calculating ROI, implications of, 64–66
    expertise, 65
    other's data, use of, 66
    ROI, positive, 65–66
    waiting until later, 65
    wasteful number crunching, 64
Numbers, over-reliance on, 72

O

Object-oriented methodology, 8–10
    Booch, 9
    Coad, Yourdon, 9–10
    Jacobson, 10
    key relationship, 9
    Rumbaugh object modeling technique,
        10

Old care, computers analogy, 39–41
Online training, 174–175
Onshore, offshore outsourcing myths,
        127–130
Open source platforms, 45–46
    Linux, 46
Organization commitment, for quality, 138
Other's data, use of, 66
Outsourcer
    contract, 199–201
    culture, 198–200
    selecting, managing, 197–204
    time barriers, 198–200
Outsourcer management, 200–203
    goals, 202–203
    methods, 201–202
    tasking, 202–203
Outsourcer selection, 198–200
    interview, 198–199
    language, 198–200
    project definition, 198
    statement of work, 199–201
Outsourcing
    country, 208
    experiences, 210
    governments, role of, 63
    human factors, 63
    in-house SQA, 204
    IT-enabled, business process
        outsourcing, differences, 63
    language, 208–209
    offshoring, 62–63
    standards bodies, 209–210
Outsourcing companies, 207–208
Outsourcing vendor, what to look for in, 242

P

Payback period, 87
Peaks, valleys in demand, with global
        software development, testing,
        111
People resources, 196–197
Performance, product readiness and, 189
Performance indicators, 138–139
Performance objectives, 71–72
Personal strategies, with global software
        development, testing, 118–120
Platform independent services, future
        developments, 34

Political issues, with global software development, testing, 124
Poor working conditions, with global software development, testing, 129
Portfolio, management, 70–71
Present value, net, 87–88
Privacy, software, with global software development, testing, 129–130
Processes, methodologies, 92
Product line model, 55–60
　evolutionary approach to product line, 58
　implementing product line, 59–60
　nonapplication of product lines, 58
　revolutionary approach to product line, 59
Product readiness, 184–197
　data migration, 189
　functionality/features, 185–188
　localization, 188
　performance, 189
　reliability, 188–189
　supportability, 189
　usability, 188
Project management tools, with global software development, testing, 111–112
Prototyping methodology, 6
　limitations of, 6
Proximity, software consumers, marketplaces, 110

Q

Quality, software, testing, 133–180
　applied ROI, 143–152, 161–164, 174–175
　calculating ROI of, 160–161
　calculating testing ROI, 152–155
　calculating training ROI, 169–174
　continuous software testing, 139–140
　costs, 142–143
　factors for ROI calculation, 157–160
　internationalization, 155–164
　localization, 155–164
　measuring training, factors for, 167–169
　metric *versus* measure, new international standard, 140–142
　myths, software quality, testing, 133–136
　organizational measures, 138–139
　quality, maximizing, 133–142

　risk, minimizing, 133–142
　software inspection techniques, 136–138
　software testing, 142–155
　software training ROI, 164–178
　summary, 175–178
Quality assurance, testing process, 239–242
　certification, 242
　inspection, 241
　planning, 240
　stages, 240
　testing, 241
Quantification difficulty, 101–103
　business values, 102
　competitive pressures, 102–103
　market share, brand equity, 102
　regulatory environment, 103
　support, serviceability cost, 103
Query builder tool, 219–220

R

Rate of return, internal, 86–87
Rational ClearQuest, 223
Readiness of product, 185–189
Reciprocity, with global software development, testing, investment laws, 124
Refining cost savings model, 155–156
Regulatory environment, quantification difficulty, 103
Release candidate certification guidelines, 203–204
Reliability, product readiness and, 188–189
Remote conferencing, with global software development, testing, 113
Resource allocation, measurement process, 141
Resource requirements, 195–197
Responsibility shift, with global software development, testing, 127–128
Returns on investments, *ROI*
Risk, cost profile, missing, 75–76
Roadmap, testing, 184–187
ROI analysis, preparation, 71–74
　assumptions, 72–73
　investments, 73
　measurements, 74
　numbers, over-reliance on, 72
　performance objectives, 71–72
　stakeholder buy-in, 73–74
　timelines, 71

S

Sales force automation application, 89–90
Scalability, 82–83
Scaleable services, loosely coupled, future
    developments, 33–34
Scenarios, with global software
    development, testing, 108–109
Seamless, secure networks, 114–115
Self-aware services, future developments, 33
Serviceability cost, support, quantification,
    103
Shrink wrap, 193–194
Six Sigma, ROI, 97–99
    control chart, 98
    defects, 98
    defects per million opportunities, 97
    define, measure, analyze, improve,
        control, 97
    design for Six Sigma, 97
    methodology, value of, 99
    Pareto chart, 98
    statistical process control, 97–98
Sizing, deployment readiness and, 190
Software, inspection techniques, 136–138
Software development, proliferation of,
    44–46
    J2EE, 45
    J2SE, 45
    Java platforms, 45
    Linux, 46
    Microsoft platforms, 44–45
    mobile operating system, 46
    mobile platforms, 46
    open source platforms, 45–46
Software development lifecycle, 183–184
    analyzing, 183
    designing, 183
    implementation, 184
    maintaining, 184
    recognizing problem, 183
    testing, 184
Software development ROI, 79–106
    applied ROI, 90–103
    baseline ROI, 84–91
    business model, 81–82
    business values, 102
    calculating total cost of ownership, 93–94
    capability, maturity model, 94–96
    competitive pressures, 102–103
    components of ROI, 85–88
    cosourcing, 92

    customers, priority of, 82–83
    data collection for ROI, 88–90
    definition of ROI, 85
    deliverables, financial view of, 84
    discount rate, internal rate of return,
        86–87
    eXtreme programming ROI, 99–100
    factor, 86
    interfaces neutral to technology, 84
    ISO 9001, 96–97
    market share, brand equity, 102
    methodologies, 94–99
    mythical 1000 percent ROI, 88–89
    net benefit, 86
    net cost, 86
    net present value, 87–88
    Pareto chart, Six Sigma, 98
    payback period, 87
    percentage, 86
    phases of, 90–92
    quantification difficulty, 101–103
    regulatory environment, 103
    repeatable capability, maturity model, 95
    sales force automation application, 89–90
    scalability, 82–83
    Six Sigma, 97–99
    statistical process control, Six Sigma,
        97–98
    support, serviceability cost, 103
    timeframes of ROI, 88
    total cost of ownership and, 93–94
    training, 91
    Web services ROI, 100–101
Software development skills as commodity,
    62
Software inspection techniques, 136–138
    automated code inspection, 137–138
    manual code inspection, 137
    testing, inspection, 136–137
Software maturity models, proliferation of,
    47–60
    capability maturity model, 47
    capability maturity model integrated,
        48–50
    change management, 52
    configuration management, 51
    continuous quality improvement, 47
    control objectives for information
        technology, 53–54
    defect classification, prevention models,
        48

evolutionary approach to product line, 58

implementing product line, 59–60

incident management, 52

information technology infrastructure library, 50–53

nonapplication of product lines, 58

product line development, reuse model, 48

product line model, 55–60

release management, 53

revolutionary approach to product line, 59

security, configuration, 51

service desk management, 52–53

Six Sigma quality model, 47–48

software inspection process, 48

software process models, 47–48

statistical process control, 48

Software process models, 47–48

  capability maturity model, 47

  continuous quality improvement, 47

  defect classification, prevention models, 48

  product line development, reuse model, 48

  Six Sigma quality model, 47–48

  software inspection process, 48

  statistical process control, 48

Software quality, testing, 133–180

  applied ROI, 143–152, 161–164, 174–175

  calculating ROI of, 160–161

  calculating testing ROI, 152–155

  calculating training ROI, 169–174

  continuous software testing, 139–140

  costs, 142–143

  factors for ROI calculation, 157–160

  internationalization, 155–164

  localization, 155–164

  measuring training, factors for, 167–169

  metric *versus* measure, new international standard, 140–142

  myths, software quality, testing, 133–136

  organizational measures, 138–139

  quality, maximizing, 133–142

  risk, minimizing, 133–142

  software inspection techniques, 136–138

  software testing, 142–155

  software training ROI, 164–178

  summary, 175–178

Software reuse, application trends, 32

Software testing, 142–155

Software training ROI, 164–178

  business value, 166

  older models of training, 166–167

  resources, 166

  selecting, 167

Spiral methodology, 4–5

  feasibility determination, 5

  initial operational capability milestone, 5

  lifecycle, 5

  risk exposure assessment, 5

Stakeholder buy-in, 73–74

Stakeholders, continuous testing, 140

Standards bodies, 209–210

Statement of work, outsourcer, 199–201

Strategic vision, missing, 74

Success criteria for global software development, testing, 115–120

Support, serviceability cost, quantification, 103

Supportability, product readiness and, 189

Support infrastructure, deployment readiness and, 190

T

Talent pool, diversified, with global software development, testing, 109–110

Tangible ROI savings, 152–154

Taxation laws, with global software development, testing, 125

Team communication, hurdles for, 208

Teams, development, diverse, 41–42

Technical training, availability of, 61–62

Technology, as global enabler, in global software development, testing, 111–115

Test design tools, 148–149

Testing

  applied ROI, 143–152, 161–164, 174–175

  calculating ROI of, 160–161

  calculating testing ROI, 152–155

  calculating training ROI, 169–174

  continuous software testing, 139–140

  costs, 142–143

  designed into software development, 139–140

  factors for ROI calculation, 157–160

  internationalization, 155–164

  localization, 155–164

  measuring training, factors for, 167–169

metric *versus* measure, new international
standard, 140–142
myths, software quality, testing, 133–136
organizational measures, 138–139
quality, maximizing, 133–142
risk, minimizing, 133–142
software, 133–180
software inspection techniques, 136–138
software testing, 142–155
software training ROI, 164–178
summary, 175–178
TestRunner tool, 220
1000 percent ROI, mythical, 88–89
Timeframes of ROI, 88
Timelines, 71
Timing, incorrect, 75
Tools
automation, 91–92
eXtreme programming ROI, 99–100
techniques for, 99–101
Web services ROI, 100–101
Total cost of ownership
calculating, 93–94
calculating total cost of ownership, 93–94
ROI, 93–94
steps to calculate total cost of ownership,
94
Training, 91
factors for measuring, 167–169
post-training factors, 168–169
during training factors, 167–168
Training ROI, calculating, 169–174
administrative costs, 170–171
baseline ROI, 173
bottom-line benefits, 173
case, 173–174
marketing costs, 171
net benefits, 171–173
net costs, 170–171
participant costs, 171
top-line benefits, 172

Twenty-four-hour software development
cycle, with global software
development, testing, 109

U

Unicode
defined, 227
technical overview of, 227–228
Usability, product readiness and, 188

W

Waiting until later, 65
Wasteful number crunching, 64
Waterfall methodology, 2–3
limitations, 3
WebLOAD 41, 218–219, 232
Web services development, 26
design, 27
development, 27
execution, 27
lifecycle of Web services, 26–28
management, 28
SOAP, deployment in, XML applications,
27
testing, 27
Web services development future, 33–34
agile services, 33
easy to upgrade services, 33
loosely coupled scaleable services, 33–34
platform independent services, 34
self-aware services, 33
write once use anywhere, 33
Web services ROI, 100–101
net benefit, 101
net cost, 101
Wireless Web interface, 215
World as software consumer, 62
Write once use anywhere, future
developments, 33